URBAN HERITAGE AND SUSTAINABILITY IN THE AGE OF GLOBALISATION

Urban Heritage and Sustainability in the Age of Globalisation

Edited by Lilia Makhloufi

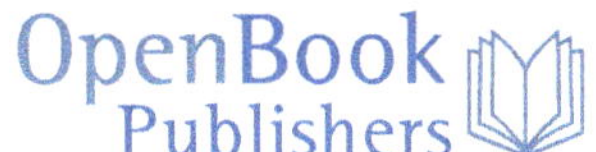

https://www.openbookpublishers.com

All external links were active at the time of publication unless otherwise stated and have been archived via the Internet Archive Wayback Machine at https://archive.org/web

Any digital material and resources associated with this volume will be available at https://doi.org/10.11647/OBP.0412#resources

ISBN Paperback: 978-1-80511-340-9
ISBN Hardback: 978-1-80511-341-6
ISBN Digital (PDF): 978-1-80511-342-3
ISBN Digital eBook (EPUB): 978-1-80511-343-0
ISBN Digital (HTML): 978-1-80511-344-7

DOI: 10.11647/OBP.0412

Cover image: Algiers, Algeria, Architectural and Urban Heritage. Photograph by Lilia Makhloufi (2016). All rights reserved.
Cover design by Jeevanjot Kaur Nagpal

Contents

Je dédie ce livre à mes parents,
pour m'avoir appris à me consacrer au travail intellectuel avec courage et détermination.
Qu'ils trouvent ici le témoignage de ma profonde reconnaissance.

This publication is a result of the research project 'Tangible and Intangible Heritage: Architecture, Design and Culture', conducted by Prof. Dr. Lilia Makhloufi and Prof. Dr. Ammar Abdulrahman, members of the Arab-German Young Academy of Sciences and Humanities (AGYA). The research project was funded by the Arab-German Young Academy of Sciences and Humanities (AGYA) based in the Berlin-Brandenburg Academy of Sciences and Humanities (BBAW) in Germany.

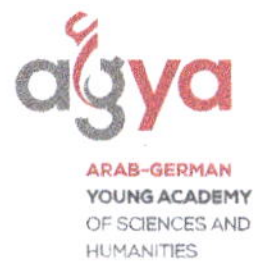

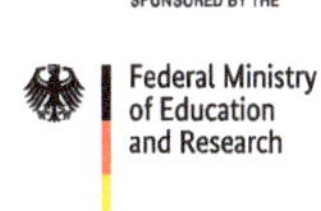

Scientific and Review Committees

All chapters have been evaluated by an international scientific committee and an international review committee consisting of researchers from various academic backgrounds.

Scientific coordinator and chair of the scientific and review committees

Dr. Lilia Makhloufi, Ecole Polytechnique d'Architecture et d'Urbanisme (EPAU), Algiers, Algeria. Member of the Arab-German Young Academy of Sciences and Humanities (AGYA), Berlin, Germany

Scientific committee members

Prof. Lalla Btissam Drissi, LPHE-Modeling & Simulations, Faculty of Science, Mohammed V University, Rabat, Morocco (AGYA Alumna)

Prof. Ahmad Sakhrieh, Mechanical and Industrial Engineering Department, School of Engineering, American University of Ras Al Khaimah, 10021, United Arab Emirates. Mechanical Engineering Department, the University of Jordan, Amman 11942, Jordan (AGYA Alumnus)

Dr. Alaa Aldin Alchomari, Islamische Abteilung an der Uni Tübingen, Tübingen, Germany

Dr. Honey Fadaie, Department of Architecture, Faculty of Art and Architecture, Roudehen Branch, Islamic Azad University (RIAU), Roudehen, Tehran, Iran

Dr. Fanny Gerbeaud, Higher National School of Architecture and Landscape Architecture (ENSAP), Bordeaux, France. PAVE Research Centre, Bordeaux, France

Dr. Ikram Hili, University of Sousse, Tunisia (AGYA Member)

Dr. Nibal Muhesen, Cultural heritage expert at the Directorate general of antiquities and museums (DGAM), Damascus, Syria, and researcher at the University of Copenhagen, Denmark

Review committee members

Prof. Khalid El Harrouni, Ecole Nationale d'Architecture, Rabat, Morocco

Prof. Assia Lamzah, Institut National d'Aménagement et d'Urbanisme, Rabat, Morocco

Dr. Ammar Abdulrahman, Institute for Ancient Near Eastern Studies of the Freie Universität Berlin, Germany (AGYA Alumnus)

Dr. Safa Achour, National School of Architecture and Urbanism of Tunis, Tunisia

Dr. Carmen Antuña Rozado, Senior Scientist, VTT Technical Research Centre of Finland, Helsinki, Finland

Dr. Aline Barlet, Higher National School of Architecture and Landscape Architecture (ENSAP), Bordeaux, France

Dr. Honey Fadaie, Department of Architecture, Faculty of Art and Architecture, Roudehen Branch, Islamic Azad University (RIAU), Roudehen, Tehran, Iran

Dr. Fanny Gerbeaud, Higher National School of Architecture and Landscape Architecture (ENSAP), Bordeaux, France. PAVE Research Centre, Bordeaux, France

Dr. Nibal Muhesen, Cultural heritage expert at the Directorate general of antiquities and museums (DGAM), Damascus, Syria, and researcher at the University of Copenhagen, Denmark

Ms. Maryam Mirzaeii, Department of Architecture, Faculty of Art and Architecture, Roudehen Branch, Islamic Azad University (RIAU), Roudehen, Tehran, Iran

Notes on Contributors

Amany Abdelsadeq S. Hussein is an independent urban researcher with eleven years of experience as an architect and urban practitioner. She was a researcher for the Waikindi Initiative, a Nubian youth-led initiative aimed at reviving Nubian heritage and promoting knowledge of Nubian culture among Egyptians. Her professional experience as an urban practitioner has acquainted her with the interrelationship between physical and social aspects of urban policies and their impact on people's everyday lives. Her main research interests are sustainable urban development, urban policies and cultural sustainability.

ORCID ID: 0000-0001-5083-7405

Safa Achour is an architect with a master's degree in architecture. As a doctoral student, she gained teaching experience at the University of Manouba in Tunis, Tunisia. Upon completing her doctorate of science in architecture with the highest honours in 2015, she continued teaching in addition to working as a researcher. In 2017, she was promoted to assistant professor at the National School of Architecture and Urbanism of Tunis, where she has also served as the director of studies since December 2020. In June 2023, she obtained her postdoctoral degree (habilitation) with accreditation to supervise research.

ORCID ID: 0000-0003-4791-2579

Sura AlHalalsheh is an architect/conservator. She earned her bachelor's degree in architecture from Jordan University of Science and Technology in 2003, and in 2019, obtained a master's degree in architectural conservation from the German Jordanian University through a scholarship funded by the German Government. She led conservation projects in collaboration with several international agencies that covered archaeological, historical, and Modern Heritage sites, involving the design and execution of multiple intervention levels in heritage sites, empowering local communities through heritage conservation, and formulation of diverse conservation guidelines. Her continuing research on the Heritage of Modernity builds upon her master's thesis, employing new methodologies to address this understudied subject.

ORCID ID: 0000-0003-2872-461X

Aline Barlet is an environmental psychologist with a doctoral degree in psychology—behavioural sciences and social practices and a master's degree in architectural and urban acoustics. She is co-director of the GRECCAU Research Centre, as well as a lecturer at Ecole Nationale Supérieure d'Architecture et de Paysage (ENSAP) in Bordeaux. Her research and teaching focuses on sustainability issues, comfort and atmospheres, particularly in the fields of territorial consultation, energy and environmental transition. Her contribution to the present volume draws upon her work as a researcher for the redivivus project 'Recuperating the Modern Movement through Sustainable Development: Lessons, Adaptations and Resourcefulness in Everyday Spaces'.

ORCID ID: 0000-0002-2794-6117

Athar Chabchoub is an architect pursuing an academic career path. After her master's degree, obtained with honors in 2013, she joined in the same year, the teaching staff of the National School of Architecture and Urbanism of Tunis (ENAU) in parallel with her research career as a doctoral student. Holding a doctoral degree in architectural sciences since 2019, her dissertation explores thermal comfort and its impact on the energy consumption of colonial and contemporary buildings in Tunis. She is currently engaged as a Faculty lecturer, researcher and coordinator of the LaRPA research laboratory (PAE3C research team, ENAU).

ORCID ID: 0000-0002-9295-9731

Khalid El Harrouni is a full professor of civil engineering and computational mechanics and UNESCO Chair *'Education and Research on Sustainable and Bicoclimatic Urban Planning and Architecture'*. As the deputy director of research at Ecole Nationale d'Architecture (ENA) in Rabat, Morocco, he is responsible for the Doctoral Studies Centre 'Architecture and Related Disciplines' and serves as scientific coordinator for the research theme 'Sustainability in Architecture and Urbanism'. He is also the editor-in-chief of *African and Mediterranean*

Journal of Architecture and Urbanism and an expert member of the two International Council on Monuments and Sites (ICOMOS) International Scientific Committees on the Analysis and Restoration of Structures of Architectural Heritage, and Energy and Sustainability. He has more than thirty-five years of research and professional experience in civil engineering, urban planning, building energy efficiency, advanced computational techniques, and heritage architecture.

ORCID ID: 0000-0002-3391-6889

Honey Fadaie is an assistant professor in the Department of Architecture at the Roudehen Branch of the Islamic Azad University in Iran, where she has taught as a board member for the past fifteen years. She has been studying Persian gardens since 2008, focusing on their sustainability and the traditional landscapes in hot and arid regions. Her current research interests include the concept of sustainability in Iranian tangible heritages.

ORCID ID: 0000-0003-4523-6028

Fanny Gerbeaud is an architect with a doctoral degree in sociology. Formerly an assistant lecturer at Ecole Nationale Supérieure d'Architecture et de Paysage (ENSAP) in Bordeaux, she now works as a research engineer at the PAVE Research Centre. She studies processes of architectural appropriation in the context of metropolitanisation and informal settlements, focusing on sustainability and architectural heritage issues. She participates in the French Ministry of Culture research programmes 'The Architectural Culture of the French People' and 'Recuperating the Modern Movement through Sustainable Development: Lessons, Adaptations and Resourcefulness in Everyday Spaces' (redivivus project).

ORCID ID: 0009-0005-4665-5234

Fakher Kharrat is a professor of architecture specialising in the study and restoration of historical monuments and cultural heritage conservation. Currently the director of the School of Architecture and Urbanism of Tunis and head of the Research Laboratory in Heritage and Architecturology (LaRPA), he has participated in various international projects related to architectural heritage as well as its conservation and enhancement.

ORCID ID: 0000-0002-1431-0523

Lilia Makhloufi is an architect and urban planner. She obtained her magister's degree in urban planning in 2003, and her doctorate of science degree in territory planning in 2009 and her postdoctoral degree (habilitation) with accreditation to supervise research in 2019. As a teacher and researcher, she worked at the University of Constantine, the University of Jijel and since 2010 at Ecole Polytechnique d'Architecture et d'Urbanisme (EPAU) in Algiers. She is also a member of the Arab-German Young Academy of Sciences and Humanities (AGYA), based in the Berlin-Brandenburg Academy of Sciences and Humanities (BBAW) in Germany. Her main research experience and international collaborations are related to housing projects, public spaces, cities and sustainability.

ORCID ID: 0000-0002-8778-5132

Caroline Mazel is an architect and lecturer at Ecole Nationale Supérieure d'Architecture et de Paysage (ENSAP) in Bordeaux, as well as a researcher and member of the PAVE Research Centre. In 2003, she founded Médiarchi, an organisation which partners with local authorities to develop awareness-raising initiatives related to architecture. Her activities focus on the Modern Movement, its diverse expressions and its social and humanist vocation. As a 'mediating architect', she is involved in shaping professional practices in architecture in addition to participating in the redivivus project.

ORCID ID: 0009-0001-4451-5343

Maryam Mirzaei holds a bachelor's degree in architecture and a master's degree in the restoration of historical buildings. Her research interests focus on Iranian tangible and intangible heritage, museum studies, the history of urban planning, and religious minorities in Iran. In addition to lecturing at various Iranian academic institutions, she works as an architect and interior designer for several engineering companies in Tehran. Her research focuses on the history of architecture and urban planning in Tehran, a subject on which she has lectured and written extensively, notably publishing several articles as well as a 2020 monograph on Tehran's Si-ye Tir Street.

ORCID ID: 0009-0008-4677-9335

Irina Oznobikhina holds a master's degree in philosophical anthropology from the National Research University Higher School of Economics in Moscow and is currently an independent researcher and sound artist. Specialising in affect and atmospheres as theorised in the new phenomenology, her additional research interests include sonic ecology, urban studies and sound studies.

ORCID ID: 0000-0001-5363-4515

Maiss Razem is a LEED AP architect with a doctorate in architecture from the University of Cambridge, funded by the Islamic Development Bank's Cambridge International Scholarship. She obtained her bachelor's degree in architectural engineering from Jordan University of Science and Technology and her master's degree in architecture from Virginia Tech University. She has worked on numerous urban rehabilitation and heritage conservation projects as part of her experience at TURATH Architecture and Urban Design Consultants in Jordan and taught at several Jordanian universities. Her research interests include sustainable building design, visual research methods and disciplinary intersections between architecture, heritage conservation, sociology, anthropology and environmental sciences. She currently works as an assistant professor at Al Hussein Technical University in Amman, Jordan.

ORCID ID: 0000-0002-8258-6417

Ousama Rumayed is a senior civil engineer, expert in cultural heritage, particularly in safeguarding cultural heritage threatened by damage and erasure due to armed conflicts. He served at the Directorate General of Antiquities and Museums (DGAM) in Syria. With over two decades of professional experience, he has held various positions, including IT Director and tutor at the Institute of Archaeology and Museums, deputy national co-manager for the Cultural Tourism Development Programme, and heritage expert and member of the Interim Steering Committee, working on the establishment of an ICOMOS National Committee in Syria. As a doctoral candidate in History at Pázmány Péter Catholic University in Budapest, his research focuses on the historical urban development of Palmyra, post-war cultural resource management and documentation using the Geographic Information System (GIS) approach. Currently, he is an academic volunteer at the Netherlands Institute for the Near East (NINO) in Leiden, Netherlands.

ORCID ID: 0000-0002-2183-2872

Mrinalini Singh is a conservation architect from New Delhi, India. She completed her bachelor's degree in architecture in 2018 at K. R. Mangalam University in Gurgaon, followed in 2020 by her master's degree in architecture with a specialisation in built heritage at the Sushant University's School of Art and Architecture. A conservation architect for a World Monuments Fund project to safeguard twentieth century modern heritage, her research interests centre around India's unexplored culture and heritage. Mrinalini is currently working as an assistant professor at Apeejay Institute of Technology- School of Architecture and Planning (AIT-SAP), Greater Noida, India.

ORCID ID: 0000-0002-9861-3061

Devashree Vyas earned her bachelor's degree in architecture from Mumbai University and has since worked primarily on projects related to heritage conservation, particularly within urban civic fabrics. She also achieved a master's degree in the World Heritage Studies programme at Brandenburg Technical University Cottbus-Senftenberg in Germany. She is currently affiliated with Ancestry Deutschland and works on digitisation of archives.

ORCID ID: 0009-0002-0500-9197

List of Illustrations

List of Tables

Preface

Lilia Makhloufi

This work is the outcome of the academic research project titled 'Tangible and Intangible Heritage: Architecture, Design and Culture',[1] which I have had the privilege of directing under the sponsorship of the Arab-German Young Academy of Sciences and Humanities (AGYA) based in the Berlin-Brandenburg Academy of Sciences and Humanities (BBAW) in Germany. This research project has resulted in two distinct volumes. The first volume, *Tangible and Intangible Heritage in the Age of Globalisation,* analysed and compared heritage in different contexts from an interdisciplinary perspective.[2]

The second volume, *Urban Heritage and Sustainability in the Age of Globalisation*, also presents a comparative and interdisciplinary analysis of heritage, but with an exclusive focus on the urban context. It comprises the work of PhD students, professors and practitioners from an array of disciplines, including architecture, civil engineering, urban planning, sociology and philosophical anthropology. The themes analysed by these researchers and practitioners originating from Egypt, France, India, Iran, Jordan, Morocco, Russia, Syria and Tunisia, contribute to the literature on urban heritage and sustainability.

As the scientific coordinator and the chair of the scientific and review committees, I would like to thank AGYA and the contributors to this volume as well as the scientific and review committee members for their commitment throughout the review process to enhancing the

1 The project was run under grant 01DL20003 from the Federal Ministry of Education and Research (BMBF).

2 Lilia Makhloufi (ed.), *Tangible and Intangible Heritage in the Age of Globalisation* (Cambridge, UK: Open Book Publishers, 2024), https://doi.org/10.11647/OBP.0388

submissions. Their active contribution and insightful recommendations on theoretical and practical approaches to heritage have been crucial to the publication project's success.

Dr. Lilia Makhloufi
Scientific coordinator
Scientific and review committees Chair

Introduction
Urban Heritage and Sustainability

Lilia Makhloufi

Urban heritage, with its tangible and intangible components, is of vital importance. It is a source of social cohesion, cultural diversity, collective memory and identities for present and future generations. Over the centuries, this urban heritage has been subjected to significant pressure due to continuous and dynamic urbanisation. As a result, many historic cities have been neglected, resulting in the loss of old buildings, cultural identities and economic resources needed to improve basic facilities.

This book offers a comparative and interdisciplinary analysis of heritage in the urban context, making a valuable contribution to the expanding body of heritage studies. The assessment examines architectural, urban and cultural parameters, studying past and present built environments and considering political constraints and economic difficulties.

The ideology of globalisation suggests that, sooner or later, it will be impossible to escape from a uniform way of life, where certain common needs are met, with cities following similar patterns of construction. In response, scholars have analysed the past and present conditions to reach viable solutions for the future of urban heritage and its sustainability in cities around the globe.

Indeed, this urban heritage was built according to a previous way of life, incorporating a set of principles that form the basis of sustainable urban planning. These principles provided long-term benefits for indoor and outdoor thermal comfort, which can be passed on to future generations. In this book, seventeen researchers from various

 https://doi.org/10.11647/OBP.0412.00

disciplines—such as architecture, civil engineering, urban planning, sociology and philosophical anthropology—share their approaches to heritage, with perspectives on cities in the Middle East, North Africa, South Asia and Western Europe. Exploring various aspects of this far-reaching topic, they enrich the debate on the past, present and future of urban heritage in their respective countries and beyond.

Our scientific collaboration on this book has generated insightful exchange with the objective of redefining the concept of heritage through interdisciplinary and intercultural reflections. The contributors examine urban and architectural heritage, investigating urban components over time and discussing socio-cultural challenges and opportunities. They analyse the conditions of the past in order to inform the present and the future. As a result, this book features case studies from Egypt, France, India, Iran, Jordan, Morocco, Syria and Tunisia, which are organised into twelve chapters structured according to the themes outlined below.

The first part of the book presents insights from architects and civil engineers into the urban development processes of historical cities in India, Syria and Iran. Through the lens of urban history, they study heritage over time and discuss the cultural challenges and opportunities of both the past and present.

Indeed, urban history proceeds from the land, which can be considered the very foundation of the city. In Chapter One, Devashree Vyas analyses the urban development of Mumbai, India, a city originally established on an archipelago of seven islands. Focusing on the typologies of the city's constituent heritage, the author examines its colonial, post-colonial and contemporary heritages in order to shed light on collective identities in the context of widespread urban development and heritage conservation difficulties.

Chapter Two analyses the urban development of Palmyra, Syria, where historical heritage has been severely damaged by conflict. The war in Syria wrought devastation upon numerous significant archaeological sites and monuments dating from the Prehistoric, Byzantine, Roman and Islamic periods. Against this backdrop, Ousama Rumayed focuses on the post-war period, outlining the recovery policy to preserve the city's archaeological park and monuments. Through a Strengths, Weaknesses, Opportunities and Threats (SWOT) analysis, the author identifies internal and external factors favourable to securing the future of this heritage and harnessing its vast cultural and socio-economic potential.

In Chapter Three, Maryam Mirzaei examines historical, architectural and urban development process in the Iranian capital of Tehran. She focuses specifically on Si-ye Tir, one of the city's most historically significant streets, reflecting on its rich religious heritage encompassing Zoroastrian, Jewish, Christian and Islamic traditions. Examining this heritage over time, she highlights the unique cohesiveness of this syncretic urban environment.

The book's second part features the contributions of architects, sociologists and civil engineers who offer their perspectives on traditional neighbourhoods in Jordan, France and Morocco. With an emphasis on rehabilitation projects, these authors explore the urban transformation of neighbourhoods and the lived experiences of their inhabitants.

Chapter Four presents a case study on the historical neighbourhood of Lweibdeh in the Jordanian capital city of Amman. Amidst the profound rehabilitation of the physical landscape, Maiss Razem and Sura AlHalalsheh consider the interactions between this old neighbourhood and the local communities that inhabit it. Here, the transect walk method brings to light various resources valued by these communities, such as shared values, social interactions and stakeholder networking dynamics.

In Chapter Five, Fanny Gerbeaud, Aline Barlet and Caroline Mazel examine the modern neighbourhoods of Mériadeck and Pontet-Lamartine in Bordeaux, France, focusing on local communities' commitment to the physical and moral rehabilitation of these suburban areas. Architectural, environmental and social surveys demonstrate inhabitants' involvement in preserving their residential heritage and their efforts to create sustainable urban heritage by adapting their practices and perceptions.

Chapter Six sheds light on the densification of old neighbourhoods, which affects many historic cities in North Africa. Khalid El Harrouni describes and analyses the rehabilitation process of the old city of Fez, Morocco, including its main stages and components over the last thirty-five years. This case study reveals the constraints governing sustainable conservation as well as best practices and dynamic approaches to safeguarding the urban heritage of old neighbourhoods, including expansive stakeholder participation and social engagement in housing rehabilitation, particularly in the case of housing units at risk of collapse.

In the third part of the book, architects share their perspectives on old buildings in Tunisia and Iran, reflecting on climatic objectives. Focusing on old cities, they examine the forms and contents of urban networks, housing, infrastructure and urban spaces such as streets, squares, and gardens in light of contemporary environmental concerns.

In Chapter Seven, Safa Achour emphasises the importance of the traditional heritage and morphology of the old town of Tunis. She examines the sustainability of this medina in terms of urban design and outdoor thermal comfort, providing urban planning recommendations for preserving its cultural heritage, social life and urban spaces.

Chapter Eight also concerns thermal comfort in the context of Tunis, evaluating its interior rather than exterior aspect. Athar Chabchoub and Fakher Kharrat analyse the city's colonial heritage, offering a comparative study of indoor thermal comfort in two downtown buildings representing the colonial and contemporary periods. Focusing on the physical, psychological and physiological aspects of comfort, they investigate the thermal performance and energy consumption of these structures. The results of this analysis demonstrate that the preservation of both traditional and colonial buildings is imperative for the sustainable conservation of urban heritage given contemporary environmental concerns.

In Chapter Nine, Honey Fadaie focuses on Persian gardens, assessing selected pavilions according to climatic objectives and design parameters. She reflects on the many varieties and forms of these structures, which are designed according to environmental specificities in different regions of Iran. The results of this analysis reveal various passive cooling strategies inextricably linked to the geometrical shape of the gardens which enable these extroverted residential buildings to maximally benefit from fresh air flow during the hot seasons in arid Iranian regions. These features distinguish Persian garden pavilions as a unique element of sustainable heritage based on endogenous construction systems conducive to interior comfort.

The fourth and final part of the book brings together architects, urban planners and philosophical anthropologists. The contributors offer their perspectives on historic landscapes in India and Egypt, reflecting on conservation challenges and atmospheres in old cities.

Chapter Ten turns to the walled city Delhi, India, where Mrinalini Singh analyses the area of North Shahjahanabad, revealing a cultural heritage comprising rich historical, social, economic, religious and architectural values. She evaluates urban regeneration as a tool for developing and managing this historic urban environment and considers the city's assets and potential as a basis for sustainability. This heritage thus becomes more than a static assortment of buildings and urban spaces, focalising dynamic social, economic and cultural spheres that continually drive it towards its full potential.

In Chapter Eleven, Amany Abdelsadeq S. Hussein investigates Port Said, located at the Mediterranean end of the Suez Canal in Egypt. Her analysis draws upon UNESCO's 2011 Recommendation on the Historic Urban Landscape, which integrates heritage conservation strategies within the wider framework of city development. The application of this approach as a tool for the conservation and management of historic areas in Port Said entails consideration of cultural, social and economic values and their dynamic interactions. It also explores the possible adjustment of current local policies to achieve real urban heritage preservation.

Chapter Twelve, the final chapter of the book, offers theoretical insights into the atmospheres of historic cities, furnishing reflections on authenticity, sense of place and other concepts central to contemporary issues of urban heritage and conservation explored in the preceding chapters. Irina Oznobikhina elucidates the emotive aspect of dynamic urban landscapes, demonstrating that old city atmospheres are not limited to sacred architecture and monuments or their historical value but also encompass local identities and cultures on a deeper spatial and atmospheric level.

Evaluating the chapters of this book from a comparative perspective yields a wealth of insights spanning theories and practices, both from architectural and urban perspectives.

Indeed, traditional architecture in North African old towns constitutes an inexhaustible source of lessons concerning energy saving and a sustainably built environment. However, the traditional buildings in these historic cities are subjected to several architectural transformations to fit an international style that does not correspond to

Mediterranean climate specificities. The latter is characterised by two distinct periods: the hot and dry period and the temperate and rainy period, with a significant temperature contrast and relatively high humidity, observed throughout the year, especially in the summertime.

Similarly, several historic cities in the Middle East are subjected to geographic, social and economic pressures. This architectural heritage undergoes profound alteration of its landscape due to the construction of many high-rise buildings to the detriment of historic buildings, destroyed despite their high architectural value and European and Islamic characteristics.

Decolonising architecture means liberating it from the historical legacy of colonialism and the resulting built framework and physical features, with the objective of conceiving 'culturally appropriate' projects. It involves reevaluating the architectural processes that dominated the construction techniques and materials during colonial rule, by working with the people who occupied these countries at the time of their contact with the outside world, while redefining their cultural identities, and while prioritising their local knowledge.

In this book, the contributors do not focus on the concept of decolonisation and its contemporary architectural and urban production. They concentrated instead on common approaches to solving issues related to heritage conservation, emphasising the local specificities of historic cities, as well as the role of civil society and public and private stakeholders in the conservation process.

In this sense, the methodologies used in the chapters emerge as especially promising for heritage studies because they provide valuable insights into the most important urban, architectural and cultural aspects of the Middle East, North Africa, South Asia and Western Europe and their impact on historical cities' past, present, and future. For instance, SWOT analyses could be an effective tool in recovery processes and heritage management, while transect walks and social surveys can be valuable alternatives in participatory sustainable planning processes and heritage conservation.

Moreover, the contributors emphasised common threats and constraints, related to the local aspects of contemporary cities and their sustainability. For instance, the planning of suburban areas was intended to improve the quality of modern life in opposition to traditional cities.

However, these modern neighbourhoods are perceived today as energy-consuming residential spaces, primarily due to the increased presence of motor vehicles.

In the era of energy transition, traditional urban fabrics are regaining value as urban heritage symbols of density and proximity. However, the sustainability of these areas is under scrutiny due to concerns about buildings' energy consumption, urban heat islands and lack of accessibility.

Today, old neighbourhoods at the 'human scale' are recognized for their value as urban heritage exemplifying density. Moreover, eco-neighbourhoods are developing on the outskirts of cities, based on traditional urban heritage, with lower buildings in smaller housing estates.

These contributors from different disciplines and countries have come together to share the latest knowledge on urban heritage and sustainability according to specific localisations, geographic and climatic distinctions, as well as people and stakeholder engagement with heritage conservation.

The COVID-19 pandemic posed considerable challenges in the course of this book's publication, necessitating that all editorial and related processes be carried out via email among contributors in different countries and time zones. Nevertheless, in navigating these obstacles and realising the completion of the project, I gained profound insights into different but complementary research on urban heritage and diverse theoretical and operational approaches that all aim to develop and foster a human-centric culture of heritage. I hope that this book will have a similar impact on the readership of Open Book Publishers.

I. HISTORIC HERITAGE: URBAN DEVELOPMENT AND SOCIAL EFFECTS

1. Mumbai: A Metropolis Forged in Lasting Fragments of *Urbs Prima in Indis*

Devashree Vyas

Through a partly chronological narrative of the city of Mumbai, this chapter explores the term 'old city' in correlation with the diverse eras of the city's history, focusing on typologies of physical and built heritage that have defined its changing landscape and continue to be a part of the global metropolis. The city's physical and social transformation encompasses tangible and intangible manifestations of various indelible heritage-making practices associated with its people, but disparities are evident in the prominence accorded to some aspects of heritage in the academic and professional discourse on the city.

Through a focus on four distinctive instances of built heritage in Mumbai, this chapter highlights inequities in conservation approaches, and offers possible explanations. The examples are chosen based on their significance in key components of Mumbai's built fabric and urban growth patterns and their expression of intangible heritage embedded within the tangible. This discussion underscores the general inattention to intangible cultural heritage within the policy and legislative systems governing heritage in Mumbai, despite the growing importance of the subject in global discourses and intrinsic presence in the city itself. Central to the idea of the 'old city' is the need to identify the old within it. This chapter posits that the prevailing notion of heritage in the city derives from non-contextual and colonial influences, leading to the blatant under-recognition of its heritage elements and the misrepresentation of its values.

 https://doi.org/10.11647/OBP.0412.01

This chapter recognises the extensive complexities associated with heritage discourses related to a city like Mumbai, with centuries of dynamic history and abiding relevance to many global trends and domains of knowledge. While acknowledging that the act of drawing attention to disparities in conservation approaches is at once an attempt to preserve an 'old city' and insufficient for the holistic conservation of such cities universally, this chapter attempts to shed light on the situation through the illustrative examples presented in the subsequent sections.

The Changing Landscape of Mumbai and an Array of Built Heritage

If heritage constitutes a field of contestation, the battle in Mumbai begins with the land.[1] Among the earliest records of the region constituting the present-day area of Mumbai is its mention as 'Heptanesia', a name introduced by Ptolemy in AD 150.[2] The designation referred to the archipelago of seven islands which once made up the city—Colaba, Old Women's Island, Bombay, Mazagaon, Parel, Worli and Mahim. The oldest known inhabitants of these islands are the *Kolis*, a community of agricultural practitioners and fisherfolk. To date, their presence is felt in the city through their residential settlements called *Koliwadas*, situated in various locations, constituting an important element of the city's built heritage. Subsequent influences on this built fabric include the Buddhist, Hindu and Muslim dynasties originating from various regions in the Indian subcontinent which settled in Mumbai, followed by colonial powers—mainly the Portuguese and the British. According to Nakamura, 'These embattled, enmeshed, and accumulated histories have marked the landscape with rock-cut caves, temples, mosques, churches, water tanks, forts and urban forms that now make up the more monumental aspects of the urban landscape of Mumbai'.[3] Recognising

1 Carolyn Nakamura, 'Mumbai's Quiet Histories: Critical Intersections of the Urban Poor, Historical Struggles, and Heritage Spaces', *Journal of Social Archaeology*, 14 (2014), 271–95, under the section entitled 'From the Seven Isles to Mumbai: A History of Struggle and Its Effacement', https://doi.org/10.1177%2F1469605314539419

2 José Gerson da Cunha, *The Origin of Bombay* (New Delhi: Asian Educational Services, 1993).

3 Nakamura, 'Mumbai's Quiet Histories', under the section entitled 'From the Seven Isles to Mumbai: A History of Struggle and Its Effacement'.

the vast diversity of that has arisen from these various contexts, the scope of this chapter is limited to specific aspects of heritage. These include the forts of Mumbai and the British colonial architecture, in terms of tangible heritage, as well as the associated cultural and memory-making practices that form the foundation of the city's intangible heritage.

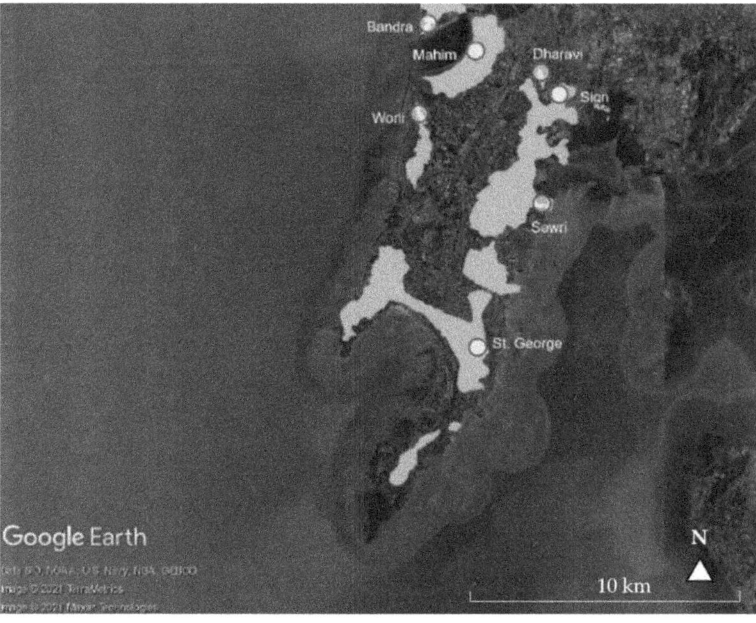

Fig. 1.1 Graphical representation superimposed on the Mumbai mainland satellite image and locations of forts. Author's illustration, based on Google Earth (2021), CC BY-NC-ND.

The forts of Mumbai, located in different parts of the city, are among the earliest physical traces integral to the historical narrative of Mumbai's evolution, that is, its transformation from the archipelago of seven islands to its defined landmass today. Eleven forts were constructed throughout the history of Mumbai, built and controlled by various dynasties spanning from the twelfth to the eighteenth century. Archival maps of the city, as indicated above, illustrate that each fort was situated along the sea or riverine coasts of individual islands, reflecting the defensive and protective strategies of fort architecture. These forts have played a central role in land and sea skirmishes between the numerous dynastic and colonial powers in Mumbai and the larger struggle to maintain power over the seven islands between the indigenous Marathas and the colonial Portuguese and British Empires, which has been entrenched in associated discourses.[4] The British gained control of the Bombay islands in 1661[5] and, subsequently, the northern regions of Salsette. The Hornby Vellard engineering project commenced in 1782 and aimed at uniting the islands into a single mass.[6] The significance of the forts cannot be overstated in their moulding of the history of Mumbai. Today, however, they remain in varying states of ruin, with some sites and structures facing illegal encroachments and with little to no interpretation onsite. Therefore, the evident apathy regarding the conservation of these forts remains a matter of concern, as it overlooks their instrumental role in defining Mumbai's subsequent narrative and their lasting imprints on the city's built fabric.

Contrastingly, the wave of British colonial architecture that followed, interspersed with Neo-Classical, Victorian Gothic and Indo-Saracenic styles, is thought to have 'created the nostalgic character of Mumbai's historic centre'.[7] This architecture continues to hold a very prominent position in the heritage discourse of the city.

To better understand the British Empire and its intent to establish Mumbai as the first urban city in India (*urbs prima in Indis*), it is essential to explore the impact of colonisation on the built environment and the socio-cultural dynamics of a colonised area. These dynamics are governed by the convergence of the colonisers' habitat characteristics with the local context. In other words, the layout and architecture of Mumbai that emerged as a result of British colonial governance bears significant resemblance to the Victorian Era of London.[8] The underlying power dynamics rooted in colonialism, including the colonial power's need to assert dominance and the inherent differences between the coloniser and the colonised, especially in order to 'rouse the awe and

---

4 Bhalchandra V. Kulkarni, *Mumbai Parisaratil Arthat Ekekalchya Firanganatil Kille* (Mumbai: Maharashtra State Directorate of Archaeology and Museums, 2009).

5 The Editors of Encyclopaedia Britannica, 'History of Mumbai' (2015), *Britannica*, https://www.britannica.com/place/Mumbai/History (para 3 of 10).

6 Sharada Dwivedi and Rahul Mehrotra, *Bombay: The Cities Within* (Bombay: Eminence Designs Pvt. Ltd., 2001).

7 Joe Bindloss, 'Mumbai's Deco Dreams: 2000 Years of Architecture in India's Metropolis' (6 March 2018), *Lonely Planet*, https://www.lonelyplanet.com/articles/mumbais-deco-dreams-2000-years-of-architecture-in-indias-mega-metropolis

8 Melanie D'Souza, 'Colonial Architecture: From Bombay to Britain' (2013), *Academia*, https://www.academia.edu/16435215/Colonial_Architecture_From_Britain_to_Bombay

wonder of the subject population',[9] form the basis for the architectural character of the city in the nineteenth century.

In the second half of the nineteenth century, a growing sense of disillusionment with the existing architectural policies induced a greater interest in understanding and adapting indigenous Indian architectural craftsmanship. This was exemplified by the incorporation of Indian motifs in colonial buildings, as seen in the Chhatrapati Shivaji Maharaj Terminus (formerly Victoria Terminus) and the Brihanmumbai Municipal Corporation building.[10] This blend of European architecture with elements of Indian origin came to be recognised as the Indo-Saracenic style and remains largely unique to Mumbai. However, despite the incremental representation of Indian craftsmanship and structural techniques in later examples like Chhatrapati Shivaji Maharaj Vastu Sangrahalaya (formerly Prince of Wales Museum) and the Gateway of India, the architecture itself remained conceptually European, lacking true synthesis with Indian architecture. Over time, this style gradually faded away.[11]

The nineteenth and twentieth centuries saw the rise of industrial textile mills, bringing forth 'new meanings of citizenship for workers'.[12] The prevailing perception of heritage in Mumbai centres around the colonial architectural heritage, notably the monumental Gothic, Neo-Classical and Victorian Gothic structures constructed mainly in the nineteenth century. This perspective, however, undermines the distinctive urban patterns that evolved in Mumbai through the tenement housing, neighbourhoods and streets associated with mill lands and workers. These patterns in socio-cultural formations that are 'central to the identity and memory of generations',[13] and yet the heritage elements remain under-recognised today. Once recognised as 'neoliberal visions of urban development',[14] the heritage of the mills has been significantly eroded through commercial and residential real estate developments.

9 Samita Gupta, 'Some Indian Influences on Colonial Architecture in Bombay', *Bulletin of the Deccan College Research Institute*, 47/48 (1988), 99–108 (p. 99).

10 Ibid., p. 100.

11 Ibid., p. 102.

12 Mark Frazier, 'The Political Heritage of Textile Districts: Shanghai and Mumbai', *Built Heritage*, 3 (2019), 62–75 (p. 62), https://link.springer.com/content/pdf/10.1186/BF03545744.pdf

13 Ibid., p. 62.

14 Ibid.

The mill districts shaped the city's structure, influencing transportation and settlement patterns, as well as served as loci of ideological and political currents pivotal to the Indian independence movement. While the preservation of certain mill structures through adaptive reuse has been proposed, the focus remains on the tangible rather than the intangible heritage. That is, conserving the structures and the lands takes precedence over memory-making experiences and records of individuals and their intrinsic lived experiences.[15]

In sharp contrast to the characteristics, attributes and conservation approaches associated with mill district heritage, Mumbai's Art Deco heritage, which dates back to the 1930s and 1940s, has seen an incremental rise in recognition in recent decades. The Art Deco architectural style 'offered a means of expressing a local yet cosmopolitan statement of modernity, a complicated one that bore witness to the city's continuing place within commercial and cultural economies of Empires'.[16] In the post-war context of Mumbai, it represented growth and 'aspirations for the city to be modern, sophisticated and cosmopolitan'.[17]

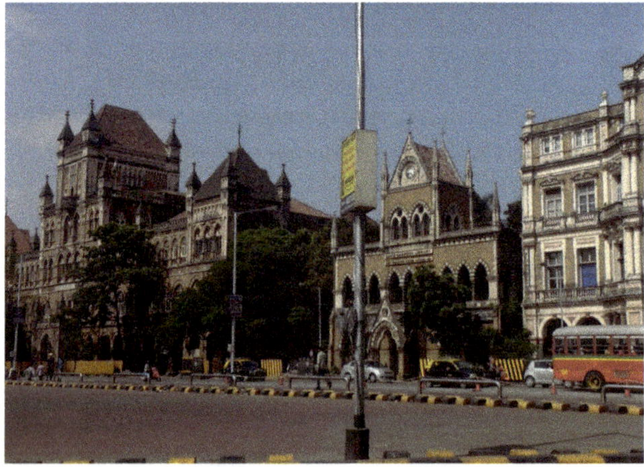

Fig. 1.2 Examples of buildings in Victorian Gothic architecture—Elphinstone College, David Sassoon Library and Army Navy Building (Kala Ghoda). Author's photograph, 2018, CC BY-NC-ND.

15 Manish Chalana, 'Of Mills and Malls: The Future of Urban Industrial Heritage in Neoliberal Mumbai', *Future Anterior*, 9 (2012), 1–15.

16 Michael Windover, 'Exchanging Looks: "Art Dekho" Movie Theatres in Bombay', *Architectural History*, 52 (2009), 201–32 (p. 202).

17 Clarissa Pelino, 'Built Heritage and Multiple Identities in Mumbai: Material Culture and Conservation Practices', in *Art and Economics in the City: New Cultural Maps, Urban Studies*, ed. by Caterina Benincasa, Gianfranco Neri and Michele Trimarchi (Bielefeld: transcript, 2019), pp. 69–82 (p. 69).

Reflecting further on the extensive discourses surrounding Art Deco, Benton *et al.* argue that its foundation in new technologies and its promotion of social change reinforce the style's pragmatism as an 'address to the "individualism" of desire' and a 'stand for democratic values'.[18] This may align with the contextual milieu of Mumbai during the emergence of Art Deco architecture within the cityscape. Therefore, the cultural significance of Art Deco heritage encompasses its representation of the social context at the time, defining the city's identity and leaning towards political independence from British colonial rule while attempting to establish a stable middle ground.

Observable Disparities in Conservation Approaches

Recognising the importance of retaining, interpreting and even preserving built heritage associated with the nuances of a colonial past, this chapter aims to explore an observable imbalance in the nature of heritage protection accorded to varying heritages. A comprehensive framework of tangible and intangible aspects may be ascribed to heritage within Mumbai and its old city. Even when focusing on architectural typologies such as pre-colonial forts, colonial public buildings in Victorian Gothic and Indo-Saracenic styles, mill districts and Art Deco buildings, the disparity in preservation approaches is evident.

The Burra Charter, widely considered a groundbreaking approach towards defining, redefining and interpreting heritage and related concepts, was adopted by the International Council on Monuments and Sites (ICOMOS) (Australia) and periodically updated. This framework afforded a definite identity to the interpretation of heritage through its definition of the term 'cultural significance',[19] emphasising values for past, present and future generations in terms of aesthetics, historicity, science, society and spirituality. Evaluating cultural significance in this regard, the aforementioned typologies, which constitute the focus of built heritage within Mumbai, may be considered intrinsic to the city's heritage discourse. However, there is a clear distinction in the extent to which governance-based conservation approaches in

18 Charlotte Benton, Tim Benton and Ghislaine Wood, *Art Deco 1910–1939* (London: V&A Publishing, 2015), under 'The Style and the Age'.

19 Australia ICOMOS, *The Burra Charter: The Australia ICOMOS Charter for Places of Cultural Significance with Associated Guidelines and Code on the Ethics of Co-existence* (Burwood: Australia ICOMOS, 2000).

Mumbai encompass each typology. For instance, the forts of Mumbai have been subject to insensitive preservation measures with little to no onsite interpretation and are constantly threatened by increasing illegal encroachment. Meanwhile, the post-colonial buildings of the British Empire are periodically restored and maintained adequately. While the forts' respective timelines and the functional differences of the two typologies suggest the need for distinctive approaches, based on variations in structural and aesthetic integrity, a cursory glance at each fort indicates concerning levels of neglect. The forts, despite their state of ruin, possess considerable potential for conveying the city's historical narrative through interpretive media and could conceivably serve as cultural and recreational areas in the space-starved city of Mumbai. Intervention from the responsible authorities would help ascertain their due place in the city's fabric.

Addressing further the lacunae within the governmental administration of heritage in Mumbai, the Mumbai Heritage Conservation Committee is the municipal body responsible for framing regulations and approving permits for work associated with heritage structures. Currently, it has no framework for institutional governance or the documentation of intangible heritage at the city level. Thus, when comparing the conservation statuses of the mill heritage and Art Deco structures in Mumbai, the latter is supported by citizen-driven initiatives, which have enabled recognition, interpretation and documentation.

The Art Deco Mumbai Trust has undertaken extensive documentation efforts to map Art Deco heritage within the city, situating it within the global context and supporting the nomination and subsequent management of the World Heritage Site, the Victorian Gothic and Art Deco Ensembles of Mumbai. There is, however, an evident disparity in terms of civic privilege and resources between the respective communities associated with Art Deco structures and mill heritage. The former includes resident-owners and experts with long-standing connections to the sites and a deep understanding of the concepts of architecture and heritage. Hence, there is an imbalance between people's heritage and the heritage deemed sufficiently valuable to receive protection withing the formal framework governing Mumbai's heritage. The 'old city' of Mumbai exists not only in the monuments showcasing aspects of its glorious past, but also in the ruins that redefined its physical existence and the residences of its working population, which extended the city's boundaries and shaped its urban patterns. Therefore, within the ambit of this chapter, it is posited that a profound understanding of Mumbai, the 'old city', encompassing its diversity, will not only reflect its heritage but also guide its future growth.

Pondering the Lacunae in the Heritage Discourses of Mumbai

> The conservation-development debate comes into play in full force at this level, with the scarcity of housing, pressures from real estate, and political loggerheads with conservation needs.[20]

The built heritage of Mumbai, a tangible manifestation of its broader heritage landscape, conveys a continuity dating back centuries. Nevertheless, it can readily be regarded as under constant threat, resulting from consequences of the city's metropolitan and global character. The transformative impact of globalisation and the incremental influx of migrants to the city from elsewhere in the nation have placed considerable pressures on the city's land and existing infrastructure, effectively engendering a conflict between the desire to conserve of the city's older elements and the necessity of development to support the city's growing population.[21]

As Bahatia claims, 'It is essential to recognise the layered growth of cultures and traditions within the built environment before further developing our metropolitan areas'.[22] Since Mumbai's inception, resident populations, shifts in power relations and demographic fluctuations have led to significant changes and varying narratives within the city's historical context, which have left a variety of imprints on its built environment and socio-cultural dynamics. Heritage and heritage sites also hold value for the city through their contributions to individual

---

20 Meha Mathur, 'Heritage Laws: British Bulwarks Well Preserved' (21 August 2020), *The Leaflet*, https://www.theleaflet.in/heritage-laws-british-bulwarks-well-preserved/#

21 Harshad Bhatia, 'Banganga: The "Whole" as a "Part" in Metropolitan Mumbai', *Journal of Architectural Conservation*, 7 (2001), 72–87 (p. 72), https://doi.org/10.1080/13556207.2001.10785287

22 Ibid., p. 73.

societal and global well-being. Therefore, the civic discourse regarding heritage must be redefined to encompass its cultural and societal value beyond historical and aesthetic significance.

A root cause behind the concerning state of heritage conservation in Mumbai is the evident sense of indifference among citizens and authorities. This can be observed through various examples, from the hazardous fires over the years that have led to the destruction of entire structures due to negligent electrical retrofitting in old buildings, to numerous instances of crude facade treatment while preserving historic buildings. Due concern for heritage conservation from governmental authorities is thus observably lacking.[23] This apathy is perpetuated through the existing Development Control and Promotion Regulations—2034, which govern development, construction, maintenance and preservation within the city.[24] These regulations are overwhelmingly focused on incentivising built-up areas and facilitating the conduct of business in real estate development. The civic government uses these policies to integrate the heritage-centric Mumbai Heritage Conservation Committee function. While initiatives and pertinent decisions regarding the conservation of built heritage constitute a part of the Committee's activities, the systematic framework lacks an understanding of the concept of heritage, its ability to create meaning within society and its contribution to public well-being. A closer examination of this framework reveals that the legacy of the legislation governing the preservation of Mumbai's built heritage is colonial.

The Ancient Monuments Preservation Act of 1904, enacted during British colonial rule under the helm of Alexander Curzon, laid the foundations for heritage preservation in India. While the Government of India has introduced subsequent acts at the national and state level in the post-independence era, the definitive basis continues to resonate with the ideology imposed by the British colonial government. For

23 Sharad Vyas, 'Govt Apathy, Law Undermine Preservation of Heritage Buildings' (10 February 2011), *Times of India*, https://timesofindia.indiatimes.com/city/mumbai/govt-apathy-law-undermine-preservation-of-heritage-buildings/articleshow/7464144.cms

24 Brihanmumbai Municipal Corporation, *Development Control and Promotion Regulations—2034* (Mumbai: Brihanmumbai Municipal Corporation, 2017), pp. 351–55 http://www.udri.org/wp-content/uploads/2017/03/DCPR_English2034.pdf

instance, monuments are considered part of a settlement rather than isolated structures within their cultural context,[25] and non-monumental heritage buildings with 'unique architectural features, historical significance or a cultural connect with the city of neighbourhood'[26] are under-recognised.

The 1995 Heritage Regulations for Greater Bombay, a milestone in the country's heritage trajectory, introduced provisions and grading systems for the protection of all heritage buildings, including monuments of national importance and residential structures and settlements of local cultural significance. However, the Development Control and Promotion Regulations—2034 have now diluted these protections in the interests of real estate development, further undermining the Mumbai Heritage Conservation Committee's role.

The ideology underlying this equation can be traced back from ideas of holistic conservation and may be attributed to the notion of 'Authorised Heritage Discourse'[27] (AHD), which asserts the existence of an authorised heritage discourse established through the dominant influence of the Western Eurocentric perspective over the professional realm of heritage. Professional heritage practitioners are recognised as expert authorities at the exclusion of the people and communities who define the heritage intended to be preserved and protected. Tendencies toward the authorised heritage discourse also exist within the systematic framework of Mumbai's approach to conservation, largely as a result of the colonial influence that shaped the city, its heritage and its perception of heritage. Monumental buildings aligned with predefined and prominently Western notions of aesthetic appeal are prioritised over other distinctive examples of heritage of and for the masses. This discourse, which disregards the cultural significance and relevance of certain examples and aspects of heritage objects and practices, has become so ingrained that non-monumental buildings are rarely perceived as heritage by the general populace.

---

25 Mathur, 'Heritage Laws'.

26 Ibid.

27 Laurajane Smith, *Uses of Heritage* (London and New York: Routledge, 2006).

Unexplored Discourse: Intangible Cultural Heritage in Mumbai

While there is limited scholarship on non-monumental built heritage in Mumbai, there is virtually none discussing intangible heritage in the city. Numerous traditions intrinsic to Mumbai have remained largely unchanged through centuries of transformation and development, including festivals and religious practices, exemplified by *Narali Purnima*[28] (ritual offerings of coconuts to the sea) and the worship of indigenous deities like the *Khoklaai*[29] (prayers dedicated towards recovery and healing from a cough). Given that 'the AHD defines heritage as material, non-renewable and fragile',[30] intangible cultural heritage concepts are excluded from the prevalent approaches and discourse surrounding heritage conservation, attested to by its conspicuous absence from the policies and practices governing heritage in Mumbai.

This chapter, through its exploration of Mumbai's heritage, supports the notion that 'all heritage is intangible'.[31] Delving deeper into this chapter's focused typologies of built heritage, intangible cultural associations with each typology become apparent.

The forts of Mumbai, long recognised for their role in the city's history of conquests, have since also become communal and recreational spaces inviting public engagement and interaction. The forts at Bandra and Sewri have noteworthy recreational value due to their locations and have also become emblematic of civic activism for the efforts to protect them in recent history. This indicates a cultural significance defined not solely through historical events but also by their continued presence.[32]

The question of British colonial architecture raises concerns about notions of 'colonial nostalgia'.[33] Reviving colonial symbols is recognised

28 Nilesh Bane, 'Heritage beyond Brick and Mortar' (7 September 2018), *Observer Research Foundation*, https://www.orfonline.org/expert-speak/43802-heritage-beyond-brick-mortar/

29 Ibid.

30 Laurajane Smith, 'Intangible Heritage: A Challenge to the Authorized Discourse?', *Revistad'Etnologia de Catalunya*, 40 (2014), 133–42 (p. 135), https://www.raco.cat/index.php/RevistaEtnologia/article/download/293392/381920/0

31 Ibid., p. 141.

32 NAGAR, *A Rejuvenation Plan for the Historic Forts of Mumbai: A Tribute to Our Rich and Varied Heritage* (Mumbai: NAGAR, 2019).

33 William Cunningham Bissell, 'Engaging Cultural Nostalgia', *Cultural Anthropology*, 20 (2005), 215–48.

as problematic, with the potential to perpetuate the discourse of colonialism.[34] The continuous engagement of Indian citizens and Mumbai residents with British colonial architecture form part of the memory-making processes which connect layers of intangible heritage to the built heritage. For this reason, these buildings hold cultural significance beyond the colonial discourse. However, it is also necessary to establish a contextual discourse that will eliminate the removal of colonial discourse. In other words, while the historic colonial buildings may be preserved, their interpretation must be redefined to include their dissonant past and the populace's diverse interactions with these structures since and currently.

A further dichotomy in recognising intangible heritage associations lies in the relevance to the community at the centre of the discourse. Heritage oriented around the mill history is mapped through mill lands and *chawls*, the predominate form of housing within the mill districts. Its architecture consists of habitable rooms and serviceable communal areas for each *chawl*, with a central courtyard or *verandah*. Despite architectural documentation, there is little record of the memories and cultural aspects of community life within these spaces.[35]

The collective region comprising the mill districts of Parel, Tardeo, Byculla and Lalbaug were called 'Girangaon', which translates to the 'village of mills' in Marathi, the regional language. The region encompassed a 'culture that both maintained the practices of villages from which the residents came and new hybridities',[36] which resulted from interactions between migrant workers and their families from different parts of India. While the name 'Girangaon' still exists in the city's geographical vocabulary, the closure of mills in the 1980s initiated an arduous process of transforming the mill lands, complicated by ownership disputes. Cultural traces of 'community-organized drama, troupes, theatres and gymnasia'[37] were imbibed in the city's intangible cultural heritage, persistent yet unrecorded.

In contrast, an extensive and growing repository of research and memories is associated with Art Deco architecture in Mumbai, which

34 Charlotte M. Echtner and Pushkala Prasad, 'The Context of Third World Tourism Marketing', *Annals of Tourism Research*, 30 (2003), 660–82.

35 Frazier, 'Political Heritage', p. 67.

36 Ibid., p. 69.

37 Ibid.

may be attributed to citizen-led initiatives.[38] This is further indication of disparities in the processes of memory-making, fuelled by privilege and power dynamics. These factors determine which narratives are documented, shared and by whom, resulting in the neglect and gradual erosion of other narratives over time.

Such instances, where the integrity of specific heritage is compromised, are not limited to the typologies or communities under consideration here, as indeed, the authoritative discourse prevails across heritage concepts relevant to Mumbai. For instance, individuals and families in the Parsi ethnoreligious community in Mumbai were once patrons of significant buildings during the British colonial era, indicating efforts to integrate 'Indian and British art, design, and culture'.[39] While these buildings are duly preserved as parts of the city's historic district and neighbourhoods, elements of Parsi heritage are losing their heritage value. The proposed infrastructural development of the city's metro railway has repeatedly threatened the structural integrity of the community's *Agyaaris* (fire temples).[40] The continuity of ceremonial practices, especially funerary traditions, also faces challenges owing to the absence of the city's vulture populations.[41] Furthermore, there has been a decline in the presence of Irani cafes, quiet, unassuming landmarks in the city's bustling culture over the past few decades.[42] The dichotomy in the perception and preservation of heritage through the selective gaze and presence of those who shape the discourse remains readily apparent in Mumbai's heritage landscape.

---

38 Art Deco Mumbai Trust, 'Research | Art Deco' (2020), *Art Deco Mumbai*, https://www.artdecomumbai.com/research/#all

39 Nicole Vance, 'Integrators of Design: Parsi Patronage of Bombay's Architectural Ornament' (master's thesis, Brigham Young University, 2016), https://scholarsarchive.byu.edu/etd/6053

40 Manthank Mehta, 'Mumbai: Parsi Community Gets Partial Relief; Metro Station to Shift Away from Fire Temple' (28 January 2019), *Times of India*, https://timesofindia.indiatimes.com/city/mumbai/mumbai-parsi-community-gets-partial-relief-metro-rail-authority-informs-sc/articleshow/67728206.cms

41 Bachi Karkaria, 'Death in the City: How a Lack of Vultures Threatens Mumbai's "Towers of Silence"' (26 January 2015), *The Guardian*, https://www.theguardian.com/cities/2015/jan/26/death-city-lack-vultures-threatens-mumbai-towers-of-silence

42 Karen Dias, 'In Pictures: Mumbai's Dying Irani Cafes' (20 March 2014), *Al Jazeera*, https://www.aljazeera.com/gallery/2014/3/20/in-pictures-mumbais-dying-irani-cafes

Conclusion: Whose Heritage? Recognising the 'Old City' of Mumbai beyond its Tangible Fabric

Mumbai's distinctive character as 'a palimpsest of different political regimes, economical ways of production, and architectural styles'[43] gives rise to varying notions of formally and informally identified heritage, where the former is represented in the systemic framework, and the latter remains unrecognised. In Mumbai, urban history begins at the amalgamation of its seven islands, the conjoined mass that now harbours a megapolis. The identity of the islands, despite centuries of change, endure. The dramatically transforming cityscape of Mumbai is at once an 'old city' and grappling with increasing levels of urbanisation, competing with global trends while retaining much of its built heritage and traditional character among its population. These kaleidoscopically interwoven notions of heritage, both tangible and intangible, are indicators of evolving patterns. As an integral part of 'people's cognitive landscapes',[44] they are foundational to memory associated with heritage concepts, and yet are presently undervalued in the city's conservation approach.

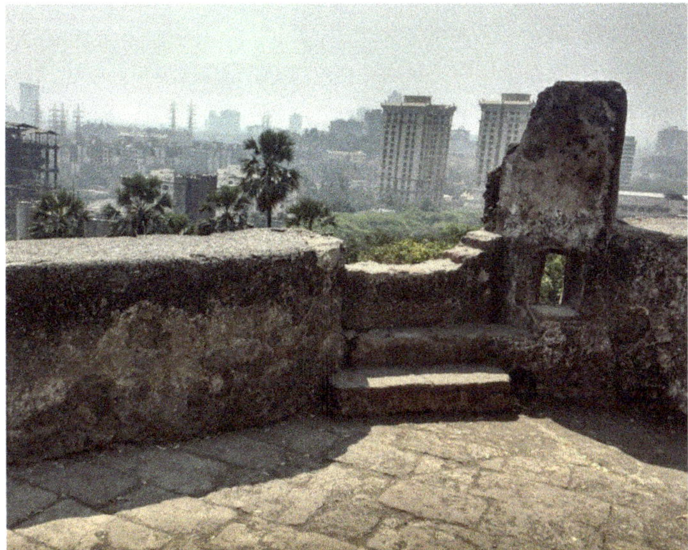

Fig. 1.3 View from Sion Fort, a representation of how the forts remain a part of the original islands before Mumbai's landmass was transformed entirely. Author's photograph, 2017, CC BY-NC-ND.

43 Pelino, p. 71.
44 Ibid., p. 70.

The instances covered within the scope of this chapter and beyond demonstrate that although the metropolitan city of Mumbai possesses centuries of history, epitomising the idea of the 'old city', its transformative and regenerative processes over time are also an intrinsic part of its contemporary heritage. The rapidity of this transformation, however, has also led to a significant loss of heritage, due primarily to an innate discourse aligned with the AHD. This has been a cause of misrecognition and misrepresentation of the heritage itself, consistently challenging its identity as an 'old city'.

The legislative structures governing heritage in Mumbai comprise a limited representation of heritage. While some citizens have appreciably taken on the onus of preserving and articulating the value of their heritage, this opportunity remains limited to those with the capacity to do so, often owing to their positions of privilege. The four typologies explored in this chapter, while not exhaustive, collectively highlight the city's diverse heritage amid the prevailing concerns of urban development and conservation.

The forts of Mumbai, remnants of an earlier form of the city itself, continue to invite the engagement and appreciation of citizens and yet remain ignored and endangered. The colonial structures, representing a sense of grandeur and monumentality, are duly preserved, but their interpretive narrative omits the connections with Indians in their construction and usage. The mill districts were instrumental in shaping the city's industrial identity and resultant growth patterns. Nevertheless, the abandoned structures have been removed on account of their low real estate value, and their lived spaces have suffered a loss of identity, replaced with conventional and even unhealthy tenements for the residents without recording the nature of the community spaces they once encompassed. The Art Deco heritage is an example of due resurgence, while highlighting the role of power dynamics in producing such examples. Throughout these considerations, the notion of intangible cultural heritage remains absent from the formal structures.

In these typologies, there is a transfusion of colonial, post-colonial and contemporary heritages, identified separately yet melded together in perception and interpretation today. Mumbai, and its identity as the 'old city', demands consensus on understanding its historical layers. The nuanced scope of heritage includes tangible, intangible, monumental, non-monumental, glorious and dissonant aspects. The land of Mumbai has undergone centuries of profound transformation, encompassing within its borders narratives of a vibrant, diverse populace. The new subsumes the old, becoming both a part of and participant in the ongoing evolution of what eventually become the old. This cycle endures, as it always has.

Bibliography

Art Deco Mumbai Trust, 'Research | Art Deco' (2020), *Art Deco Mumbai*, https://www.artdecomumbai.com/research/#all

Australia ICOMOS, *The Burra Charter: The Australia ICOMOS Charter for Places of Cultural Significance with Associated Guidelines and Code on the Ethics of Co-existence* (Burwood: Australia ICOMOS, 2000).

Bane, Nilesh, 'Heritage beyond Brick and Mortar' (7 September 2018), *Observer Research Foundation*, https://www.orfonline.org/expert-speak/43802-heritage-beyond-brick-mortar/

Benton, Charlotte, Benton, Tim and Wood, Ghislaine, *Art Deco 1910-1939* (London: V&A Publishing, 2015).

Bhatia, Harshad, 'Banganga: The "Whole" as a "Part" in Metropolitan Mumbai', *Journal of Architectural Conservation*, 7 (2001), 72–87, https://doi.org/10.1080/13556207.2001.10785287

Bindloss, Joe, 'Mumbai's Deco Dreams: 2000 Years of Architecture in India's Metropolis' (6 March 2018), *Lonely Planet*, https://www.lonelyplanet.com/articles/mumbais-deco-dreams-2000-years-of-architecture-in-indias-mega-metropolis

Bissell, William Cunningham, 'Engaging Cultural Nostalgia', *Cultural Anthropology*, 20 (2005), 215–48, https://doi.org/10.1525/can.2005.20.2.215

Brihanmumbai Municipal Corporation, *Development Control and Promotion Regulations—2034* (Mumbai: Brihanmumbai Municipal Corporation, 2017), http://www.udri.org/wp-content/uploads/2017/03/DCPR_English2034.pdf

Chalana, Manish, 'Of Mills and Malls: The Future of Urban Industrial Heritage in Neoliberal Mumbai', *Future Anterior*, 9 (2012), 1–15.

da Cunha, José Gerson, *The Origin of Bombay* (New Delhi: Asian Educational Services, 1993).

Dias, Karen, 'In Pictures: Mumbai's Dying Irani Cafes' (20 March 2014), *Al Jazeera*, https://www.aljazeera.com/gallery/2014/3/20/in-pictures-mumbais-dying-irani-cafes

D'Souza, Melanie, 'Colonial Architecture: From Bombay to Britain' (2013), *Academia*, https://www.academia.edu/16435215/Colonial_Architecture_From_Britain_to_Bombay

Dwivedi, Sharada and Mehrotra, Rahul, *Bombay: The Cities Within* (Bombay: Eminence Designs Pvt. Ltd., 2001).

Echtner, Charlotte M. and Prasad, Pushkala, 'The Context of Third World Tourism Marketing', *Annals of Tourism Research*, 30 (2003), 660–82, http://dx.doi.org/10.1016/S0160-7383(03)00045-8

Editors of Encyclopaedia Britannica, 'History of Mumbai' (2015), *Britannica*, https://www.britannica.com/place/Mumbai/History

Frazier, Mark, 'The Political Heritage of Textile Districts: Shanghai and Mumbai', *Built Heritage*, 3 (2019), 62–75, https://link.springer.com/content/pdf/10.1186/BF03545744.pdf

Gupta, Samita, 'Some Indian Influences on Colonial Architecture in Bombay', *Bulletin of the Deccan College Research Institute*, 47/48 (1988), 99–108.

Karkaria, Bachi, 'Death in the City: How a Lack of Vultures Threatens Mumbai's "Towers of Silence"' (26 January 2015), *The Guardian*, https://www.theguardian.com/cities/2015/jan/26/death-city-lack-vultures-threatens-mumbai-towers-of-silence

Kulkarni, Bhalchandra V., *Mumbai Parisaratil Arthat Ekekalchya Firanganatil Kille* (Mumbai: Maharashtra State Directorate of Archaeology and Museums, 2009).

Mathur, Meha, 'Heritage Laws: British Bulwarks Well Preserved', 21 August 2020), *The Leaflet*, https://www.theleaflet.in/heritage-laws-british-bulwarks-well-preserved/#

Mehta, Manthank, 'Mumbai: Parsi Community Gets Partial Relief; Metro Station to Shift Away from Fire Temple' (28 January 2019), *Times of India*, https://timesofindia.indiatimes.com/city/mumbai/mumbai-parsi-community-gets-partial-relief-metro-rail-authority-informs-sc/articleshow/67728206.cms

NAGAR, *A Rejuvenation Plan for the Historic Forts of Mumbai: A Tribute to Our Rich and Varied Heritage* (Mumbai: NAGAR, 2019)

Nakamura, Carolyn, 'Mumbai's Quiet Histories: Critical Intersections of the Urban Poor, Historical Struggles, and Heritage Spaces', *Journal of Social Archaeology*, 14 (2014), 271–95, https://doi.org/10.1177%2F1469605314539419

Pelino, Clarissa, 'Built Heritage and Multiple Identities in Mumbai: Material Culture and Conservation Practices', in *Art and Economics in the City: New Cultural Maps, Urban Studies*, ed. by Caterina Benincasa, Gianfranco Neri and Michele Trimarchi (Bielefeld: transcript, 2019), pp. 69–82.

Smith, Laurajane, *Uses of Heritage* (London and New York: Routledge, 2006), https://doi.org/10.4324/9780203602263

Smith, Laurajane, 'Intangible Heritage: A Challenge to the Authorized Discourse?', *Revistad'Etnologia de Catalunya*, 40 (2014), 133–42, https://www.raco.cat/index.php/RevistaEtnologia/article/download/293392/381920/0

Vance, Nicole, 'Integrators of Design: Parsi Patronage of Bombay's Architectural Ornament' (master's thesis, Brigham Young University, 2016), https://scholarsarchive.byu.edu/etd/6053

Vyas, Sharad, 'Govt Apathy, Law Undermine Preservation of Heritage Buildings' (10 February 2011), *Times of India*, https://timesofindia.indiatimes.com/city/mumbai/govt-apathy-law-undermine-preservation-of-heritage-buildings/articleshow/7464144.cms

Windover, Michael, 'Exchanging Looks: "Art Dekho" Movie Theatres in Bombay', *Architectural History*, 52 (2009), 201–32, https://doi.org/10.5749/futuante.9.1.0001

2. Urban Development of Palmyra, Post-war Damage Assessment and Recovery Policy

Ousama Rumayed

Introduction

Between 2015 and 2017, the Islamic State of Iraq and Syria (ISIS) twice occupied Syria, wreaking deliberate devastation which systematically targeted archaeological monuments without any regard for their cultural, historical, and socio-economic significance. The city of Palmyra, inscribed on the United Nations Educational, Scientific and Cultural Organization (UNESCO) World Heritage List in 1980, tragically found itself on the List of World Heritage in Danger in 2013, alongside five other sites in Syria.

ISIS carried out a systematic campaign to destroy Palmyra's architectural monuments in an attempt to obliterate the site's history, resulting in severe damage to several parts of the ancient city. Specifically, Palmyra's historical park, home to the most significant and magnificent ancient monuments, experienced massive explosions that destroyed many important historical monuments and left others in a state of partial destruction.

In addition to targeting archaeological sites, this violence was also directed at museum staff, facilities, and Palmyra residents, many of whom were displaced during the conflict. All of these events pose a considerable risk to the city's tangible and intangible heritage.

 https://doi.org/10.11647/OBP.0412.02

Recognizing the importance of Palmyra's revival, there is an urgent need for a recovery plan integrating the master planning process, science-based conservation strategies, and the leveraging of effective partnerships. This plan should aim to provide lasting heritage protection while remaining sufficiently flexible to address the complex challenges posed by this site.

Before any far-reaching proposal can be made for post-war reconstruction, it is essential to collect ample information about each of the archaeological site's monuments as well as about its historical development, urban style, and construction materials. This knowledge is integral to preserving Palmyra's authenticity and identity, which must be a priority in all reconstruction, restoration and preservation initiatives.

Historical Background

Palmyra, an iconic archaeological site with evidence of human settlement since the Palaeolithic and Neolithic eras, is one of the important cultural centres of the ancient world. Located in the heart of Syria, its geographical foundation is a natural spring at a mountain crossing in the desert of the Levant. This spring gave rise to a green oasis that became a place of rest between Iraq and the Levant and a caravan station between the Arabian Gulf and Persia and the Mediterranean Sea. It grew steadily along the trade routes, marking the crossroads of several civilisations.[1]

The history of Palmyra dates back to the late third millennium BC. The name 'Palmyra' appears on a plastered clay tablet found in Cappadocia (Anatolia) and in the documents of the Mari kingdom from the reign of Hammurabi in the eighteenth century BC, as well as in Assyrian records dating back to the twelfth century BC.[2]

1 Eid Mari, 'Palmyra as an Important Station on the Caravan's Road During the Second Millennium', in *Palmyra and the Silk Road, International Colloquium, Palmyra, 7–11 April 1992* (Damascus: DGAM, 1996), pp. 135–37.

2 Warwick Ball, *Rome in the East, The Transformation of an Empire* (London: Routledge, 2000), p. 74.

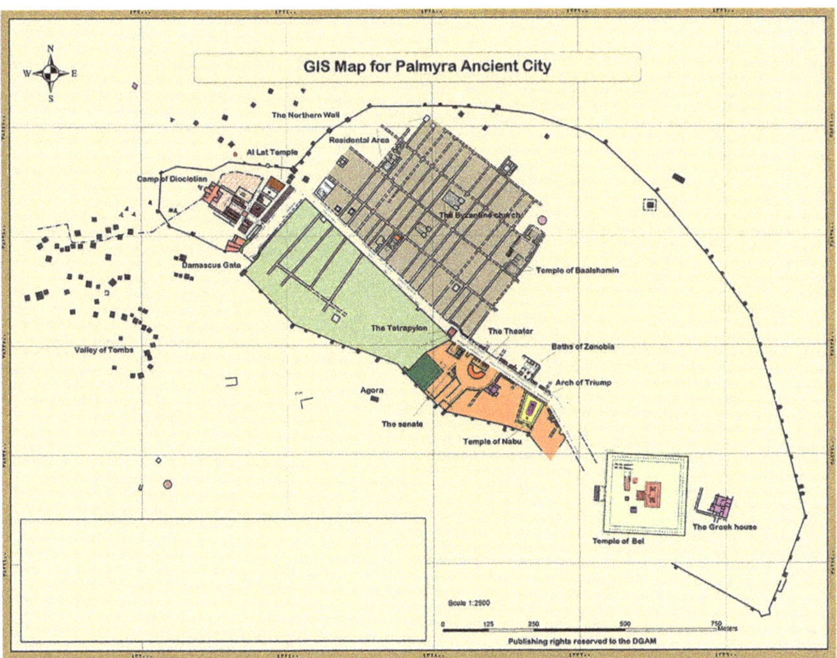

Fig. 2.1 Documentation Palmyra by GIS, IT Department. GIS Map by Directorate General of Antiquities and Museums-DGAM, 2014, CC BY-NC-ND.

Palmyra became renowned in the Greco-Roman period during the reign of Odaenathus (AD 252–268), who defeated Shapur, the Persian king, in AD 265. Rome granted him the title of Reformer of the East and the Vice Emperor, with command over the armies in natural Syria. He also assumed the title of King of Kings.[3]

Following Odaenathus's murder, his wife, Queen Zenobia, took the throne on behalf of her son, Wahb Allāt, who was eight years old at the time of his father's death. Zenobia established independence from Rome and ruled over the entire East, from the Gulf and the Levant to Egypt and Anatolia. In AD 271, her armies occupied Syria and Asia Minor, extending her domain to the Bosporus Strait. She and her son adopted the titles of the Roman emperors, which Roman Emperor Aurelian considered a challenge to his authority. He deployed his army

3 Nathanael J. Andrade, *Zenobia, Shooting Star of Palmyra* (London: Oxford University Press, 2018), pp. 117–20.

to confront Zenobia, forcing her armies to retreat in AD 273–274. After a brutal siege, Palmyra fell, and Aurelian seized its territories.[4]

In the Umayyad period, Palmyra regained its prominence due to its location between the two al-Hier palaces of Hisham ibn Abd al-Malik.[5] However, it lost its status when the Abbasid relocated the caliphate's capital from Damascus to Baghdad. In the early tenth century AD, Palmyra was struck by a major earthquake that destroyed many of its buildings and most of its inhabitants died beneath the rubble.[6]

Palmyra went into decline after the Tamerlane invasion of the Levant and the destruction of the cities of the Euphrates with which Palmyra had traded.[7]

Architectural and Urban Planning of the Ancient Zone

The city developed during the Greco-Roman period, extending from the Temple of Bel to the Afqa spring and encompassing the oasis and the tombs outside the city walls. The hard limestone used to build the facades of the buildings was brought from stone quarries located ten kilometres north of the city.

Practical Methods and Techniques

Palmyra's urban plan did not follow the Roman orthogonal scheme, unlike the neighbouring city of Dura-Europos. Instead, Palmyra adopted a local urban plan better suited to the high temperature, winds and topography of the terrain, allowing the city to expand beyond its oasis. This was not a disadvantage as many Greco-Roman cities followed their own urban patterns, even Rome itself.

Establishing a new urban settlement included the construction of a broad north-to-south street intended to replace the old convoy route.[8]

4 Javier Teixidor, *A Journey to Palmyra* (Leiden: Koninklijke Brill NV, 2005), p. 220.

5 Emanuele E. Intagliata, *Palmyra after Zenobia 273–750. An Archaeological and Historical Reappraisal* (Oxford: Oxbow Books, 2018), p. 85, https://doi.org/10.2307/j.ctt2272712

6 Michael Sommer, *Palmyra: A History* (New York, London: Taylor & Francis, 2018), p. 220.

7 Adnan Bounni, *Palmyre. Histoire, Monuments et Musée* (Damascus: n.p., 1982), pp. 120–30.

8 Salim Abdulhak, 'Palmyra in the Architecture and Urbanism of the First Centuries AD', in *Palmyra and the Silk Road*, pp. 224–26 (p. 224).

This transverse street had a portico on its eastern and western sides. It originated in the south at the Damascus Gate and the oval area behind it, known as the Oval Forum. Inscriptions on its columns indicate that the transverse street had both commercial and religious functions.[9]

Given that the western residential area was bordered by underground tombs and rocky highlands, its inhabitants had to expand their settlement eastward. To procure freshwater from the spring, they devised a system for conveying water through an underground canal.[10]

The second settlement area was established to the east, at the junction where convoys travelling from the east encountered those coming from the Levant. This was where the public square, the Agora, and its warehouse were constructed.[11]

The grand colonnade is a prime example of a structure representing a major artistic development. The grand monumental colonnaded street, with its covered side passages and subsidiary cross streets, together with the major public buildings, constitute an exceptional illustration of architecture and urban planning at the peak of Rome's expansion and engagement with the Eastern world.[12]

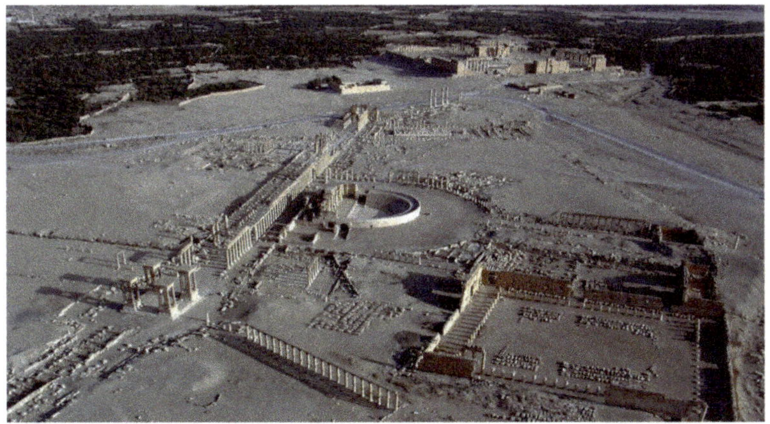

Fig. 2.2 Palmyra landscape aerial view. Photograph by DGAM, Archive, CC BY-NC-ND.

9 D. Wielogsz, 'Tadmor nel deserto. La città greco-romana', in *Siria: Dalle antiche città-stato alla primavera interrotta di Damasco*, ed. by M. Giudetti (Milan: Jaca Book, 2006), pp. 41–60.

10 Abdulhak, 'Palmyra in the Architecture and Urbanism of the First Centuries AD', pp. 224–26.

11 Ibid., pp. 263–85.

12 Sommer, *Palmyra: A History*, p. 171.

The main colonnaded street, with secondary perpendicular colonnaded streets, connected the major public landmarks, including the Temple of Bel, the Agora, the Theatre, Diocletian's Camp, other temples and the urban quarters. Architectural ornaments, including unique examples of funerary sculpture, combined Greco-Roman art with indigenous elements and Persian influences, resulting in a profoundly original style. Outside the city's walls lie remnants of a Roman aqueduct and immense necropolises.[13]

Palmyra's architecture exhibited creativity and was adapted to local conditions and constraints. It was neither strictly Hellenistic nor Roman, but instead represented a combination of urbanisation and originality.[14]

The Urban Situation in Palmyra Since 2013

Terrorism Damage

Palmyra was designated a national heritage site in 1934 and later recognized as a World Heritage site in 1980. Unfortunately, in 2013, it was added to the list of World Heritage sites in Danger, joining five other endangered sites in Syria. On 21 May 2015, the situation in and around Palmyra worsened dramatically when ISIS militants launched an attack on the ancient city, with uncertain consequences.

The city faced an imminent threat to its archaeological heritage as well as to its very survival. The destruction of Palmyra would be a catastrophic loss for all of Syria, erasing an important part of the nation's history. Moreover, Syrian cultural heritage suffered even greater damage and destruction when organised armed groups of antiquities looters spread throughout the ancient city in the summer of 2013. They conducted various illegal excavations and thefts, engaging in the systematic destruction of dozens of archaeological sites, hills and tombs.[15] During 23–27 March 2016, the Syrian armed forces launched a military operation to retake the city and establish control.[16]

13 Ball, *Rome in the East*, p. 74.

14 Malcolm Colledge, 'Roman Influence in the Art of Palmyra', in *Palmyra and the Silk Road*, pp. 363–71.

15 Maamoun Abdulkarim, *The Syrian Cultural Heritage in Palmyra Faces Challenges and Risks* (Damascus: DGAM, 2015).

16 DGAM, *Ancient City of Palmyra is Being Restored* (Damascus: DGAM, 2016).

Palmyra was re-occupied by ISIS militants on 11 December 2016 and liberated again by Syrian forces on 1 March 2017. During the 2015–2017 period, the ancient city of Palmyra witnessed the confirmed destruction of many significant landmarks and monuments in a series of major cultural, scientific, and human losses. The following examples illustrate the damage inflicted on Palmyra's cultural heritage.

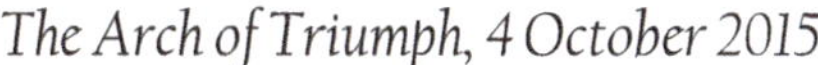

The Arch of Triumph, 4 October 2015

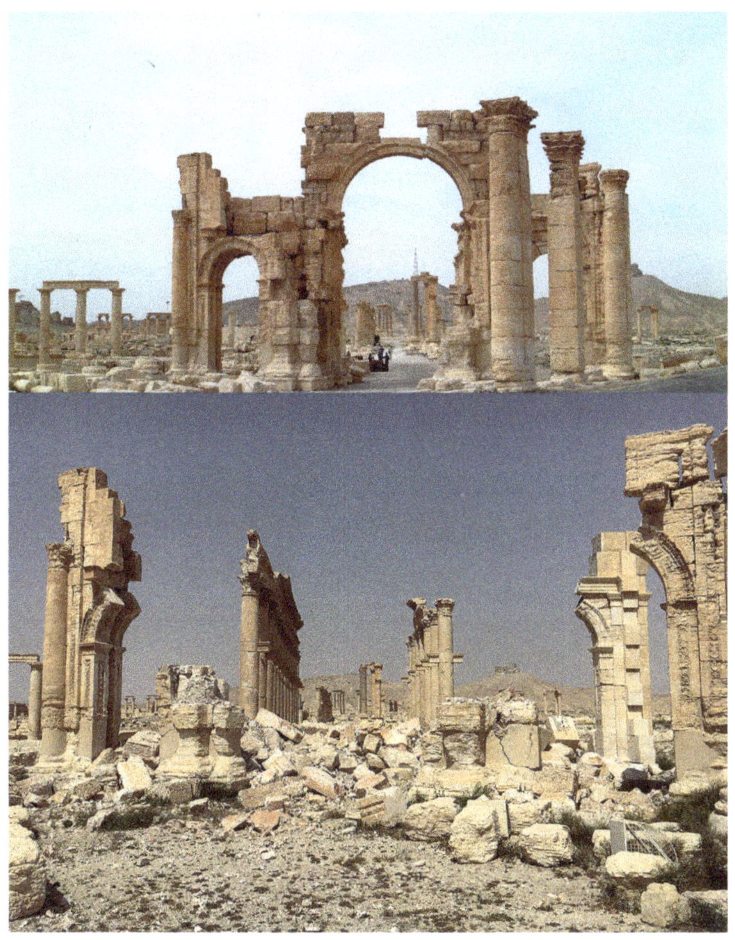

Fig. 2.3 The Arch of Triumph. Damage assessment of Palmyra. Photographs by DGAM, 2017, CC BY-NC-ND.

The Arch of Triumph, also known as the Monumental Arch, is one of the most famous monuments of Palmyra. The uniqueness of this Arch derives from the way the arch transitions between its northern and the southern facades. It also boasts unique ornamentation, with detailed decorative carvings of floral and leaf patterns.

The collapse of its middle spans destroyed the central arch and smaller flanking arches, leaving the columns on all sides standing.[17]

Temple of Baal-Shamin, 23 August 2015

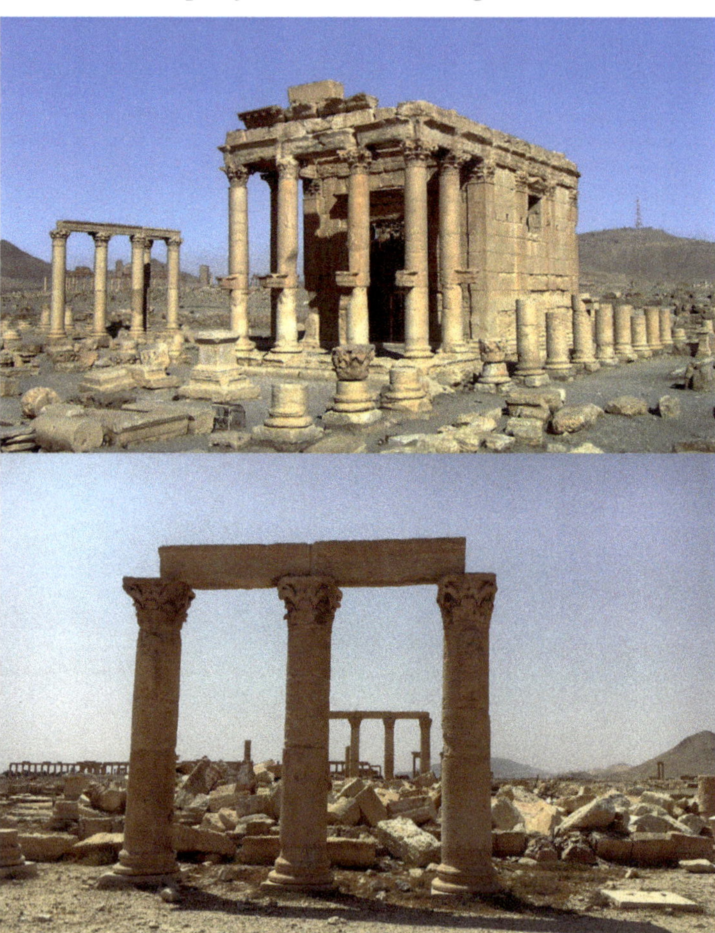

Fig. 2.4 Temple of Baal-Shamin. Damage assessment of Palmyra. Photographs by DGAM, 2017, CC BY-NC-ND.

17 DGAM, *ISIS Destroys the Arch of Triumph in Palmyra* (Damascus: DGAM, 2015).

The temple of Baal-Shamin, a deity associated with rain and fertility, is located in the northern quarter of the ancient city, northeast of Tetrapylon. The temple is built atop the ruins of an earlier temple and is composed of two courtyards with a cella (10×20 metres) and porticoes. Exemplary of second-century Romano-Syrian architecture, the temple's cella forms a triangular truss above six adorned columns.

Although the temple's cella was destroyed, the northern and southern columns just next to the cella survived the explosion and remained in good condition.[18]

The Cella of Temple of Bel, 28 August 2015

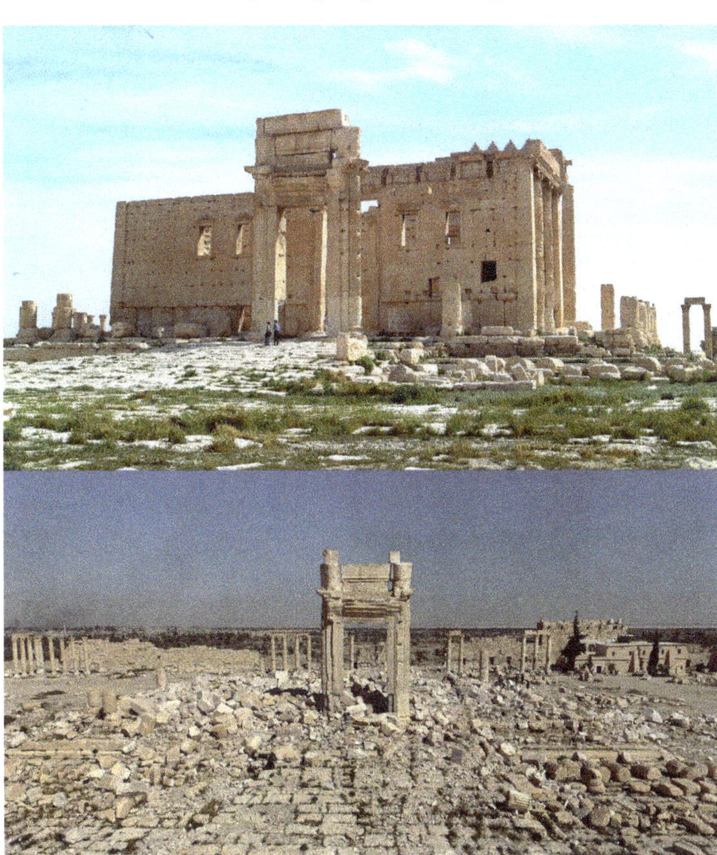

Fig. 2.5 The cella of Temple of Bel. Damage assessment of Palmyra. Photographs by DGAM, 2017, CC BY-NC-ND.

18 DGAM, *Palmyra: ISIS Blown up Baal-Shamin Temple* (Damascus: DGAM, 2015).

The Temple of Bel is considered one of the most famous religious temples in the ancient East. The temple was surrounded by a sanctuary (205×220 metres) composed of 375 columns. The cella, which only priests were allowed to enter, was situated in the middle of the sanctuary.

Unfortunately, the cella was destroyed, its stones reduced to small fragments scattered around the site.[19]

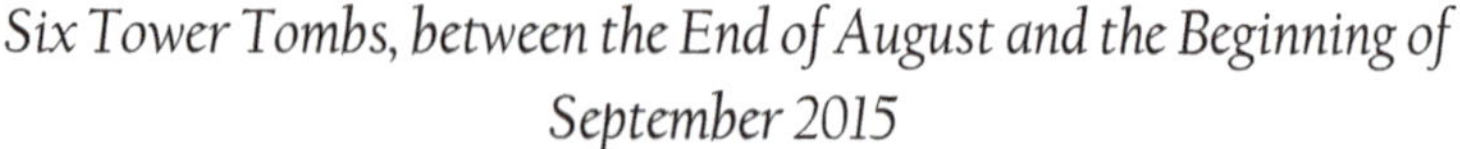

Six Tower Tombs, between the End of August and the Beginning of September 2015

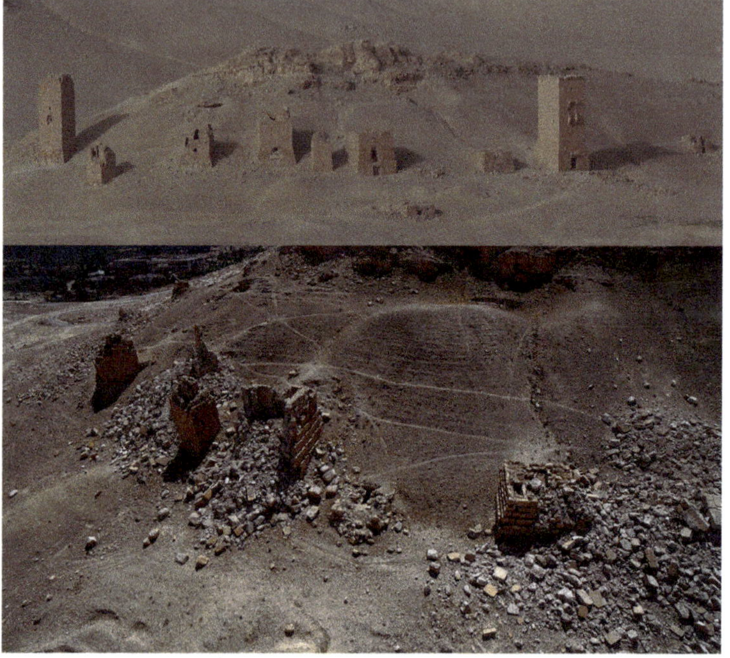

Fig. 2.6 Six tower tombs. Damage assesment of Palmyra. Photographs by DGAM, 2017, CC BY-NC-ND.

Among the tomb types of Roman Syria are the curious 'tower tombs' of Palmyra, which are unparalleled in the Roman architecture of the Western Empire. Documentation efforts have revealed approximately 180 tower tomb structures in various states of preservation that are still identifiable. The American Schools of Oriental Research (ASOR), based

19 DGAM, *ISIS Setting up Explosives and Destroying the Sella of Bel Temple in Palmyra* (Damascus: DGAM, 2015).

at Boston University, published an update on the situation in Palmyra, including satellite imagery showing six tower tombs in the city that had been completely destroyed by ISIS militants.[20]

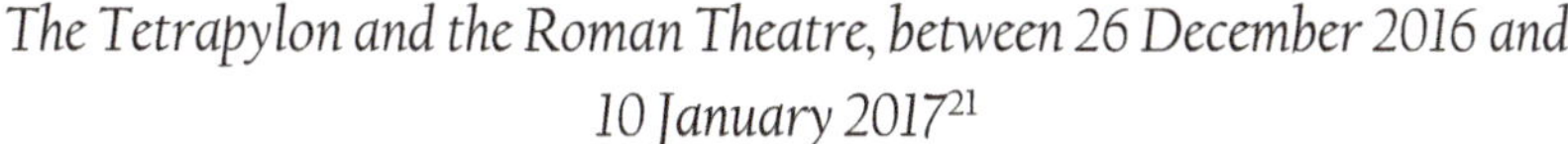

The Tetrapylon and the Roman Theatre, between 26 December 2016 and 10 January 2017[21]

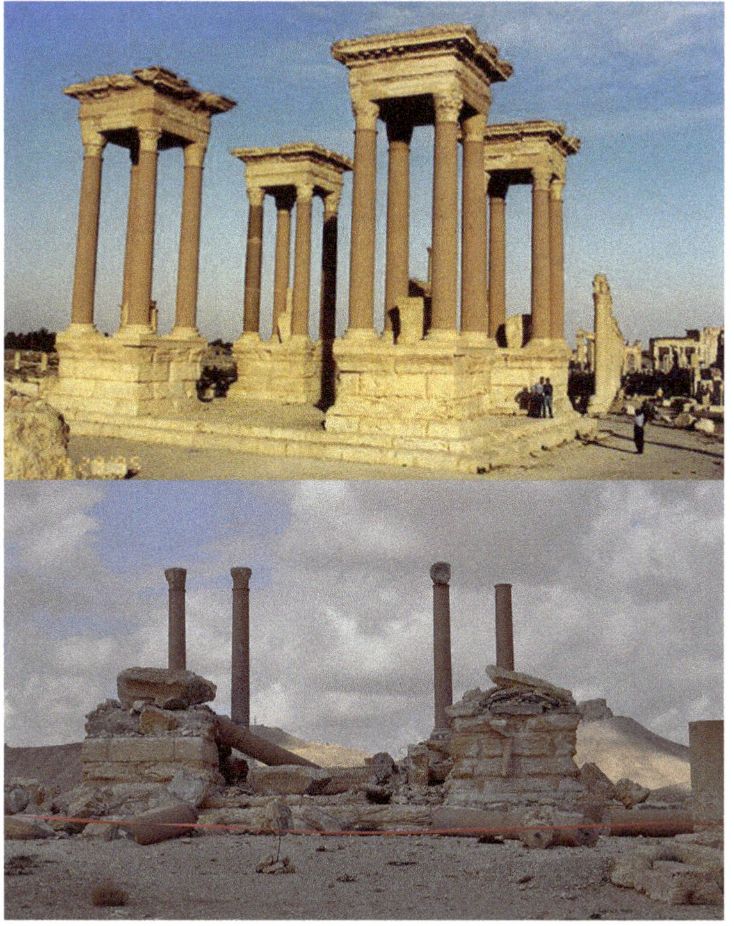

Fig. 2.7 The Tetrapylon. Damage assessment of Palmyra. Photographs by DGAM, 2017, CC BY-NC-ND.

20 DGAM, *Satellite Imagery of 6 Tower Tombs in Palmyra Destroyed by ISIS* (Damascus: DGAM, 2015).

21 DGAM, *New Destruction at Palmyra: Tetrapylon and the Roman Theater* (Damascus: DGAM, 2015).

The Tetrapylon stands on an oval square in the middle of the colonnade street to the northwest. It comprises four square blocks (10×10 metres), each seventy-five centimetres high, supporting four two-meter granite Corinthian columns. These sets of columns uphold a decorative ceiling. The Tetrapylon served a purely ornamental purpose, designed to conceal the ten-degree incline of the colonnade street.[22]

Notably, fifteen columns of the Tetrapylon are replicas. The original ceiling was destroyed, while the bases of the columns are intact and four are still standing in place.[23]

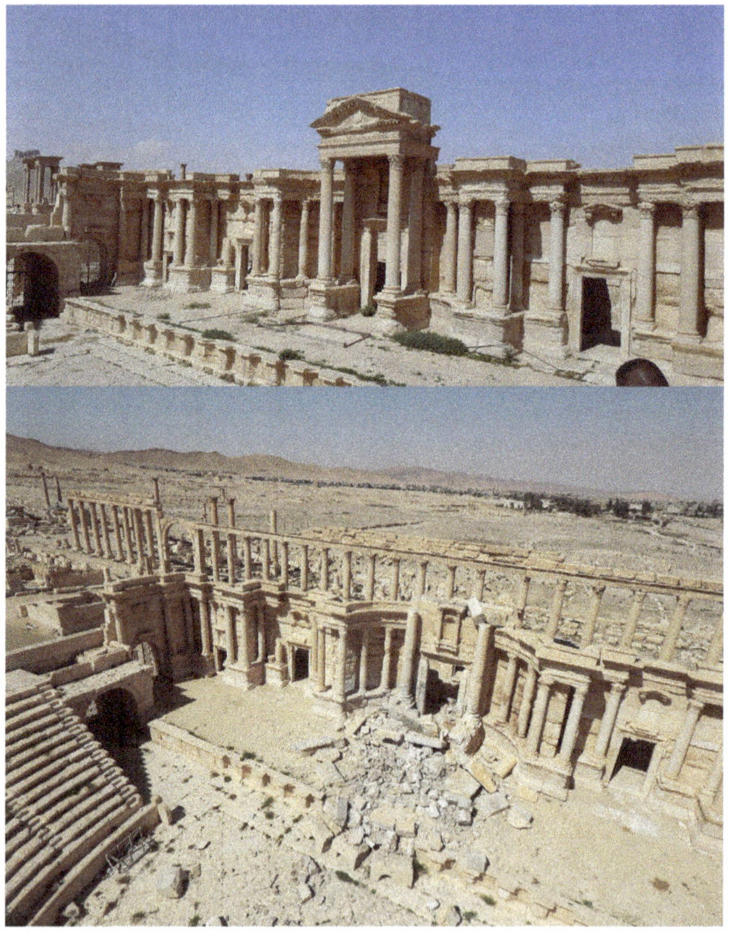

Fig. 2.8 The Roman theatre. Damage assessment of Palmyra. Photographs by DGAM, 2017, CC BY-NC-ND.

22 Iain Browning, *Palmyra* (London: Chatto & Windus, 1979), p. 132.

23 DGAM, *Latest News from Palmyra* (Damascus: DGAM, 2017).

The theatre is located on the left side of the colonnade street between the Tetrapylon and the Triumphal Arch. It has a semi-circular design stretching fifty meters, with thirteen levels of tiered seating for the audience and a facade that stands behind a rectangular platform (9.5×45.5 metres), which is 1.95 metres above the orchestra pit.

During the ISIS occupation of the city in January 2017, the theatre was damaged, resulting in the destruction of a portion of the upper niche in the facade and partial damage to the platform.

The Citadel of Palmyra

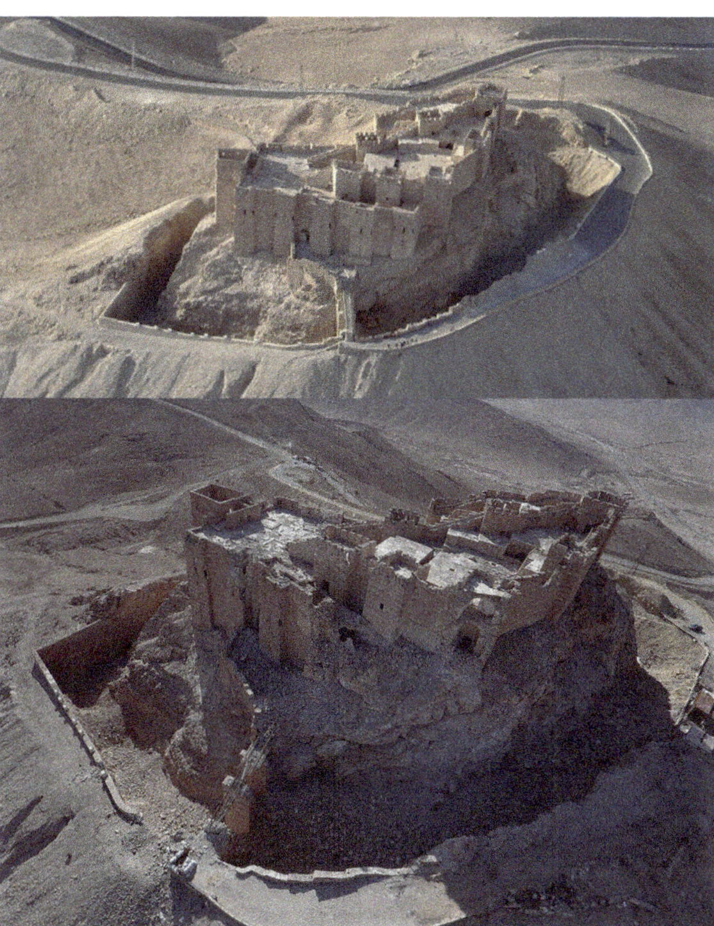

Fig. 2.9 The Citadel of Palmyra. Damage assessment of Palmyra. Photographs by DGAM, 2017, CC BY-NC-ND.

The Palmyra Citadel contained a series of self-contained interior units with a regular outer envelope, completely vaulted inside on different horizontal planes and surrounded by defensive perimeter walls. There were no large open spaces inside, where sectors and rooms with different functions were arranged along central passageways. The original construction included eight towers connected by a defensive wall, forming a roughly triangular perimeter envelope.[24]

On 21 September 2015, rocket attacks caused extensive damage to the castle's outer walls, affecting twenty-five percent of its walls.

Palmyra's Current Urban Situation

In wartime, cities must adapt to the circumstances of conflict. This necessitates certain changes in order to maintain control over and defend territories. During a visit to Palmyra in 2017, after the city's liberation, it was observed that the road adjacent to the archaeological site was used by tanks and military vehicles. In the past, flying over Palmyra was restricted to protect the city's heritage from any vibration caused by planes.

Moreover, the appearance of Palmyra itself has been altered by shelling, clashes and mine explosions during clearance operations. The military presence within the city, intended to ensure its security, has led to major changes in the structure of the archaeological site and its surroundings. For instance, new infrastructure was constructed to facilitate transportation between Palmyra citadel and Al Badya Police Station in the modern city located to the east of the northern tombs.

The new road, visible in satellite imagery, was constructed between 1 September 2012 and 14 November 2013 and remained in use until 26 October 2014. Extending from where the original road to the citadel branches toward the communications mast, the new road cuts through the north-western and northern necropolises down to the tarmac road on the eastern edge of the modern town of Tadmur. The road is approximately 2.4 kilometres long, with a secondary section stretching 580 metres.[25]

---

24 Janusz Bylinski, 'Qal'at Shirkuh at Palmyra: A Medieval Fortress Reinterpreted', *Bulletin d'études orientales*, 51 (1999), 151–208.

25 UNITAR, *Satellite-Based Damage Assessment to Cultural Heritage Sites in Syria* (n.p.: UNITAR, 2014), https://unosat.web.cern.ch/unitar/downloads/chs/FINAL_Syria_WHS.pdf

The 20 February 2014 image shows several site disruptions which occurred prior to ISIS occupation. Banks have been erected along the site's border with the modern town and up the western ridge toward the fortress.

A clearing with surrounding banks has been created below the fortress hill, just west of the southwest corner of the racetrack. There are rectangular and circular banked enclosures on and partly inside the racetrack. A wide straight track has been bulldozed diagonally from the museum to the southern ridge of the fortress, where it branches, with one part leading up to the fortress road and another to the hill behind the Diocletian Camp, where a defensive position and possibly a tank are visible. Finally, a deep trench, seventy metres long and walled on three sides (apart from the northwest), has been dug from northwest to southeast just south of the Nabo Temple.[26]

The primary danger of this path stems from its location, as it passes through an area containing numerous ancient tombs. Reports indicate that archaeological remains along its trajectory, specifically tomb foundations, were removed during its construction.

Some archaeological stone blocks have been relocated for defensive purposes. Additionally, levees of various heights have been created in multiple locations near the archaeological site. This has not only altered the site's appearance but may also have led to the clearance of certain archaeological layers.

Recovery Vision and Planning

This vision sets out the methods and techniques that should be applied in accordance with the international charters and guidelines adopted for the technical conservation and ongoing care of the Palmyra World Heritage Site. The 'Recover Plan' requires a long-term approach to projects, with due consideration accorded to proper conservation techniques, economic concerns and the need to raise social awareness about management and care.

The plan should represent an integrated process of master-planning, scientific conservation, community involvement and the establishment

26 Torbjørn Preus Schou, *Catalogue of Archaeological Site Integrity Violations in Syria 2010–2016* (Syria: *Shirīn*–Syrian Heritage in Danger: An International Research Initiative and Network, 2016), p. 18.

of effective partnerships. It must serve to provide enduring protection while remaining sufficiently flexible to address the challenges posed by the site.[27]

Vision

The vision for Palmyra's recovery is the starting point for planning the site's future. The recovery of Palmyra must be approached in a way that balances the evolving functional needs of the community with the overriding commitment to preserving the historical, environmental and symbolic significance of the site.[28]

Three paradigm shifts have been recognised as crucial.

- First, the importance of considering the economic, social, and environmental dimensions of sustainability during the reconstruction of the historic urban area was underscored.
- Second, understanding the heritage as a 'living urban context', or 'a historic urban landscape', as formalised in 2011 by the Recommendation on the Historic Urban Landscape (HUL), was emphasised, albeit before this document was officially issued.
- Third, a clear indication for reconstruction has been formulated in the context of the heritage definition criteria for relisting in the 2018 Warsaw Recommendation on Recovery and Reconstruction of Cultural Heritage.

Key Objectives

1. Conserving the Heritage and Memory of the Site

The most pressing objective is to identify the monuments needing urgent repair, take temporary security measures for consolidating them, document their current condition and develop projects for their restoration. Several other urgent initiatives are required in order

27 DGAM, *State Party Report, on the State of Conservation of the Syrian Cultural Heritage Sites* (Damascus: DGAM, 2020), p. 7

28 Ibid., p. 8.

to safeguard the historical values and enable the restoration of both the monuments and the urban fabric. In particular, the following interventions are urgently needed:

a) *Consolidation of damaged buildings:* Restoring the majority of the destroyed buildings and structures requires studies, design work and careful reconstruction practices, which will take time. These restorations will only be possible in the mid- and long term. Therefore, it is essential and urgent to consolidate the structures to prevent further collapses and prepare for future restoration work.

b) *Protection of ruins:* The ruins of buildings and structures scheduled for later intervention must be effectively protected and enclosed to prevent the removal of materials and decorative elements. Conservation plans should define the main conservation, excavation and presentation strategies and include provisions on urban development regulations and visitor arrangements.

2. Empowering the Local Community

Intangible cultural values rooted in community life were also severely impacted during the conflict. The displacement of people and communities, the destruction of religious and cultural institutions and local facilities, and the collapse of markets for cultural goods and services have affected age-old cultural values and practices.

A full understanding of the post-conflict situation is necessary to define policies and actions. To achieve this, a map of all the city's existing cultural assets should be created, to include all cultural, social and economic resources, community centres and local skills.

This activity will facilitate stakeholder engagement in the reconstruction and recovery process and optimize the use of local cultural and technical resources.

Developing civic engagement tools is essential to foster participation, mobilise the population and speed-up the reconstruction and recovery process. Potential initiatives include the following:

- Organising local awareness campaigns to inform the population about the progress of works and initiatives and rally support for projects of collective interest.
- Promoting participation mechanisms to involve local associations and communities in the decision-making process in order to fully incorporate the views and needs of the population.
- Conducting training and capacity-building workshops focused on local communities and their empowerment.
- Facilitating technical and on-the-job training programs to build local capacities with regard to construction and restoration works, surveying activities, documentation management and cultural initiatives management.
- Supporting cultural community projects involving the resident population and displaced persons to foster dialogue and social inclusion.
- Promoting youth programs in collaboration with schools and universities to encourage engagement, entrepreneurship, and artistic initiatives among young people.
- Organising cultural programs and initiatives aimed at preserving and reviving local traditions.[29]

The plan's development must be discussed and negotiated with professional planners, technical experts, civil society organisations, NGOs, other representative bodies and affected citizens and businesses.

3. Developing Short- and Long-term Integrated Emergency Preventive Conservation

In planning and implementing the reconstruction and recovery of Palmyra, the 2011 UNESCO Recommendation on the Historic Urban Landscape provides a foundational approach. Particular attention is given to the following aspects:

---

29 UNESCO, *Recommendation on the Historic Urban Landscape* (Paris: UNESCO, 2011), p. 24.

- Understanding the complex layering of historical typologies and morphologies.
- Preserving the sense of place and visual relationships in historic areas, open spaces and the urban skyline.
- Safeguarding traditional expressions and values, as well as the related crafts and cultural industries.
- Respecting the diversity of expressions and identities of different communities.

A project master plan alone cannot address all aspects of the site before conservation efforts are initiated to prevent further deterioration. This study identifies the following prerequisite tasks:

- Establishing conservation procedures for defining priorities, roles and the selection of implementing partners.
- Developing a short-term emergency and preventive conservation plan for urgent repairs, prioritising monuments at immediate risk due to structural problems.
- Implementing documentation, publication procedures, scientific and archival research and inventory procedure studies to gain a better understanding of buildings and acquire precise information on matters such as structural resistance.
- Securing projects for the comprehensive conservation of monuments and the redesigning and improvement of existing infrastructure.[30]

Recovery Plan Policy

Strengths, Weaknesses, Opportunities and Threats (SWOT) analysis is a strategic planning technique designed for use in the preliminary stages of the decision-making processes and can be used to evaluate the strategic position of recovery plan policy. It is intended to specify the objectives of the recovery plan policy and identify the internal and external factors that facilitate or hinder the achievement of the stated objectives.

30 DGAM, *State Party Report*, p. 7.

Table 2.1 Characteristics of the Palmyra site within the framework of SWOT analysis.

Strengths	**Weaknesses**
(1) Extensive national support for the plan (2) Global scientific repute and appeal to national and international donors (3) Preserved cultural landscape	(1) Conservation issues with certain monuments (2) Absence of comprehensive conservation planning (3) Lack of resources, expertise and workmanship (4) Insufficient data (5) Inaccessibility of previous reports (6) Lack of suitable accommodation and working conditions (7) Economic constraints (8) Absence of a local antiquities department
Opportunities	**Threats**
(1) Attracting national and international funds and resources (2) Generating employment (3) Promoting the educational and cultural values of the site's archaeological landscape (4) Increasing local and public awareness and interest in the site (5) Enhancing conservation through monitoring, diagnosing and restoration (6) Developing technical capacities (7) Fostering international technical cooperation (8) Improving governance and policies for the site	(1) Decreased financial support. (2) Poor technical infrastructure (3) Lack of sustainable management and future planning (4) Insufficient management system for the monuments, which are a part of the World Heritage Property[31]

31 Ibid., p. 9.

Recovery Plan Tools

Informed by the SWOT analysis, several tools and strategies emerge that can be of use in the development of an immediate conservation program to prevent further deterioration of Palmyra's heritage pending a long-term recovery plan. In terms of knowledge and planning, databases of archaeological and architectural documentation as well as the legal and administrative aspects of the reconstruction and recovery plan should be created, in addition to an up-to-date database of cultural heritage damage assessments in the ancient city. Additionally, comprehensive cultural mapping should be undertaken, encompassing cultural infrastructure, organisations, activities and industries, accompanied by technical for all necessary restoration and rehabilitation works.

At the regulatory level, building and zoning codes must be modified based on reconstruction and recovery efforts. A specialised office should be established to expedite the issuance of permits and oversee an effective inspection process for building safety certification. At a later stage, a comprehensive management plan for the World Heritage Site should be drafted, implemented and adequately monitored.

Financial tools which could be utilised in these processes include innovative, guaranteed microcredit systems as well as special heritage conservation incentives and the harnessing of international partnerships and cooperation.

Master Plan

The master plan provides a vision and framework to guide the recovery phase. It establishes the identity, history, authenticity and outstanding value of the site, defining the objectives and outlining the scope, projected costs and expected outputs of the project.

The master plan aims to articulate the conservation and presentation priorities and principles and integrate conservation, presentation and development policies. It should specifically focus on guiding medium and long-term decisions on the site's restoration, reconstruction, rehabilitation and regeneration.

Furthermore, based on public consultations, a restoration 'philosophy' should be adopted, adhering to international restoration standards and approaches and supported by international expertise.

The plan should aim to facilitate public and private initiatives in areas in need of rehabilitation by creating suitable conditions for the investment of funds by private actors and the financial system.[32]

The vision, guiding principles, goals, and strategies outlined in the master plan should be based on the following principles:

- A successful vision for post-war reconstruction depends on a broad scientific consensus at the national and international levels, including among national authorities with members of scientific advisory boards, International Council on Monuments and Sites (ICOMOS), UNESCO and experts who participated in the archaeological missions at the site.
- Effective archiving and documentation are essential to fully understanding the site's needs.
- Urgent intervention must be undertaken, accounting for external factors such as looting.
- Damage evaluation must include an analysis of techniques and an assessment of materials science, encompassing both existing monuments and all conservation intervention proposals and materials.
- Diagnosing and surveying the archaeological site, the oasis, and the surrounding areas are necessary.
- Efforts to garner national and international financial and technical support are essential.
- Rebuilding the site's image is crucial to mobilise and raise awareness among Palmyra residents concerning conservation issues and the importance of their shared heritage.[33]

Conclusion and Lesson Learned

Recently, several World Heritage Sites and historically significant urban areas have been affected by disasters or conflicts. Recent examples include cities like Katmandu in Nepal, Port-au-Prince in Haiti, and

32 Municipality Administration Modernization (MAM), *Palmyra Region Strategic Action Plan a Strategy for Sustainable Development* (Syria: n.p., 2009), p. 199.

33 DGAM, *State Party Report*, p. 9.

Christchurch in New Zealand, struck by natural disasters, as well as cities like Beirut in Lebanon, Sarajevo in Bosnia and Herzegovina and Timbuktu in Mali, affected by conflict. These cases can serve as valuable references in devising a recovery plan for Palmyra.

The reconstruction and recovery plan for Palmyra must draw upon the experience gained in the last decades in addressing the needs of urban communities and historic urban areas affected by crises. The objective is to preserve the heritage values that constitute the most important legacy and source of identity of this World Heritage Site, while maintaining a balance between place-based and people-based policies. In other words, physical reconstruction should not be undertaken without full citizen participation and the implementation of policies to support the livelihoods of the original population.

Actively engaging the population in the reconstruction process is the key to mobilising the technical skills and financial commitments needed for a speedy recovery. While addressing humanitarian needs must be a priority, especially in the early phases after a crisis, the reconstruction and recovery process should begin by restoring essential monuments and urban areas that play a significant role in community life.

As historic cities emerge from armed conflicts, they struggle with the imperative to foster reconciliation within their communities, particularly where crises have impacted the core of local identities. The recovery of cultural heritage emerges from a common vision, which is then linked to the broader vision of post-war reconstruction. This should seek not only to revitalize economic and social development but also to foster an environment of peace to avert the outbreak of renewed violence. The reconstruction of the Mostar Bridge in Bosnia and Herzegovina after its destruction in 1993 exemplifies the value of heritage reconstruction in reconciling communities and rebuilding local identity.

Ultimately, the vision for Palmyra's recovery should entail establishing an effective management system and developing a master plan for reconstruction and recovery. This should be guided by a flexible strategy and SMART objectives, which should be specific, measurable, achievable, relevant and time-bound. SWOT analyses can be a valuable tool in recovery processes and heritage conservation, contributing to effective and equitable program implementation.

The reconstruction and recovery of Palmyra is a major challenge for the Syrian people and their government. Substantial effort and financial resources are required to restore monuments, rebuild urban infrastructure, stimulate a sustainable economy and rehabilitate social life and societal cohesion.

Bibliography

Abdulhak, Salim, 'Palmyra in the Architecture and Urbanism of the First Centuries AD', in *Palmyra and the Silk Road, International Colloquium, Palmyra, 7–11 April 1992* (Damascus: DGAM, 1996), pp. 224–26.

Abdulkarim, Maamoun, *The Syrian Cultural Heritage in Palmyra Faces Challenges and Risks* (Damascus: DGAM, 2015).

Andrade, Nathanael J., *Zenobia, Shooting Star of Palmyra* (London: Oxford University Press, 2018).

Ball, Warwick, *Rome in the East, The Transformation of an Empire* (London: Routledge, 2000).

Bounni, Adnan, *Palmyre. Histoire, Monuments et Musée* (Damascus: n.p., 1982).

Browning, Iain, *Palmyra* (London: Chatto & Windus, 1979).

Bylinski, Janusz, 'Qal'at Shirkuh at Palmyra: A Medieval Fortress Reinterpreted', *Bulletin d'études orientales, Institut Francais du Proche-Orient*, 51 (1999), 151–208.

Colledge, Malcolm, 'Roman Influence in the Art of Palmyra', in *Palmyra and the Silk Road, International Colloquium, Palmyra, 7–11 April 1992* (Damascus: DGAM, 1996), pp. 363–71.

Directorate General of Antiquities and Museums-DGAM, *ISIS Destroys the Arch of Triumph in Palmyra* (Damascus: DGAM, 2015).

DGAM, *ISIS Setting up Explosives and Destroying the Sella of Bel Temple in Palmyra* (Damascus: DGAM, 2015).

DGAM, *New Destruction at Palmyra: Tetrapylon and the Roman Theater* (Damascus: DGAM, 2015).

DGAM, *Palmyra: ISIS Blown up Baal-Shamin Temple* (Damascus: DGAM, 2015).

DGAM, *Satellite Imagery of 6 Tower Tombs in Palmyra Destroyed by ISIS* (Damascus: DGAM, 2015).

DGAM, *Ancient City of Palmyra is Being Restored* (Damascus: DGAM, 2016).

DGAM, *Latest News from Palmyra* (Damascus: DGAM, 2017).

DGAM, *State Party Report, on the State of Conservation of the Syrian Cultural Heritage Sites* (Damascus: DGAM, 2020).

Intagliata, Emanuele E., *Palmyra after Zenobia 273–750. An Archaeological and Historical Reappraisal* (Oxford: Oxbow Books, 2018), https://doi.org/10.2307/j.ctt2272712

Mari, Eid, 'Palmyra as an Important Station on the Caravan's Road During the Second Millennium', in *Palmyra and the Silk Road, International Colloquium, Palmyra, 7–11 April 1992* (Damascus: DGAM, 1996), pp. 135–37.

Municipality Administration Modernization (MAM), *Palmyra Region Strategic Action Plan a Strategy for Sustainable Development* (Syria: n.p., 2009).

Schou, Torbjørn Preus, *Catalogue of Archaeological Site Integrity Violations in Syria 2010–2016* (Syria: *Shirīn*–Syrian Heritage in Danger: An International Research Initiative and Network, 2016).

Sommer, Michael, *Palmyra: A History* (New York, London: Taylor & Francis, 2018).

Teixidor, Javier, *A Journey to Palmyra* (Leiden: Koninklijke Brill NV, 2005).

UNESCO, *Recommendation on the Historic Urban Landscape* (Paris: UNESCO, 2011).

United Nations Institute for Training and Research (UNITAR), *Satellite-Based Damage Assessment to Cultural Heritage Sites in Syria* (n.p.: UNITAR, 2014), https://unosat.web.cern.ch/unitar/downloads/chs/FINAL_Syria_WHS.pdf

Wielogsz, D., 'Tadmor nel deserto. La città greco-romana', in *Siria: Dalle antiche città-stato alla primavera interrotta di Damasco*, ed. by M. Giudetti (Milan: Jaca Book, 2006), pp. 41–60.

3. The Urban Development of Si-ye Tir Street in Tehran

Maryam Mirzaei

Introduction

Historic city centres are regarded as cultural heritage, with the potential to attract regional, national and international tourists. They not only bolster the tourism industry but also promote indigenous and regional culture and identity.

Unsustainable urban development and rapid, reckless changes have negatively impacted the physical appearance of cities in Iran, damaging urban heritage and its intrinsic values. This has led to the erosion of parts of the collective memory of city inhabitants. The old city of Tehran, the Iranian capital, has undergone these dramatic changes throughout its history.

To revive and conserve historical memory and to develop tourism, it is crucial to identify and preserve historic city centres. However, few relevant studies have been conducted on the old city of Tehran. Therefore, this chapter explores one of Tehran's historical and cultural streets, widely known as Si-ye Tir and Mirza Kuchak Khan. This street is a vibrant and dynamic part of Tehran and is presented as an example of the capital's cultural, religious and social fluctuations.

Running from north to south, this street intersects four major east-west streets (Imam Khomeini, Colonel Sakhaei, the Islamic Republic and Neauphle-le-Château). These intersections have divided the street into three parts, each of which has had various names in past, such as Bagh-e Jenab-e Amin al-Soltan St., Ghazzagh-Khaneh St., Ghavam al-Saltaneh St., Farrokh St., Raphael St., Marshal Stalin St., and No-Bahar St.

 https://doi.org/10.11647/OBP.0412.03

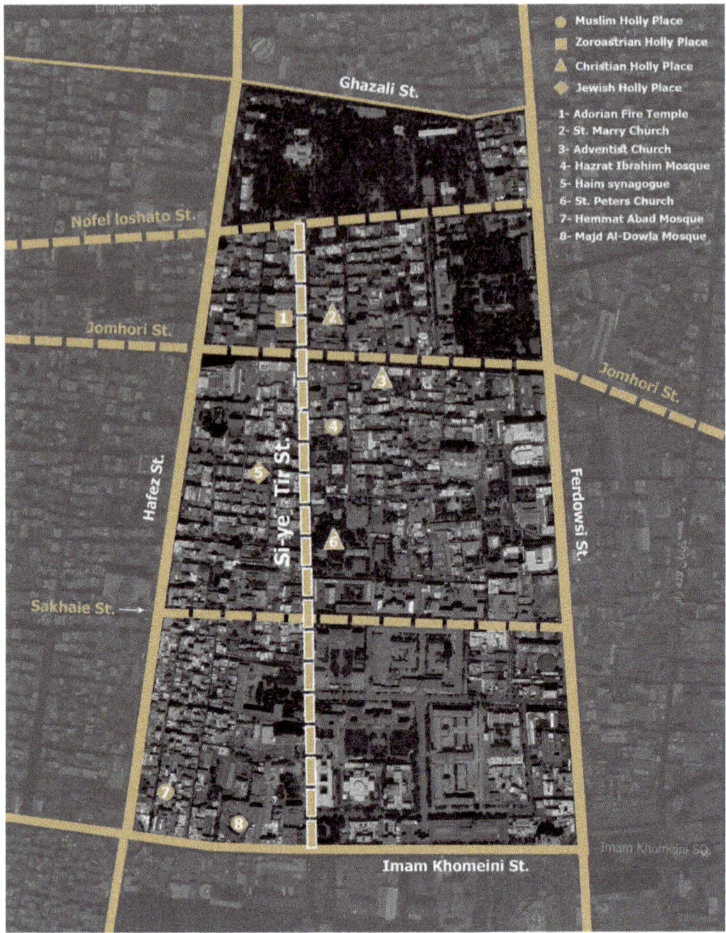

Fig. 3.1 Map of the case study district—sanctuaries of four religions. Author's illustration, based on Google Maps (2018), CC BY-NC-ND.

A relatively coherent literature on this district and street has been compiled through the consultation and comparison of available sources, including:

- Written sources: early printed volumes, travellers' reports, memoires of prominent figures, newspapers, magazines, books and essays.
- Archives: historical documents and formal letters.
- Visual sources: maps, photos and paintings.

- Oral sources: interviews, records of the reminiscences of the residents, observations and memories.
- Field observations: visiting historical sites and re-examination of inscriptions.

The Significance of Si-ye Tir Street

Si-ye Tir Street, located in the heart of Tehran, is nearly 150 years old, dating back to the reign of Nasser al-Din Shah Qajar (r. 1848–1896), the fourth Qajar king of Persia. The street has become a popular tourist destination, attracting both local residents and travellers to Tehran.

One of the key features which sets it apart from many other streets is that it houses sanctuaries of four religions: Zoroastrianism, Judaism, Christianity and Islam. Along its 1280-metre stretch, 350 metres are dedicated to one fire temple, one synagogue, three churches and a mosque. Additionally, two more mosques are also located along the length of the street. The coexistence of these sacred sites is a testimony to the peaceful relationship between various religious communities who have lived in harmony since the establishment of the street. This street also accommodates foreign institutions like the British and Russian Embassies and American, Russian and German schools. The diverse religious minority groups and cultural communities living on this street have endowed it with dynamic characteristics.

Some of the oldest buildings in Tehran were built on this street, namely the National Museum of Iran (the city's first public museum building), the National Library (the first library building in Tehran), the Adorian Temple (Tehran's first fire temple), the Industrial College of Iran and Germany (the city's first industrial college), the Jamshid Jam School (the first Zoroastrian educational institution in Tehran), the State Hospital (Tehran's first modern hospital servicing the general public), the Faculty of Conservation and Reparation of Historical-Cultural Artifacts (the first research facility for historical reparation in the city), as well as the first street-food hub in Tehran, among others.

The History of Si-ye Tir and Mirza Kuchak Khan Street

Tehran's historical significance dates back to the Safavid era. Under Shah Tahmasb the First (1524–1576), the first fortification was built around the city, encompassing four gates connecting the city to its suburbs. Tehran was first declared the capital of Iran during the Qajar period, hence the link between Tehran's history and that of the Qajar dynasty.

With population growth and the expansion of construction, the gardens inside the fortifications were soon transformed into houses and mansions. The need for space even led to discussions of expanding construction beyond city walls. However, even two decades after Naser al-Din Shah's coronation, Tehran remained confined within Shah Tahmasb's fortress, divided into five districts: Arg, Oudlajan, Bazar, Sanglaj and Chal Meydan.

As the population gradually increased, the city was unable to accommodate new inhabitants. Consequently, by the regal order of Nasser al-Din Shah in 1867, a plan was initiated to expand the city in four directions. This plan was the basis for a new irregular polygonal fortification. In addition to expanding the five existing districts, this development gave rise to a new district called Dowlat in the northern part of the fort of Tehran. Present-day Si-ye Tir and Mirza Kuchak Khan streets were located in this newly established district and the surrounding plats were possessed one by one.

Before the construction of the new fortification, Meydan-e Mashq, a military training ground dating back to the Fath Ali Shah Qajar era (1797–1834), was one of the first facilities developed in this zone, beyond Tehran's walls. It was located at the southern end of what would become Si-ye Tir street. During the reign of Nasser al-Din Shah, this field was developed and renovated several times. A Russian-style barracks was later constructed to the north, known as Ghazzagh-Khane (Cossak House), which was in use prior to urban development.[1]

A few years before Nasseri's urban development, the British Embassy bought a plat outside the city, on the other side of what would become Si-ye Tir Street. The new British Embassy would later be constructed on this property. This building, which was the first constructed in the European style, has been preserved to this day and is one of the most important monuments in this area.[2]

1 Amir Bani Massoud, *Contemporary Iranian Architecture* (Tehran: Century Architecture Publishing, 2012), p. 107.

2 Mohsen Motamedi, *Historical Geography of Tehran* (Tehran: University Publishing Center, 2002), pp. 257–60.

Following the destruction of the old fortress and the construction of Naseri's fortress, urban development accelerated in the new district and on present-day Si-ye Tir Street. In 1867, by order of Nasser al-Din Shah, the Marizkhane Dowlati (State Hospital), the first modern public hospital in the city, was constructed at the southern end of the street in a large plat in the west of Meidan-e Mashgh. The original building was small and no longer exists, while subsequent buildings erected on the plat continue to operate as a public hospital, now called Sina Hospital.[3]

After the new development, the upper class began moving to the newly established district of Dowlat, including a number of religious minorities, such as Armenians. The British government's policies supporting Christians motivated Armenians to settle in the vicinity of the British Embassy, a trend that accelerated in the late 1880s. As the Armenian population in the Dowlat district grew, the need for certain facilities arose, such as churches and schools. Financed by Armenian donations, the Haykazian School was built along the northern part of the street, west of the British Embassy. However, the construction of a church was postponed due to insufficient funds.[4]

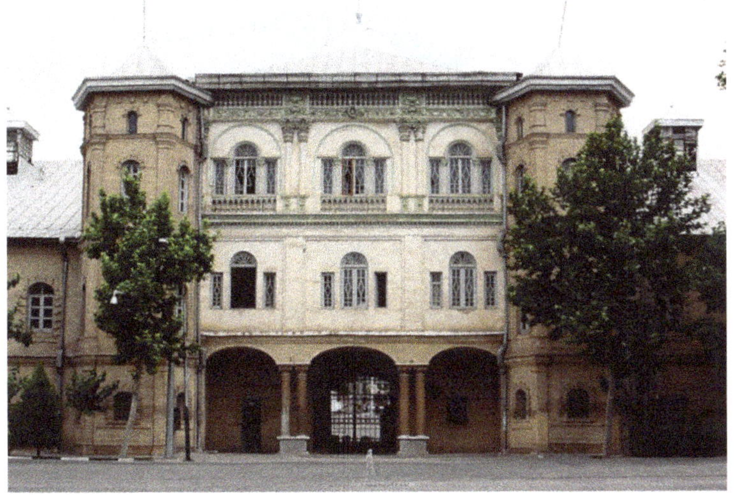

Fig. 3.2 Ghazzagh-Khane (Cossak House), Tehran. Photograph by Blondin Rikard (2014), Wikimedia, https://commons.wikimedia.org/wiki/File:Ghazzaghkhaneh_Tehran_University_of_Art.jpg, CC BY 2.0.

3 Mohsen Roustaei, *History of Medicine*, 2 vols. (Tehran: Documents Organization and National Library of the Islamic Republic of Iran, 2003), I, pp. 208, 209.

4 Hovik Minasian, 'From Haykazian School to Kooshesh High School', trans. by Garon Sarkisian, *Hoys Biweekly*, 199 (2012), 3.

The growing Armenian population in this district encouraged American protestant missionaries to relocate their church and school to the Dowlat district. Before the arrival of American missionaries in Iran, Protestantism was not common in the country, due to strict limitations in Islamic/ Iranian culture on promoting other religions. The missionaries targeted Armenian youth and teenagers in their missionary work, providing charity facilities and free education as a means of persuasion. In 1885, they purchased a large piece of land north of Meydan-e Mashgh to establish a school and a church. This location was advantageous on account of its proximity to the Armenian community and the British Embassy. The church became well-known as the Evangelical Presbyterian Church and is now affiliated with the Anglican Church of Persian-Speakers.[5]

After the Evangelical Church, Majd Al-Dowleh Mosque was the second religious building constructed in this area. This mosque was built in 1892 in the eastern part of the State Hospital. In 1905, another mosque was built in this area called Hemmat Abad Mosque, west of the public hospital (now Sina Hospital). Both mosques have been preserved in their original Qajari appearance and are still active today.[6]

In the last years of the Naseri period, Mirza Ali Asghar Khan Amin Al-Soltan,[7] Naser Al-Din Shah's prime minister, possessed a substantial piece of land north of this district, where he created a large garden and several buildings. At this complex, later named Amin Al-Soltan Park or Atabak Park, he hosted friends, relatives and foreign representatives as well as held glamorous parties.

After Amin Al-Soltan's death, the garden was purchased by Arbab Jamshid,[8] a famous Zoroastrian merchant. In 1915, the Russian Loan Bank

5 Jan Eldar, *History of the American Mission in Iran*, trans. by Soheil Azari (Tehran: Noorjahan, 1952), p. 35.

6 Abdol Hojat Hosseini Bolaghi, *History of Tehran: Central and Additions [and North]*, 3 vols. (Tehran: Maziar, 1971), I, pp. 57, 64.

7 Mirza Aliasghar Khan (1858–1907), titled as Amin Al-Soltan, was the second child of Ebrahim Amin Al-Soltan and served as prime minister to three Qajar kings: Naser Al-Din Shah, Mozafar Al-Din Shah and Mohammad Ali Shah. An Iranian of Georgian descent, he held the titles of Sahib Jam, Amin Al-Soltan and Atabak Azam. As the prime minister of Mozafar Al-Din Shah, he made two trips to Europe, espite the considerable expenses and the resulting indebtedness of Iran to foreign governments. His era could be accurately characterised as a period of concessions to external powers. Amin Al-Soltan was assassinated by adversaries in front of the house of parliament in 1907.

8 Jamshid Bahman Jamshidian, also known as Arbab Jamshidi (born in 1851 in Yazd, died 16 January 1933 in Tehran), was a prominent Zoroastrian figure in Iran

took ownership of the park as compensation for Arbab Jamshid's debts to this institute. After the Russian Revolution, the Soviet government became the deputy of the Russian Loan Bank and Atabak Park was taken over by the Soviet Embassy.[9] This area remains under the possession of the Russian Embassy, the largest embassy in Iran in terms of area.

In the late Nasseri era, citizens of Western countries took up residence in Tehran, exhibiting a heightened interest in the region and leading to the construction of several new facilities. Furthermore, the construction of European-style mansions became popular, fostering an atmosphere of Europeanism in the north of old Tehran. By 1903, this area was mainly occupied by Europeans.[10] This demographic composition made this district an appealing place for religious minorities to settle.

The ancient Iranian religion of Zoroastrianism had small communities scattered in different parts of the country. At the time, Tehran had only a limited Zoroastrian population, comprising workers from the city's bazaar. Like other minority groups, these Zoroastrians, as well as those coming from other cities, gradually relocated to this district and formed the first Zoroastrian quarter in Tehran. Consequently, the need arose for nearby educational facilities catering to this community.

In 1907, Arbab Jamshid Jamshidian sponsored the foundation of a Zoroastrian school on his property, to be the first of its kind in the city. The plat was in an alley north of Si-ye Tir Street, west of the British Embassy. It was eventually named Jamshid Jam School after its founder and continues to educate male Zoroastrian students.

Several years later, Zoroastrians built the Adorian Fire Temple in the district, the first fire temple in the district. The construction of the temple began in 1915 with the financial support of Parsis and the temple was officially opened three years later.[11]

Simultaneously with the Zoroastrian school, an Iranian-German school was established as the result of a cultural agreement between the two governments in 1907. This was part of Germany's efforts to deepen its involvement in Iranian affairs through new regional policies.

---

who introduced the country to modern banking and was the first Zoroastrian representative in the Iranian Parliament.

9 Nasser Najmi, *Dar al-Khalafah*, 2nd ed. (Tehran: Hamgam, 1988), p. 174.

10 Hasan Kariman, *Tehran in the Past and Present* (Tehran: National Iranian University Press, 1976), p. 270.

11 Faramarz Pourrostami, *Tehran Zoroastrian Association: A Century of Effort and Service* (Tehran: Forouhar Publishing Cultural Institute, 2008), pp. 243–46, 281.

The Iranian authorities chose a piece of land along the southern part of Si-ye Tir Street, northwest of Meydan-e Mashgh. This school, the first technical college in Tehran, still operates under the name of Mandegar Industrial College.[12]

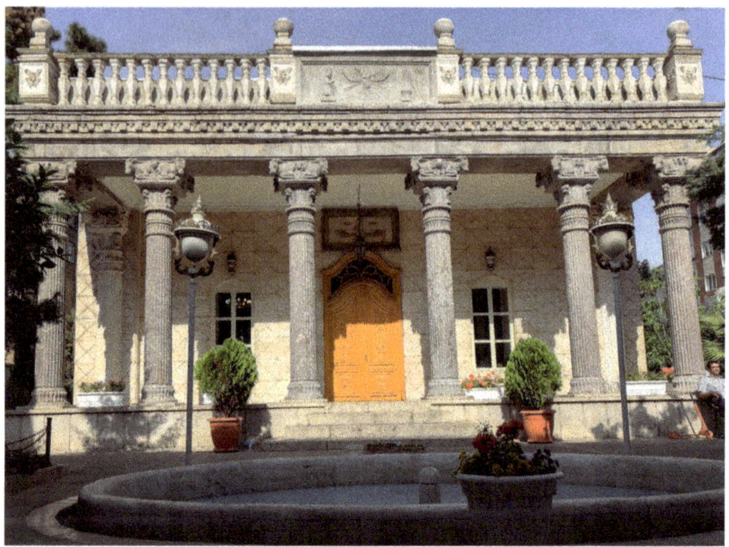

Fig. 3.3 Adorian Fire temple, Tehran. Author's photograph, 2018, CC BY-NC-ND.

Two other foreign schools were built in this area by the Russians, who wielded considerable influence in Iran at the time and were seeking to promote the Russian language. One of these schools, the Ghazagh Khaneh School, was exclusively for children of Cossack (Ghazagh) soldiers and located near the Ghazagh Khaneh. The other, known as Gimnaz or Progimnaz, was situated east of Ghazagh Khaneh and operated under the supervision of the Russian Embassy. This institute was sponsored by the Russian Loan Bank and Russian people's charity. Neither of these schools are still in operation.[13]

The garden and mansion of Ghavam Al-Saltaneh, a respected prime minister of the Qajar and Pahlavi eras, are two other notable monuments in this area. This complex contains two buildings, Biruni and Andaruni, within a garden. The Andaruni (inner) building served as living quarters

12 Parviz Salahi and Mehri Basnas, *History of Foreign Schools in Iran* (Tehran: Avae Noor, 2003), pp. 196, 197.

13 Najmi, *Dar al-Khalafah*, p. 340.

while the Biruni (outer) building housed Ghavam Al-Saltaneh's office. The garden was situated in the middle of Si-ye Tir Street, north of the American area.

The construction of this complex began in 1912 and took almost three years to complete. However, Ghavam Al-Saltaneh was unable to live at the mansion for long, as he was exiled to Europe in 1923 by Reza Khan and moved to Paris. During this period, he initially rented this property to the Egyptian Embassy but was soon forced to sell it to them in order to cover his living costs in Europe. His name remained prominently displayed on the street until the Islamic Revolution in 1979, when the name was changed to Si-ye Tir. After the Egyptian Embassy, the property was owned by the Afghanistan Embassy and later the Iranian Commerce Bank.

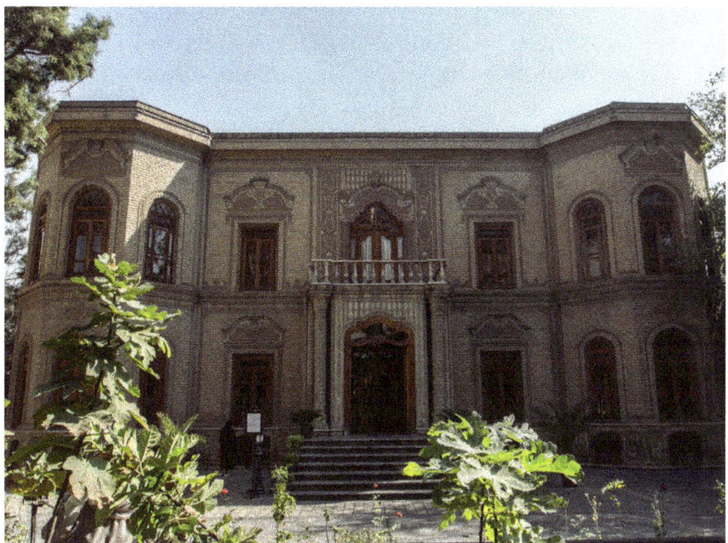

Fig. 3.4 The Glassware and Ceramic Museum of Iran (outward section of Ghavam house), Tehran. Author's photograph, 2018, CC BY-NC-ND.

Following a 1977 renovation led by the Austrian architect Hans Hollein, the outer facility of the site was transformed into the Iranian Glassware and Ceramic Museum, while its inner facility became a cultural centre and eventually the Farabi Cinema Foundation. Both buildings still operate in these capacities.[14]

---

14 Maryam Mirzaei and Ali Haeri, 'Austrian Artist Hans Hollein: Designer of Tehran Glass Museum', *Journal of Architecture and Culture*, 52 (2016), 85–90 (p. 87).

Haim Synagogue is another religious edifice located in this area. Unlike the Zoroastrians and Christians, there is no authentic information about the time of Jewish settlement in this area. After the success of the Iranian constitutional revolution in 1909, the Jewish community purchased a plat in an alley to the west of Si-ye Tir Street, opposite the American school and church. In 1913, they constructed a synagogue that would come to be known as Haim Synagogue, which is still used for Saturday worship.

Despite Iran's neutral status in the First World War, Russian and British forces occupied large parts of the country. The young Ahmad Shah, the last king of the Qajar dynasty, was unable to maintain order and stability in the country. In this context, a Qazaq officer named Reza Khan fought several wars for the country and devised reforms which helped to preserve unity and restore security. His efforts earned him the parliament's support for major change. On 31 October 1925, the parliament announced the end of the Qajar dynasty and designated Reza Shah as the first king of the Pahlavi dynasty.

To demonstrate his competence and authority, Reza Shah sought to forge a connection with the ancient Persian Empire. The predominantly Modernist approach adopted in this era led to significant improvements in various sectors of society. Many governmental and public facilities were constructed drawing clear architectural inspirations from ancient Persian motifs, which came to be known as the National style. These changes gradually transformed the traditional characteristics of Tehran. To reinforce military power, one of Reza Shah's first actions was to build several military camps outside the city. This stripped Meydan-e Mashgh oft its military function, rendering the site obsolete and insecure. As a result, in 1927, the municipality decided to create a European-style public park in its place named Bagh-e Melli (national garden).

One of the most notable structures in this garden is the Bagh-e Melli Gateway (propylaeum), commemorating Tehran's occupation during a 1921 coup attempted by Reza Shah, the war minister of Ahmad Shah at that time.

Meydan-e Mashgh was soon divided into smaller plots, which the government allocated to various state institutions. The Post Office was one of the first facilities constructed on this land, accompanied by the construction of the two-storey Iranian-British oil company office on the west side of the gateway. The Officers' Club, Police Station (Shahrbani House), Detention

Centre, Document Registration Office and Ministry of Foreign Affairs were among the buildings constructed in Meydan-e Mashq.[15]

Although welcomed by the people, Bagh-e Melli's role as a public park was short-lived. The first alteration came in 1933, when a large portion of its eastern side was designated for a museum and a library. The National Museum and the National Library, completed in 1937,[16] were designed by French architect André Godard. The National Museum was the first building constructed to serve as a modern museum in the city, and the National Library was the first intended to be a library. The National Museum still operates in this location, while the National Library, after about seven decades, was relocated to a new building outside the old city centre and is now operating as a museum. Today, the original building houses the National Science and Technology Museum on its first floor and a museum dedicated to scribing and printing on the ground level.

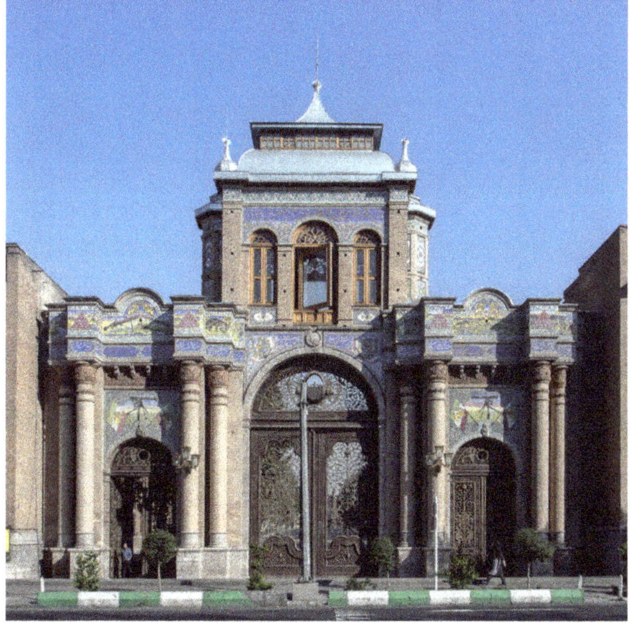

Fig. 3.5 *Bagh-e Melli*, gateway/propylaeum, Tehran. Author's photograph, 2018, CC BY-NC-ND.

15 Eskandar Mokhtari Taleghani and Ahad Valizadeh, *Practice Square* (Tehran: Cultural Research Office, 2010), p. 10.

16 Ali Asghar Hekmat, 'Notes from the Pahlavi Era: The First Interrogation', *Vahid Memoirs Journal*, 19 (1973), 13–21.

In 1940, Reza Shah ordered the construction of a new building to compliment the National Museum on the empty plat to its east. After being delayed for various reasons, the construction process was completed in 1959. This museum has had various names over the years and is now known as the Museum of Art and Archaeology of Islamic Iran, functioning as a supplement to the National Museum.[17]

During the Second World War, despite Iran taking a neutral position, allied forces occupied the country in September 1941, forcing Reza Shah's abdication. The allies agreed to transfer power to his son, Crown Prince Mohammad Reza.

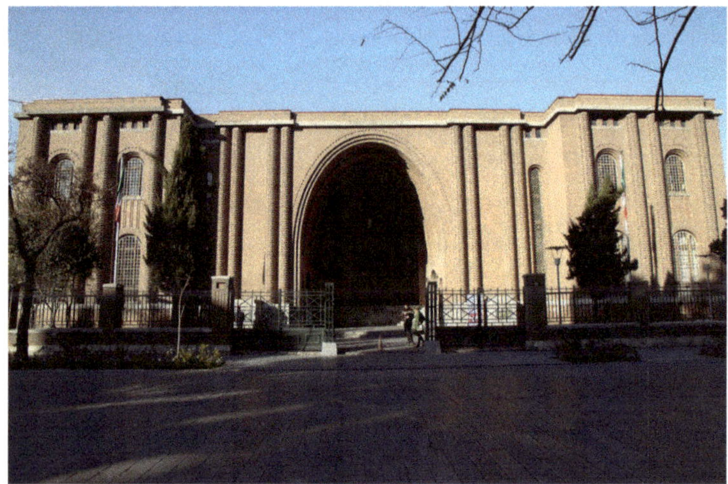

Fig. 3.6 National Museum of Iran, Tehran. Author's photograph, 2018, CC BY-NC-ND.

An important wartime event that took place in this area was the Tehran Conference, held between 28 November and 1 December 1943. The conference brought together three allied leaders—United States President Franklin D. Roosevelt, British Prime Minister Winston Churchill and Soviet Premier Joseph Stalin—for confidential negotiations in the fourth year of the Second World War. The conference, following on a previous meeting held in Cairo, was one in a series of conferences with the goal of striking an agreement on the post-war world order.[18]

17 Mohamad Reza Riazi, 'National Museum of Iran: Problems and Guidelines', *Journal of Architecture and Construction*, 38 (2014), 116–27 (p. 120).

18 Nikoli Dolgopolov, *Vartanian: The Story of the Greatest Soviet Spy in Iran*, trans. by Bashir Arshadi (Tehran: Al-Huda International Publications, 2016), pp. 38–60.

In recognition of this significant milestone in Tehran's history, the municipality decided in June 1944 to rename three streets in the capital after the three world leaders. The northern section of Si-ye Tir Street, which led to the Russian Embassy, was renamed Marchal Stalin.

St. Mary Armenian Apostolic Church, another religious building on Si-ye Tir Street, began construction in 1938, opening seven years later following its sanctification and related formal ceremonies. As previously discussed, the Armenians had planned to construct a church many years earlier, at the same time as the construction of the first Armenian school in the area, Haykazian School, and on the same plat.[19]

The third and final church in this area, built in 1949, belongs to the Seventh Day Adventists, a branch of Protestant Christianity. The Adventist Church was constructed a short distance from the Evangelical Presbyterian Church.

After the construction of this church during the late reign of the second Pahlavi king, no other religious buildings were constructed in the area. However, new schools were built in the coming years for Zoroastrian, Armenian and Muslim children. Among these were the Firuz Bahram School and Rostam Abadian Nursery School for Zoroastrian children, and the Kooshesh Davidian High School and Vache Hovsepyan Primary School for Armenian children.

The Iranian Islamic Revolution took place on 11 February 1979, marking the start of a new cultural, social, political and economic era in the country. After the revolution, Iran's relationships with European countries changed dramatically and its ties were severed with the United States. Most contracts with foreign companies were dissolved and American and European consultants left the country, along with Iranians belonging to religious or ethnic minority groups. A portion of Si-ye Tir Street's inhabitant likewise departed Iran with this wave of emigration.

In the aftermath of the Islamic Revolution, many streets in Tehran were renamed. The southern part of the street, between Imam Khomeini Square to Jomhuri Eslami Street, was designated Si-ye Tir Street in memory of the martyrs of the 1952 uprising.[20] The northern part of the

19 Shahin Hospian, 'A Brief Look at the History of Armenian Churches in Iran', *Peyman Cultural Quarterly*, 27 (2004), 52–68 (p. 54).

20 The Sie Tir uprising occurred in July 1952, when Iranians demanded Ghavam Al-Saltaneh's removal from office and the return of Dr. Mohammad Mosadeq.

street, from Jomhuri Eslami Street to Neauphle-le-Château, was named after Mirza Kuchak Khan, the revolutionary leader of Nehzat-e Jangal (the Jungle Movement) in the early twentieth century.

The third mosque and the last religious building constructed in this area, Ebrahim-e Khalil Mosque, was built in the post-revolutionary period. It was constructed in 1957 northeast of Abgineh Museum (formerly Ghavam Al-Saltaneh's house).

In this period, another museum, the Malek Museum, was constructed east of the Museum of Art and Archaeology of Islamic Iran. Several other governmental buildings in the Meydan-e Mashgh were also converted into museums, including the Post and Communications Museum in the old building of the Postal Ministry and Ebrat Museum in the former detention facility. After slight modifications, the former Ghazzagh-Khane building also came to house the University of Art.[21]

Si-ye Tir Street and its Surroundings Today

The narrative of the religious architecture and religious minorities in this area transformed after the Islamic Revolution. According to the Constitution of the Islamic Republic of Iran, Iranian Christians, Zoroastrians and Jews are the only recognised religious minorities in the country.

Within the confines of the law, these groups are free to perform their religious rites and ceremonies as well as to defer to their respective canons in matters of personal affairs and religious education. According to this principle, followers of these three faiths continue to practice their rituals in the area's various fire temples, churches and synagogues. With the exception of the Adventist Church, the minority religious centres in the district remain operational and continue to serve their followers.

While the district has seen a decrease in minority populations, with many moving to different areas or even to other countries, the religious and cultural centres of these communities continue to attract many

This led to clashes between the civilians and the military, resulting in significant casualties. Those who perished during the uprising were later declared national martyrs.

21 Maryam Mirzaei, *The Story of the Street: The Evolution of Si-Ye Tir Street* (Tehran: Gooya House of Art and Culture, 2019), pp. 77–82.

followers of these religions to the street for religious events. For schools, however, the reduced number of children living in the area has taken a heavy toll, with some schools even transformed into other facilities. For example, two Armenian schools were shuttered due to low enrolment, and three Zoroastrian schools are facing serious resource shortages.

In terms of structure, the street has maintained its historical appearance, preserving the important religious, cultural and educational edifices. While some modifications have been made to the street and several residential buildings, these have not impacted the street's overall appearance.

In 2016, the street was repaved with carpet stones, replacing the previous asphalt pavement that had been in place since its early unpaved period. This change was intended to reduce car traffic, although the street is still open to vehicles.

In the fall of the same year, a festival took place on Si-ye Tir Street, west of the Iranian National Museum, featuring a variety of ambulant food vendors, street-food stalls, fast food brands and coffee shops. After the festival, many of these food vendors remained on the street, increasing rapidly in number and giving the street a reputation as a street-food destination.[22]

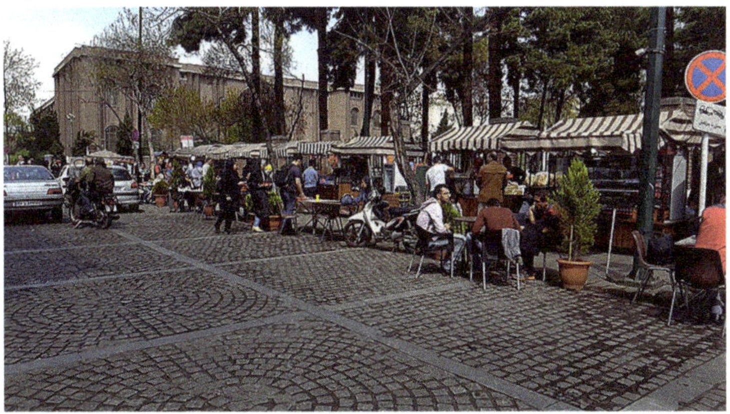

Fig. 3.7 Street food of Si-ye Tir. Photograph by GTVM92 (2017), Wikimedia, https://commons.wikimedia.org/wiki/File:30Tir_20170401_142730.jpg, CC BY-SA-4.0.

22 Ibid., pp. 82–86.

Conclusion

As places imbued with cultural heritage values, old city centres represent various historical periods with their spatial and structural characteristics. Preserving their values and interpreting their significance plays an important role in protecting the collective memories of citizens and constitutes an investment in knowledge and cultural heritage.

This chapter described and analysed Tehran's historical, architectural and urban development through the case study of Si-ye Tir Street. This major cultural landmark is the site of diverse religious heritage, encompassing Zoroastrian, Jewish, Christian and Muslim communities.

Today, the district comprising Si-ye Tir and Mirza Kuchak Khan streets is roughly 150 years old, originating during the reign of Nasser al-Din Shah Qajar. In the late Nasseri era, Western and European citizens living in Tehran left their mark on the city's landscape with the construction of various facilities and European-style mansions. This attracted religious minorities to the area, including citizens of various religious backgrounds. These communities likewise established various necessary facilities nearby, including religious, educational and service facilities, many of which are still in operation today.

Since the late nineteenth century, this street has witnessed Tehran's social, cultural and religious evolution, as a place where people from different backgrounds coexist peacefully. While some researchers believe that the constitutional revolution's success explains the concentration of religious minorities in this zone, this chapter has demonstrated that this phenomenon occurred even earlier.

In contrast to many of Tehran's old districts, which are today transformed or abandoned, the Si-ye Tir district preserves its multi-faceted historical heritage while continuing to develop. The unique dynamism and urban cohesion of this area presents enormous potential for even greater progress.

With its invaluable religious structures, museums and other priceless architecture such as the Bagh-e Melli propylaeum, this street is still the site of important cultural and social events and has the capacity to become one of Tehran's premier tourist attractions. On par with many of the world's most famous streets, Si-ye Tir boasts a vibrant nightlife and offers visitors the chance to explore, be entertained, learn, and enjoy local cuisine.

Bibliography

Bani Massoud, Amir, *Contemporary Iranian Architecture* (Tehran: Century Architecture Publishing, 2012).

Bolaghi Hosseini, Abdol Hojat, *History of Tehran: Central and Additions [and North]*, 3 vols. (Tehran: Maziar, 1971).

Dolgopolov, Nikoli, *Vartanian: The Story of the Greatest Soviet Spy in Iran*, trans. by Bashir Arshadi (Tehran: Al-Huda International Publications, 2016).

Eldar, Jan, *History of the American Mission in Iran*, trans. by Soheil Azari (Tehran: Noorjahan, 1952).

Hekmat, Ali Asghar, 'Notes from the Pahlavi Era: The First Interrogation', *Vahid Memoirs Journal*, 19 (1973), 21–13.

Hospian, Shahin, 'A Brief Look at the History of Armenian Churches in Iran', *Peyman Cultural Quarterly*, 27 (2004), 68–52.

Kariman, Hasan, *Tehran in the Past and Present* (Tehran: National Iranian University Press, 1976).

Minasian, Hovik, 'From Haykazian School to Kooshesh High School', trans. by Garon Sarkisian, *Hoys Biweekly*, 199 (2012), 3.

Mirzaei, Maryam, *The Story of the Street: The Evolution of Si-Ye Tir street* (Tehran: Gooya House of Art and Culture, 2019).

Mirzaei, Maryam and Haeri, Ali, 'Austrian Artist Hans Hollein: Designer of Tehran Glass Museum', *Tehran: Journal of Architecture and Culture*, 52 (2016), 90–85, 256.

Mokhtari Taleghani, Eskandar and Valizadeh, Ahad, *Practice Square* (Tehran: Cultural Research Office, 2010).

Motamedi, Mohsen, *Historical Geography of Tehran* (Tehran: University Publishing Center, 2002), pp. 260–67.

Najmi, Nasser, *Dar al-Khalafah*, 2nd ed. (Tehran: Hamgam, 1988).

Pourrostami, Faramarz, *Tehran Zoroastrian Association: A Century of Effort and Service* (Tehran: Forouhar Publishing Cultural Institute, 2008).

Riazi, Mohamad Reza, 'National Museum of Iran: Problems and Guidelines', *Journal of Architecture and Construction*, 38 (2014), 116–27.

Roustaei, Mohsen, *History of Medicine*, 2 vols. (Tehran: Documents Organization and National Library of the Islamic Republic of Iran, 2003).

Salahi, Parviz and Basnas, Mehri, *History of Foreign Schools in Iran* (Tehran: Avae Noor, 2003).

II. OLD NEIGHBOURHOODS: COMMUNITIES AND LOCAL PARTICIPATION

4. Sustainable Cultural Heritage through Participatory Planning: A Transect Walk in the Lweibdeh Neighbourhood in Amman

Maiss Razem and Sura AlHalalsheh[1]

Introduction

Conservation paradigms have evolved significantly over the past few decades, increasingly foregrounding multifarious interpretations of cultural heritage as an asset for future generations. Accordingly, unearthing community dynamics has been advocated in sustainable urban planning and heritage conservation as a means of surpassing formal narratives and capturing the connections between tangible and intangible heritage. In addition to providing valuable insight for planning authorities, understanding these community-based interpretations of local heritage has been argued to enable 'communities of discourse',[2] which can facilitate more sustainable forms of management and local

1 The authors thank the Friends of Lweibdeh Cultural Association (FOLCA) for nominating participants in the transect walks and for sharing their time, contacts and valuable information for the research. We thank Lweibdeh's residents and users who volunteered to share their appreciated knowledge and experiences with us.

2 Kevin Walsh, *The Representation of the Past: Museums and Heritage in the Post-Modern World* (London: Routledge, 1992), p. 158.

 https://doi.org/10.11647/OBP.0412.04

governance.[3] The recent recognition of cultural heritage's role in achieving the 2030 agenda of the United Nations UN) Sustainable Development Goals (SDGs), specifically Target 11.4, has provided governments with a broad roadmap to track implementation[4] and a more detailed toolkit for localisation.[5] Arguably, localised routes to achieve SDGs merit greater attention in the emerging economies of the Global South,[6] where rapid urbanisation can generate a sense of loss and erosion of heritage.

Considering these challenges, this chapter investigates the context of Jordan, focusing on the Lweibdeh neighbourhood in Amman. Lweibdeh, nationally recognised for its historical and cultural significance, has been attracting the attention of various stakeholders seeking to capitalise on the location's affordances. Amman and Lweibdeh have undergone fast-paced growth, necessitating prompt scholarly attention.[7] Acknowledging the need to localise SDGs, this chapter examines the method of 'transect walk' as a participatory-planning tool to explore Lweibdeh's values, which are linked to the daily experiences of the neighbourhood's inhabitants. As such, this chapter poses the question: Do 'transect walks' offer knowledge about community resources essential to conserving cultural heritage beyond conventional participatory planning? Can it qualify as a 'localised' method worthy of consideration for achieving Target 11.4, adaptable across various contexts?

In addressing these questions, the chapter first provides a literature review, examining the role of 'values' in conservation, participatory planning and sustainability discourses. It then evaluates

---

3 Andrew Hodges and Steve Watson, 'Community-Based Heritage Management: A Case Study and Agenda for Research', *International Journal of Heritage Studies*, 6.3 (2000), 231–43.

4 United Nations, *SDG Goal 11 Monitoring Framework: A Guide to Assist National and Local Governments to Monitor and Report on SDG Goal 11 Indicators* (Nairboi: United Nations, 2016), https://www.local2030.org/library/60/SDG-Goal-11-Monitoring-Framework-A-guide-to-assist-national-and-local-governments-to-monitor-and-report-on-SDG-goal-11-indicators.pdf

5 Ege Yıldırım, *ICOMOS Action Plan: Cultural Heritage and Localizing the UN Sustainable Development Goals (SDGs)* (Istanbul: ICOMOS, 2017), p. 17, https://www.icomos.org/images/DOCUMENTS/Secretariat/2017/ICOMOS_Action_Plan_Cult_Heritage_and_Localizing_SDGs_20170721.pdf

6 Harini Nagendra *et al.*, 'The Urban South and the Predicament of Global Sustainability', *Nature Sustainability*, 1.7 (2018), 341–49, https://doi.org/10.1038/s41893-018-0101-5

7 Rami Daher, 'Amman's Vanishing Legacy of Modernity', *Jordan Property*, 23 (2008), 10–21.

the underutilised ethnographic method of 'transect walks' for its analytical potential in heritage studies and SDG localisation. Third, the findings from three transect walks are presented, highlighting the various resources revealed by the walks to be valued by the local community and their potential to tap into mainstream cultural heritage for sustainable development. Finally, the chapter concludes by arguing for the method's inclusion in SDG localisation plans on account of its methodological utility in delineating local priorities for safeguarding the cultural heritage of Lweibdeh.

Literature Review

Valorising Cultural Heritage

Value is a term that appeared throughout the eighteenth and nineteenth centuries but became widespread in the twentieth century with the decline of traditional beliefs, following Friedrich Nietzsche's proclamation that 'God is dead'.[8] The term lacks a precise definition, as each discipline assigns a relative meaning. However, in the field of cultural heritage, Marta de la Torre offers the following descriptive definition:

> [...] positive characteristics attributed to heritage objects and places by legislation, governing authorities, and other stakeholders. These characteristics are what make a heritage site significant and are the reason why stakeholders and authorities are interested in it. The benefits of heritage are inextricably linked to these values.[9]

Alois Riegl was among the first to systematically classify multiple values in modern conservation.[10] More importantly, he assigned a fundamental significance to clarifying variations in the perception of these values, as

8 Luisa De Marco, 'Values in Heritage Conservation: From Museification towards Human Cohabitation', paper presented at the Values-based Decision-making for Conservation conference (Ottawa, 2005).

9 Marta de la Torre, Margaret G. H. MacLean, Randall Mason, and David Myers, 'Introduction', in *Heritage Values in Site Management: Four Case Studies*, ed. by Marta de la Torre (Los Angeles, CA: The Getty Conservation Institute, 2005), pp. 3–9 (p. 5).

10 Alois Riegl, 'The Modern Cult of Monument: Its Essence and Its Development', in *Historical and Philosophical Issues in the Conservation of Cultural Heritage*, ed.

this would decisively influence the direction of all conservation works. Cesare Brandi made a major contribution in relating the values of artistic work to the conservation process and in stressing the importance of contextuality.[11] Another pivotal development in the conservation field occurred in 1979 when the International Council on Monuments and Sites (ICOMOS) issued the Burra Charter, defining cultural significance and advocating for the consideration of all values when conserving a heritage site, without unwarranted emphasis on any one value at the expense of others.[12] Thereafter, several charters and declarations re-examined various approaches to value recognition in order to adapt conservation practice to an expanding reality.

One key concept in the evolution of heritage practice is understanding the nature of values as attributed, manifold, mutable, incommensurable and in conflict, which means that the values in heritage are never inherent: '[I]n fact, heritage places are value-neutral until they are attributed cultural value, at that point they cross into the category of heritage'.[13] Multiple values may be attributed to a place by different interested groups, which could result in a conflict between two or more values.

By 'validating the idea that heritage is valued in myriad different ways, by myriad different people and institutions with different world-views and epistemologies',[14] planning for cultural heritage sites is 'rapidly moving away from fairly authoritarian and centralized decision making toward concerns for social inclusion and involving local stakeholders and communities in dealing with the historic environment'.[15] Consequently, participatory value-centred planning is

---

by Nicholas C. Price, M. Kirby Talley Jr., and Alessandra Melucco Vaccaro (Los Angeles, CA: Getty Publications, 1996), pp. 69–83.

11 Cesare Brandi, 'Theory of Restoration 2', in *Historical and Philosophical Issues in the Conservation of Cultural Heritage*, ed. by Nicholas C. Price, M. Kirby Talley Jr., and Alessandra Melucco Vaccaro (Los Angeles, CA: Getty Publications, 1996), pp. 339–42.

12 Australia ICOMOS, *The Burra Charter: The Australia ICOMOS Charter for Places of Cultural Significance 2013* (Burwood: Australia ICOMOS, 2013), p. 4.

13 Marta de la Torre, 'Values and Heritage Conservation', *Heritage & Society*, 6.2 (2013), 155–66 (p. 160).

14 Randall Mason, 'Theoretical and Practical Arguments for Values-Centered Preservation', *CRM: The Journal of Heritage Stewardship*, 3.2 (2006), 21–40 (p. 31).

15 Willem J. H. Willems, 'Laws, Language, and Learning Managing Archaeological Heritage Resources in Europe', in *Cultural Heritage Management: A Global Perspective*, ed. by Phyllis Mauch Messenger and George S. Smith (Gainesville, FL: University Press of Florida, 2010), pp. 212–29 (p. 220).

one approach to achieving much-needed community involvement and accommodating myriad valuations.

Participatory Planning

Participatory planning may be defined as 'a categorical term for citizen power. It is the redistribution of power that enables the have-not citizens, presently excluded from the political and economic processes, to be deliberately included in the future'.[16] In general, several methods may be employed in participatory planning. According to Sherry Arnstein's 'ladder' of citizen participation, each method entails a different level of participation, ranging from manipulation at the bottom of the ladder, where a few citizens are placed on advisory boards but have no substantial influence, and ascending to full participation at the top, where citizens exercise complete control over the planning process. In the middle of this ladder is the tokenism rung, which comprises three levels of participation. The lowest level, 'informing', in most cases results in a one-way flow of information from authorities to citizens, without allowing for feedback or empowering citizens for negotiation. However, this is considered an important first step toward 'legitimate citizen participation'.[17]

Urban development projects in the Middle East, including cultural heritage management projects, fall within the tokenism rung, as observed by Luna Khirfan and Bessma Momani[18] in their investigation of several participatory projects in Amman. Based on their evaluation of methods and participant groups, they concluded that not only was participation in these projects at the lowest informing level, but that several instances of tyranny were exhibited in both method and participant selection. Seteney Shami's argument supports this finding in her book chapter 'Ethnographies of Governance', where she states that an 'unequal participation in governance becomes a given in the cities of the Middle East and is reinforced not only through political processes

16 Sherry R. Arnstein, 'A Ladder of Citizen Participation', *Journal of the American Institute of Planners*, 35.4 (1969), 216–24 (p. 216).

17 Arnstein, 'Ladder', p. 219.

18 Luna Khirfan and Bessma Momani, 'Tracing Participatory Planning in Amman', in *Order and Disorder: Urban Governance and the Making of Middle Eastern Cities*, ed. by Luna Khirfan, Kristin Good, and Martin Horak (Montreal: McGill-Queen's University Press, 2017), pp. 79–102, https://doi.org/10.1515/9780773549760-006

[method] but also by intellectual processes of exclusion [group]'.[19] She calls for a rhetorical transition from urban services to urban resources, where spaces, kinship networks, environment, neighbourly relations and other elements are all considered resources used by communities to define heritage and identity. Hence, shifting away from a conventional focus on urban services, there is a need to operationalise a participatory method that 'provide[s] a model on how to work on local issues in local ways'[20] and unearths communities' urban resources.

Cultural Heritage and Sustainable Development

The role of culture and heritage in sustainability has long been overlooked or subsumed under the 'social' pillar of the three-pillar sustainability framework. However, calls for their inclusion as a 'fourth pillar' of sustainability[21] have since been explicitly recognised in Target 11.4 to 'strengthen efforts to protect and safeguard the world's cultural and natural heritage'.

A 2019 report by the Culture2030Goal campaign offers insight into the nuanced ways culture contributes to the synergies between SDGs,[22] indicating the need to empirically illustrate culture's performative role in achieving sustainability. Evidence-based research on the interconnectedness of culture with many SDGs enriches research and policy, shedding light on SDG interdependencies that have often been overlooked. Since '[e]ffective translation of SDG indicators from the global to the national level is needed, and national governments are considered as key actors in this process',[23] the localisation of Target 11.4 has been addressed in ICOMOS's Priority Actions. Specifically,

19 Seteney Shami, 'Ethnographies of Governance: Urban Spaces and Actors in the Middle East', in *Governance on the Ground: Innovations and Discontinuities in Cities of the Developing World*, ed. by Patricia Louise Mc Carney and Richard E. Stren (Washington, DC: Woodrow Wilson Center Press, 2003), pp. 58–82 (p. 80).

20 Shami, *Ethnographies*, p. 80

21 Jon Hawkes, *The Fourth Pillar of Sustainability: Culture's Essential Role in Public Planning* (Melbourne: Cultural Development Network: Common Ground, 2004); UCLG, *Culture: Fourth Pillar of Sustainable Development* (Barcelona: United Cities and Local Governments, 2010), p. 8.

22 Culture2030Goal Campaign, *Culture in the Implementation of the 2030 Agenda* (Barcelona, Paris, Harare, Sydney, Montreal, The Hague and Brussels: United Nations, 2019), p. 105.

23 Florian Koch and Kerstin Krellenberg, 'How to Contextualize SDG 11? Looking at Indicators for Sustainable Urban Development in Germany', *ISPRS International Journal of Geo-Information*, 7.12 (2018), 464.

one of the actions' principles reflects 'making "localizing" graspable by active interaction with localities at the level of the citizen and local decision-making'.[24]

In publishing Jordan's first Voluntary National Review (VNR) for SDG implementation, eighteen working groups were formed to delineate intersections between the seventeen SDGs. In contradistinction to the other seventeen groups, the 'culture and youth' group was prevalent and intersected with all SDGs, underscoring the essential role culture plays in sustainable development. In this context, culture serves to 'strengthen the link between communities and their environments and enable vibrant cultural diversity'.[25]

In sum, the discourse on the incommensurability of cultural heritage values and the imperative of inclusive, participatory planning permeates the 'localisation' efforts of Target 11.4. Given Jordan's commitment to safeguarding its rich cultural heritage as part of SDG implementation, understanding local priorities is paramount.[26] In order for Jordan to advance in operationalising tools to achieve culture-related SDGs, heritage needs to be framed

> beyond monuments and protected areas to socio-economic aspects/integrated conservation, focusing on incorporation of heritage values into territorial development and planning policies and on partnerships with local government, civil society organizations and non-heritage stakeholders based on common interests.[27]

Method

This chapter draws upon the Rapid Ethnographic Assessment Procedures (REAP) for conservation,[28] specifically utilising 'transect walks' to understand community/place interactions. While transect walks have been used extensively in fields like agriculture to identify communities' natural resources, the method is employed in this study

24 Yıldırım, *ICOMOS*, p. 5.

25 MOPIC, *Jordan's Way to Sustainable Development: First National Voluntary Review on the Implementation of the 2030 Agenda* (Jordan: Ministry of Planning and International Cooperation, 2017), pp. 54–55.

26 Maiss Razem, 'Place Attachment and Sustainable Communities', *Architecture_MPS*, 17.2 (2020), https://doi.org/10.14324/111.444.amps.2020v17i1.003

27 Yıldırım, *ICOMOS*, p. 5.

28 Getty, *Assessing the Values of Cultural Heritage: Research Report* (Los Angeles, CA: The Getty Conservation Institute, 2002), p. 36.

to explore the cultural values of Lweibdeh's community as 'resources'. Transect walks are intended to extract local knowledge shared by community members through the unconventional emancipatory walk-and-talk approach. Several studies have emphasised the relation between walking and knowledge production, liberation and empowerment, framing 'walking as an everyday practice—or "tactic"—that can open democratic possibilities by deviating from the strategies employed by urban planners, architects and engineers to exert power over citizen behaviors'.[29] While conventional methods may be helpful in collecting comprehensive data about a place, they often fail to account for the microfeatures of the built environment. In a comparative study of seated interviews and the walk-along method, Jessica Finlay and Jay Bowman, regarding the latter, noted:

> the method stood apart from the seated interview in its ability to access reflexive and unrefined lived experiences in situ [...] The mobile interview offered rich insights into place and self: It attended to participants' rich realities [...] Participants were empowered to become the 'tour guide' and expert.[30]

In addressing the question 'How can we, as social science researchers, harness the power of place in our methodology?',[31] Anderson argues that 'talking whilst walking' can unearth memories and values of which the researched or the researcher may have been unaware. Such a method

> produces not a conventional interrogative encounter, but a collage of collaboration: an unstructured dialogue where all actors participate in a conversational, geographical and informational pathway creation. Consequently, the knowledge produced is importantly different: atmospheres, emotions, reflections and beliefs can be accessed, as well as intellects, rationales and ideologies.[32]

This chapter draws on the research potential of place-produced knowledge by employing transect walks, a method with the promising

29 Saskia Warren, 'Pluralising the Walking Interview: Researching (Im)Mobilities with Muslim Women', *Social & Cultural Geography*, 18.6 (2017), 786–807 (p. 790).

30 Jessica M. Finlay and Jay A. Bowman, 'Geographies on the Move: A Practical and Theoretical Approach to the Mobile Interview', *The Professional Geographer*, 69.2 (2017), 263–74 (pp. 267, 269).

31 Jon Anderson, 'Talking Whilst Walking: A Geographical Archaeology of Knowledge', *AREA*, 36.3 (2004), 254–61 (p. 257).

32 Ibid., p. 260.

capacity to illuminate community values and resources that conventional methods may overlook or marginalise.

Three transect walks were conducted in October 2020 by the authors, accompanied by members of the Friends of Lweibdeh Cultural Association (FOLCA). The walks covered a geographical area that had been witnessing drastic changes for several years. The method's democratic nature allowed participants to alter their paths, highlighting individual points of interest, concerns, social connections and cherished memories while staying within the pre-set area. The walks were conducted on different days and at different times to observe life in Lweibdeh from diverse temporal perspectives.

Eleven participants were involved in the walk, aged twenty-five to seventy-five. Some were not among the study's original participants but were individuals encountered during the walks—shop owners, building guards, business owners and residents—who engaged in dialogue willingly. The conversations were in Arabic, audio recorded, translated into English, and transcribed. Participants' names are anonymised and replaced with pseudonyms, and all sites mentioned by participants were photographed.

Findings

Each transect walk followed a different route within the area of Paris Square, Al-Shari'a Street and Dirar bin-Alazwar Street, as depicted in Figure 4.1. The paths passed by houses of historical and architectural significance, like the one shown in Figure 4.2. Three main places of interest, marked in Figure 4.1, emerged from the walks and discussions as representative of participants' contested values: the restaurant zone, Bsharat Church and House C. While other locations in Lweibdeh deserve equal if not greater analytical attention, these three nodes were the most frequently mentioned and referred to when participants' transcripts were coded and seemed to have spillover effects like socio-economic changes and the shaping of the heritage discourse. The walks uncovered three resources that can contribute to mainstream cultural heritage for sustainable development: community-shared values; old/new synergies and conflicts, and the voice of local knowledge; and stakeholders' networking dynamics.

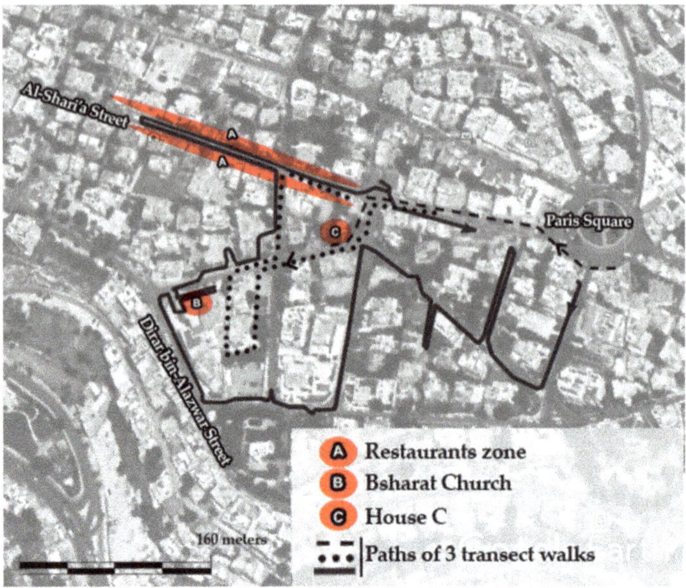

Fig. 4.1 Aerial view of part of Lweibdeh, showing the walks and places of interest. Author's illustration, based on Google Earth (2020), CC BY-NC-ND.

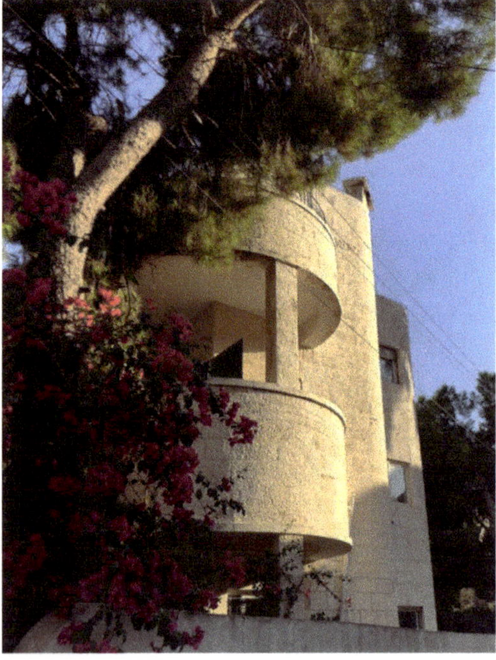

Fig. 4.2 One of Lweibdeh's houses seen while walking, featuring circular balconies. Author's photograph, 2020, CC BY-NC-ND.

Community-shared Values

The unique spirit of a place is not merely a product of its distinctive architecture and urban setting but is meaningfully constructed by its residents, visitors and workers. During the transect walks, participants led the way and conversations flowed in a non-structured manner, prompted by general questions, such as what a typical daily routine in Lweibdeh consists of.

Lweibdeh has attracted many artists, becoming a cultural and artistic destination. Bilal, an artist from FOLCA who has been working in his studio for more than ten years, shared how Lweibdeh is a source of inspiration for him:

> First thing I do when I come to my studio, I water the plants...the most important thing in Lweibdeh is to enjoy its morning and listen to Fairuz.[33] Then I paint at my studio... and I walk around Lweibdeh... and I paint outside a lot... I really like walking in Lweibdeh... especially when I like to brainstorm about ideas... See this alley, for example... It would be great to activate it and have artists painting here. (Bilal, male, 55–65)

Walking through the neighbourhood, participants noted variations in noise levels and the concentration of vehicles from one street to another, and in many conversations, associations between values and these auditory characteristics were evident. For example, Bilal appreciated one particular street, describing it as 'one of the classiest and quietest streets in Lweibdeh'. The quaint nature of the neighbourhood is changing, according to Abed (male, 25–35), who remarked that 'you would not know this street at night... Lots of cars come here and park and young people... Another life is different from daytime, and it annoys residents'. During the walk, Bilal greeted Amer, who has been a security guard at one of the houses for ten years. Amer expressed similar views:

> It is different... changed to worse... It used to be very quiet... Now a lot of inappropriate activities happening in the streets... affecting families living here that represent the history of Jordan. It used to be that when working hours are over, you will not find cars, now you find day and night there are cars and people... This has only been happening during the last five or six years. (Amer, male, 45–55)

33 Famous Lebanese singer.

While the recent transformations in Lweibdeh have been marked by highly publicized restaurant openings on Al-Sharia Street, the quiet residential quarters are attractive to non-residents. The preference for quiet over growing levels of unwanted noise had physical manifestations. Pointing to a house that had uncharacteristically high fences compared to those common at old houses, Bilal said 'some are annoyed by the noises, many "for sale" signs... And see this house, they raised their fences to block noise and night activities'.

The value of 'quietness' attached to Lweibdeh as a whole is a part of the neighbourhood's identity that is being threatened by commercial creep, as iterated by Abed:

> I used to come here every Friday when I was a student and get my books signed by writers in Paris circle... The writers used to come to Paris circle... then it stopped in 2014... because it stopped being a good place. The whole identity of Lweibdeh has vanished. There used to be a lot of activities for youth... Now I come here for a purpose to work. I come here in times I know there will not be a lot of people... The most important thing is not to enter the restaurants' zone.

Nature was a prevalent theme during the walks, with participants expressing admiration for the age of pine trees and the aromas of jasmine trees. Surrounded by trees and planters, a recently repurposed building that previously housed Pakistani and American Embassies has retained many of its original features, thanks to its new owners. The building is currently a foundation for conserving Jordan's heritage and offers local cuisine. One staff member (male, 25–35) highlighted the importance of smell as a sensory experience of Lweibdeh where 'the purpose of having these aromatic plants (lavender, verbena, Otra, basil) in this planter is for the guest to pick his favourite herbs when he drinks his tea'. While seated for a cup of verbena tea, Bilal reflected that 'you sense a high spirituality in this place... Many embassies would not have selected it unless they sensed its special character... Did you see how beautiful the trees are?'

Contrary to the aforementioned building, which is perceived to have preserved its sense of place despite recent adaptations, changes made to some buildings have elicited disapproval for their seeming disrespect for Lweibdeh's essence. Old religious buildings in Lweibdeh are part of its place identity, like Bsharat Church and Al-Sharia Mosque, of which participants spoke fondly. Thus, when, in the words of Sanad, a longtime resident, 'new changes were horrendously and ignorantly done in Al-Sharia Mosque', he acted to preserve its value:

> There used to be old pine trees and they were removed, a fountain inside that was broken and removed... They placed more glazing in efforts to modernise the mosque. When I went to pray there, I stopped them from these major renewals and sand blasting the old stone. (Sanad, male, 65–75)

In addition to alterations to old buildings, demolitions pose a threat to both tangible and intangible place values. A five-story hotel development has been temporarily halted by local residents, as it required the demolition of an old house and the cutting down of its aged trees, shown in Figure 4.3.[34] Sanad, whose home overlooks the site, is frustrated that 'they came to the most beautiful corner in Lweibdeh, to House C... If it goes away, then we will no longer have a downtown... Each tree is around fifty to sixty years old, you know... It will be erased! The view of these trees and corners is a dream and imagine replacing it with a new stone building'. Kamel, who also lives near House C, also expressed that:

> They should stay within the walls of the building, retain the spirit of the old house and keep the trees, others have turned the buildings into restaurants but kept the buildings as they are... No country can be proud of itself unless it is proud of its heritage... This is our heritage, what will remain for us as Jordan if we lose this heritage? (Kamel, male, 65–75)

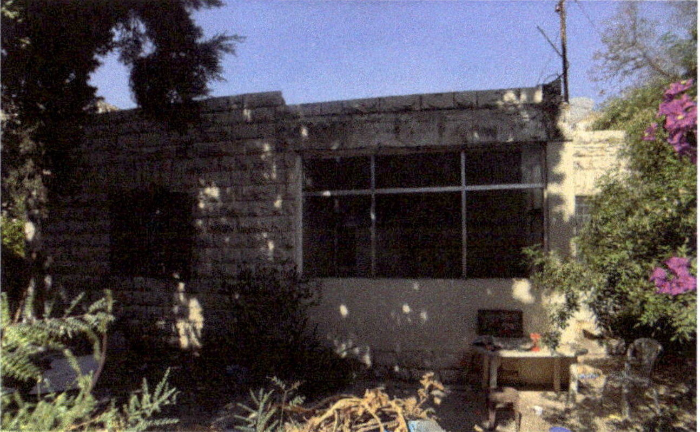

Fig. 4.3 The vacant House C in Lweibdeh. Author's photograph, 2020, CC BY-NC-ND.

34 Since the writing of this chapter, House C has been demolished, all its old trees have been cut down and the hotel project has already begun.

The walks revealed various significant values that characterise Lweibdeh according to those who interact with the neighbourhood daily. These include historical value, as for many participants the area represented both a physical and non-physical connection to the past, and an artistic value, embodied in its ability to stimulate the senses of its residents, visitors, and users. Moreover, the walks demonstrated that Lweibdeh has a strong social value stemming from the deep and enduring relationships between neighbours, a resilient sense of community and a noticeable feeling of general solidarity among original residents across social strata. Religious value, tangible and intangible, was also evident, whether in the historical religious buildings or in the coexistence between Muslims and Christians, which was noted during the walks.

One of the important values which emerged during the study is Lweibdeh's rich architectural heritage representing the legacy of modernity in Jordan. Despite the recent demolitions, the area retains research value stemming from this understudied period in Jordan's history. Several participants also highlighted the natural value of Lweibdeh; some cherished the old trees, others fought for their protection, and some viewed them as a means to attract tourists and visitors. Economic value was likewise articulated, primarily by shop owners, who expressed their desire to capitalise on the neighbourhood's cultural and aesthetic values and transform the area into a cultural hub and tourist destination.

While these sensory values were apparent from the participants, what is held dear can often be implicit, taken for granted and unacknowledged, seeming to surface only when new changes interrupt the status quo. With several new developments underway, community members, especially original inhabitants with local knowledge of Lweibdeh's multi-layered values, have emerged as essential resources for learning.

Old/new Synergies and Conflicts, and the Voice of Local Knowledge

Many residents expressed dissatisfaction with the 'restaurant zone', although others have accepted this change reluctantly. For Kamel, born and raised in Lweibdeh, restaurants 'brought the riffraff of Amman, but in the end, you say, it is like any downtown. It has a commercial centre... If you come at night, you cannot step in here'. The operating hours of these restaurants, extending late into the night, have been a nuisance for many, a sentiment which Hani reiterated:

> Why are restaurants still open till 4:00 am? What kind of productive society stays up all night smoking hookah? This is the quality of people who come here... Just look at the trash they leave in the morning, broken bottles and sometimes vandalism... The other day, some broke the glass of the barber shop. We need police presence. (Hani, male, 55–65)

The trend of transforming old shops and houses into restaurants was humorously but critically remarked upon during the walk. Bilal greeted a shop owner, praising his produce to us by saying, 'this is a place with most delicious coffee and nuts... and restaurant', to which the owner laughingly said, 'we are not a restaurant!' Jokingly, Bilal responded 'why don't you turn it into one then'. However, while this transformation of old buildings into restaurants and cafés has the potential to bring financial vitality to Lweibdeh, some locals are experiencing the effects of economic gentrification, as expressed by the security guard, Amer:

> I am happy about the increase in restaurants here, but for people like me who cannot afford it... I mean... before, I could buy cheap food from here. Now, when I want to eat, I go downtown... Eating from Lweibdeh is not economical for me anymore. I buy groceries and vegetables from downtown.

Not all of these changes are commercial in nature; new apartment buildings have also been popping up with increasing frequency, introducing a new typology of structures perceived as foreign to Lweibdeh's architectural character. As we approached the Bsharat Church, built in 1961, Abed pointed to a new apartment building. He urged us to 'look at this cultural shock... Compared to old-fashioned houses, this had a view of Jabal Amman, now it is blocked... What a view it used to be'.

Bilal shared Abed's sentiments, saying, 'it is suffocated now... Residents complained about these developments for five years, but it was done anyway'. As shown in Figures 4.4 and 4.5, the influx of apartment buildings has blocked the view from and to Bsharat Church over the last decade. While this illustrates the growing interest in investing in Lweibdeh, it conceals a narrative of contestation and struggle for power. Efforts to protect the value of the view and the significance of the church's visibility as a landmark were thwarted, as Hani explained:

> We struggled to fight against the construction of these five residential buildings... and they were built without avail. We collected 5,000 signatures to prevent them, but heritage is not a value to them (authorities)... They were built like dominos.

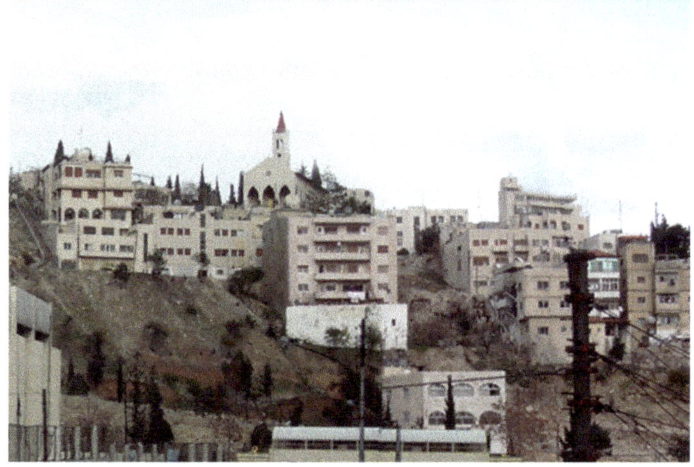

Fig. 4.4 Unobstructed view of Bsharat Church in Lweibdeh. Author's photograph, 2008, CC BY-NC-ND.

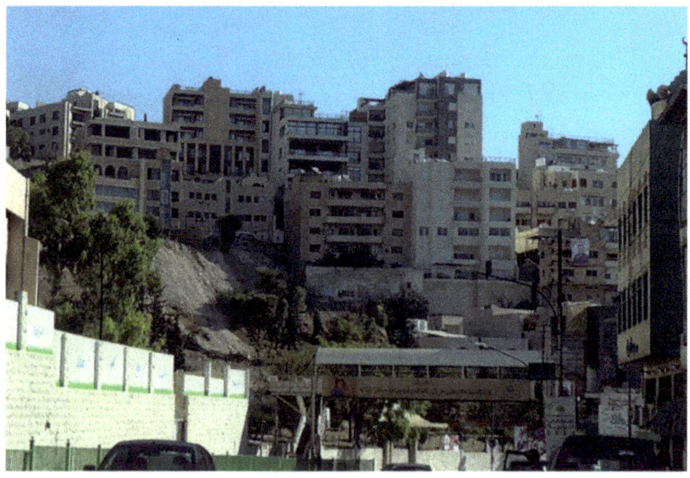

Fig. 4.5 Recent residential constructions blocking the view of Bsharat Church in Lweibdeh. Author's photograph, 2020, CC BY-NC-ND.

In navigating the balance between the old and the new, the values expressed by longtime residents appear to clash with the ambitions of newcomers. FOLCA has actively mobilised the community to defend against radical interventions, succeeding in some cases but failing in others. Many members, like Hani, have expressed frustration about the authorities' ambivalence towards the prioritisation of heritage conservation:

> The problem is when someone has a heritage house and decides to build over it without retaining the same style... We are not against progress in Lweibdeh but with responsible progress based on real study... Study the impact on the environment, people, consult people... There are people in the government who understand the meaning of heritage and heritage conservation, but they are not in the position of power... Many of their recommendations are not taken into consideration.

As conflicts arise, a democratic and participatory resolution process must focus on inclusion, where heritage experts and original residents play a pivotal role that cannot be side-lined. When we met with Dr. Rami Daher, an architect and heritage expert who works and has family roots in Lweibdeh, he perspicaciously remarked:

> Someone should be responsible for the voice of the place. Not all shop owners belong to Lweibdeh; there are old users of Lweibdeh and new users of Lweibdeh, some shop owners only care for their shops. In Lweibdeh, genuine efforts by people who are willing to stay for a long time are what will do.

This sentiment resonates with the active engagement of longtime residents, as expressed by Sanad, who, along with his neighbours, 'monitor[s] changes in neighbourhood... Many houses are purchased and demolished... If this keeps on going... no old house will remain in Lweibdeh'. Kamel and Sanad possess local knowledge that remains undocumented and untapped. One reason they are rallying against the demolition of House C is that, according to Kamel, 'it is one of the first houses that were built in Lweibdeh!'.

This community's cultural capital, as a resource, is also transforming, underscored by Kamel's remark that 'Lweibdeh has been almost emptied. The street in front of us is all cafes... People died, people moved... We are the survivors to conserve Lweibdeh'. Unlike Sanad and

Kamel, Bilal, who has been working in Lweibdeh for a decade but is not an original resident, devalued House C, claiming that there is nothing 'beautiful' about it except for the trees. The varied value judgments about House C only highlight the importance of granting the building a 'voice', according to Daher, by acknowledging the voices of the original residents and historical narratives. The lived experiences and insights of the original residents can be a resource and repository of knowledge for heritage experts. In this context, longtime residents and experts have implicit capacities to grant agency to buildings, revealing values that are usually absent from the decisions and actions of authorities.

The transect walks unearthed various attitudes towards preserving old buildings while negotiating new changes from community members, including longtime residents, experts, workers and youth. During the walks, coincidental encounters enabled face-to-face interactions with some community members who might be disinterested or excluded from participatory planning, like the security guard. Moreover, participants' diverse value judgements regarding the new restaurants and House C indicate the complexity of these divergent perspectives and invite further inquiry into why the blocking of the church from view, for example, elicited a unified synergetic response from residents.

Stakeholders' Networking Dynamics

The walks facilitated interactions among many community members and enabled participants to connect with one another. Some stakeholders shared their vision for the neighbourhood and what holds the most value for them. Rajab, a restaurant and foundation manager, shared that:

> I talked with Bilal a month ago... We want to do something fruitful since we are all passionate about Lweibdeh. Why not produce a promotional video that markets Lweibdeh as a brand? ... This film can be one minute long... and you can talk about FOLCA... I mean we are all in the same 'ditch'... My business has been here for three years and I do not know that there is FOLCA... Sociologically speaking, we as Lweibdeh community need to coordinate and unify efforts... There is architectural and social heritage here that you must introduce people to... Jasmine trees, a cup of coffee and pine trees are all part of the experience. (Rajab, male, 45–55)

While visiting the restaurant, Bilal from FOLCA also introduced Rajab to one of the association's partner organisations that 'is involved in cultural activities and empowering local communities'. Rajab's response to this was, 'so let them come and have free tea and coffee here please'. During these incidental encounters, community members shared their planned projects and ideas for collaborative efforts, acknowledging that formal channels do not seem sufficiently conducive or responsive to the community's needs. Rajab elaborated on a recent rehabilitation project planned in Lweibdeh by a heritage expert:

> The expert is a scientific, academic kind of person, and I respect and love him, and my friend. Regardless, today we are an industry that is suffering... We need promotion... This long-term plan... be it cultural, academic, scientific, book, lecture, seminar... feelings... excellent. But we need to pay salaries, electricity bills, rent. We need marketing from yesterday... We conserve heritage through heritage tourism, through maintaining its sustainability commercially through tourism... We have no shortage of academics, we have a shortage in commercial incentivisation.

Hani, a longtime resident, also described the disconnect with planning authorities. When a heritage documentation project was undertaken in Lweibdeh around ten years ago, he recalled that 'they did not consult anyone... Ideally, I should have the right to object... They cannot change anything in my neighbourhood without consulting me... I hope planning committees visit the site and ask the residents about their concerns before reaching results and decisions, but they do not do that'.

In addition to the economic promotion of Lweibdeh, the protection of heritage buildings, like House C, highlighted the desire of longtime residents for conflict resolution and investor education regarding the place's value. This eagerness for mediation was evident from Kamel's response when asked whether he was willing to meet with the investor planning to demolish House C:

> Of course... We did not get the chance; we did not ask to meet him, nor he asked to meet us... Talk to the investor he could be better than us... Learn about his vision... and we can reach a shared solution where it is satisfactory and can prevent him from losing money... I think that the investor was cheated... Maybe he did not know what he was getting into.

Throughout the walks, issues like heritage tourism, economic sustainability, participatory planning and heritage conservation emerged as embedded in the value system of the community, reflecting what matters most to them in Lweibdeh. Moreover, these conversations revealed a common desire among various stakeholders to work together to protect Lweibdeh's heritage. This underscores the need to swiftly address issues connected to residents' experiences and daily lives, the urgency of which is often beyond the grasp of 'external' planning officials. The eagerness for networking and local organisation expressed during the walks reveals a hidden social resource. Understanding these social relationships and shared interests can facilitate a more nuanced and sustainable approach to safeguarding Lweibdeh's cultural heritage which empowers local actors and is attuned to locally shared values.

Conclusion

Diverging from decontextualised universalist narratives, this chapter recognises the need to consider micro-scales in heritage and urban planning discourses. To this end, the chapter employs the resource-exploring tool of transect walks to capture contextual nuances and local perspectives. The transect walks in Lweibdeh demonstrated the method's potential to enhance sustainability at the community level in three ways. Firstly, they provided partial insights into planning practice and community interactions. The findings revealed that rehabilitation projects in Lweibdeh have followed a top-down decision-making model, confirming Khirfan and Momani's analysis[35] and supporting Shami's[36] call for alternative planning methodologies to achieve a genuinely participatory approach. Moreover, according to community members, planning authorities exhibited weak advocacy for cultural heritage issues, hindering community efforts to counter projects that lacked an understanding of the area's layered significance. This can be addressed as one of the local priorities in the SDG's Target 11.4 implementation action plan, which calls for training these officials[37] in Jordan.

35 Khirfan and Momani, 'Tracing Participatory Planning'.

36 Shami, 'Ethnographies'.

37 Pursuant to ICOMOS Action Area2: 'Offer/provide technical guidance/ support to stakeholders (particularly local governments) for integrated and sustainable

Secondly, the method shed light on the diversity of the community's heritage values and resources. Shared values, the community's ability to negotiate its past amidst ongoing changes and networking dynamics were identified as resources conducive to participatory conservation efforts in Lweibdeh. Community members, such as longtime residents, who possess local knowledge of Lweibdeh's multi-layered values were found to be essential cultural heritage resources that are underutilised if not forgotten. This chapter illustrates the importance of documenting these residents' accounts of Lweibdeh's history as well as invites inquiry into mechanisms for ensuring their voices are represented on a decision-making level. To harness existing urban resources such as social networks, neighbourly relationships, common interests and values for resolving local issues in local ways,[38] transect walks offered access to these resources and opened channels of communication for community mobilisation.

Thirdly, the tool demonstrated methodological utility compared to conventional methods such as interviews, group meetings and surveys. As an exploratory tool, its short-term and locally immersive advantages allowed researchers to observe the interactions and relationships of community members as experts in their environment. Many participants were willing to join the transect walks and even introduced additional participants. Crucially, these walks engaged and provided a platform for community members typically underrepresented in formal settings that might otherwise drown out their voices or exclude them. However, one of the shortcomings of this tool is its considerable reliance on happenstance, especially with participants determining the route. Therefore, it is recommended to use transect walks as an initial step into the community under examination, to be followed by more structured, democratic and representative participatory methods.

In capturing nuanced and diverse dynamics, this chapter argues for systematically incorporating transect walks into participatory sustainable planning processes, particularly within cultural heritage contexts. Transect walks can serve various functions and this chapter

urban planning strategies and tools, tailored to local context/ realities, in particular for using the Historic Urban Landscape (HUL) tools, heritage impact assessment and community engagement' (Yıldırım, *ICONOS Action Plan*, p. 9).

38 Shami, 'Ethnographies'.

has explored only one aspect of this method. However, based on the findings, the method has potential to serve as an urban planning tool to shed light on the value of traditional cultural fabrics and communal networks as sustainable assets, in terms of their social, economic and environmental values.

Bibliography

Anderson, Jon, 'Talking Whilst Walking: A Geographical Archaeology of Knowledge', *AREA*, 36.3 (2004), 254–61, https://doi.org/10.1111/j.0004-0894.2004.00222.x

Arnstein, Sherry R., 'A Ladder of Citizen Participation', *Journal of the American Institute of Planners*, 35.4 (1969), 216–24, https://doi.org/10.1080/01944366908977225

Australia ICOMOS, *The Burra Charter: The Australia ICOMOS Charter for Places of Cultural Significance 2013* (Burwood: Australia ICOMOS, 2013).

Brandi, Cesare, 'Theory of Restoration 2', in *Historical and Philosophical Issues in the Conservation of Cultural Heritage*, ed. by Nicholas C. Price, M. Kirby Talley Jr. and Alessandra Melucco Vaccaro (Los Angeles, CA: Getty Publications, 1996), pp. 339–42.

Culture2030Goal Campaign, *Culture in the Implementation of the 2030 Agenda* (Barcelona, Paris, Harare, Sydney, Montreal, The Hague and Brussels: United Nations, 2019).

Daher, Rami, 'Amman's Vanishing Legacy of Modernity', *Jordan Property*, 23 (2008), 10–21.

De la Torre, Marta, 'Values and Heritage Conservation', *Heritage & Society*, 6.2 (2013), 155–66, https://doi.org/10.1179/2159032x13z.00000000011

De la Torre, Marta, MacLean, Margaret G. H., Mason, Randall, and Myers, David, 'Introduction', in *Heritage Values in Site Management: Four Case Studies*, ed. by Marta de la Torre (Los Angeles, CA: The Getty Conservation Institute, 2005), pp. 3–9, https://doi.org/10.2167/jht028b.0

De Marco, Luisa, 'Values in Heritage Conservation: From Museification towards Human Cohabitation', paper presented at the Values-based Decision-making for Conservation conference (Ottawa, 2005).

Finlay, Jessica M. and Bowman, Jay A., 'Geographies on the Move: A Practical and Theoretical Approach to the Mobile Interview', *The Professional Geographer*, 69.2 (2017), 263–74, https://doi.org/10.1080/00330124.2016.1229623

Getty, *Assessing the Values of Cultural Heritage: Research Report* (Los Angeles, CA: The Getty Conservation Institute, 2002).

Hawkes, Jon, *The Fourth Pillar of Sustainability: Culture's Essential Role in Public Planning* (Melbourne: Cultural Development Network: Common Ground, 2004).

Hodges, Andrew and Watson, Steve, 'Community-Based Heritage Management: A Case Study and Agenda for Research', *International Journal of Heritage Studies*, 6.3 (2000), 231–43, https://doi.org/10.1080/13527250050148214

Khirfan, Luna and Momani, Bessma, 'Tracing Participatory Planning in Amman', in *Order and Disorder: Urban Governance and the Making of Middle Eastern Cities*, ed. by Luna Khirfan, Kristin Good and Martin Horak (Montreal: McGill-Queen's University Press, 2017), pp. 79–102, https://doi.org/10.1515/9780773549760-006

Koch, Florian and Krellenberg, Kerstin, 'How to Contextualize SDG 11? Looking at Indicators for Sustainable Urban Development in Germany', *ISPRS International Journal of Geo-Information*, 7.12 (2018), 464, https://doi.org/10.3390/ijgi7120464

Mason, Randall, 'Theoretical and Practical Arguments for Values-Centered Preservation', *CRM: The Journal of Heritage Stewardship*, 3.2 (2006), 21–40.

MOPIC, *Jordan's Way to Sustainable Development: First National Voluntary Review on the Implementation of the 2030 Agenda* (Jordan: Ministry of Planning and International Cooperation, 2017), pp. 54–55.

Nagendra, Harini *et al.*, 'The Urban South and the Predicament of Global Sustainability', *Nature Sustainability*, 1.7 (2018), 341–49, https://doi.org/10.1038/s41893-018-0101-5

Price, Nicholas C., Talley Jr., M. Kirby and Melucco Vaccaro, Alessandra, eds., *Historical and Philosophical Issues in the Conservation of Cultural Heritage* (Los Angeles, CA: Getty Publications, 1996), pp. 69–83, https://doi.org/10.2307/1506756

Razem, Maiss, 'Place Attachment and Sustainable Communities', *Architecture_MPS*, 17.1 (2020), https://doi.org/10.14324/111.444.amps.2020v17i1.003

Riegl, Alois, 'The Modern Cult of Monument: Its Essence and Its Development', in *Historical and Philosophical Issues in the Conservation of Cultural Heritage*, ed. by Nicholas C. Price, M. Kirby Talley Jr. and Alessandra Melucco Vaccaro (Los Angeles, CA: Getty Publications, 1996), pp. 69–83, https://doi.org/10.2307/1506756

Shami, Seteney, 'Ethnographies of Governance: Urban Spaces and Actors in the Middle East', in *Governance on the Ground: Innovations and Discontinuities in Cities of the Developing World*, ed. by Patricia Louise Mc Carney and Richard E. Stren (Washington, DC: Woodrow Wilson Center Press, 2003), pp. 58–82 (p. 80).

UCLG, *Culture: Fourth Pillar of Sustainable Development* (Barcelona: United Cities and Local Governments, 2010).

United Nations, *SDG Goal 11 Monitoring Framework: A Guide to Assist National and Local Governments to Monitor and Report on SDG Goal 11 Indicators* (Nairboi: United Nations, 2016), https://www.local2030.org/library/60/SDG-Goal-11-Monitoring-Framework-A-guide-to-assist-national-and-local-governments-to-monitor-and-report-on-SDG-goal-11-indicators.pdf

Walsh, Kevin, *The Representation of the Past: Museums and Heritage in the Post-Modern World* (London: Routledge, 1992), https://doi.org/10.4324/9780203075722

Warren, Saskia, 'Pluralising the Walking Interview: Researching (Im)Mobilities with Muslim Women', *Social & Cultural Geography*, 18.6 (2017), 786–807.

Willems, Willem J. H., 'Laws, Language, and Learning Managing Archaeological Heritage Resources in Europe', in *Cultural Heritage Management: A Global Perspective*, ed. by Phyllis Mauch Messenger and George S. Smith (Gainesville, FL: University Press of Florida, 2010), pp. 212–29.

Yıldırım, Ege, *ICOMOS Action Plan: Cultural Heritage and Localizing the UN Sustainable Development Goals (SDGs)* (Istanbul: ICOMOS, 2017), https://www.icomos.org/images/DOCUMENTS/Secretariat/2017/ICOMOS_Action_Plan_Cult_Heritage_and_Localizing_SDGs_20170721.pdf

5. Tackling Sustainability in Bordeaux: Bridging Modern and Traditional Neighbourhoods

Fanny Gerbeaud, Aline Barlet and Caroline Mazel

Introduction

Bordeaux embodies the traditional European heritage city. Like many cities on the old continent, it is a palimpsest that has witnessed several currents of thought on urban development patterns, comfort, modernity and ecological awareness. Today, the city comprises several urban elements reflecting these diverse perspectives as well as major societal changes that are transforming our understanding of these testaments of the past.

This chapter aims to explore the debates and periods of rehabilitation, both moral and physical, that have successively affected multifunctional districts. These districts, encompassing both traditional neighbourhoods (from the eighteenth and nineteenth centuries) and modern neighbourhoods, are now confronting the challenges of ecological transition. By elucidating the principles that governed the construction of these neighbourhoods, subsequent viewpoints, particularly those of the modern movement, and contemporary perspectives, we will demonstrate their significance in current discourses and their alignment with the goals of creating sustainable cities in the twenty-first century.

 https://doi.org/10.11647/OBP.0412.05

This chapter shares the results of a two-year joint research programme (2017–2019) conducted by the PAVE and GRECCAU Research Centres (ENSAPBx) and the University of Cincinnati (DAAP). The project focused on the perceptions of stakeholders—inhabitants, landlords and experts—of what constitutes sustainable heritage in the context of the energy transition with regard to modern housing. The research entailed stakeholder interviews, housing measurements (including hygrothermal and natural light assessments) and socio-spatial analyses, focusing on the modern neighbourhoods of Mériadeck and Pontet-Lamartine. These two neighbourhoods, despite their contrasting dimensions, typologies and locations, share urban qualities and a strong potential for change. Mériadeck (1951–1980), in the centre of Bordeaux, is characterised by deck-and-tower structures with separate circulation systems and cross-shaped towers overlooking one of France's first protected heritage areas. Pontet-Lamartine consists of twenty-eight patio row houses (1970–1971). The owner-residents of this neighbourhood are proactive in promoting their Modernist heritage and developing civic life, for example, joining forces to safeguard amenities like shops, services, shared public spaces and a park open to a rapidly densifying surrounding area.

In sharp contrast with their environment, these two neighbourhoods recently merged with the traditional city centre and the suburban fabric of the growing metropolis. Both have contributed to Bordeaux's sustainability through their distinctive designs and facilities.

This chapter first discusses the spatial and urban qualities of the traditional stone city and modern post-war neighbourhoods, as envisioned by their designers, which can be described as sustainable today. Combining both objective metrics and subjective evaluations, this research identifies specific urban features in these districts that, rather than confirming their obsolescence, demonstrate the value of these areas in terms of quality of use. It argues for an adapted definition of the sustainability goals and strategies in heritage neighbourhoods dating from and before the twenty-first century. Finally, we highlight the inhabitants' commitment to achieving the physical and moral rehabilitation of the heritage they value while addressing the challenges of sustainability on a metropolitan scale.

Bordeaux, a Heritage City with Two Faces

France's largest port in the eighteenth century, Bordeaux built its fortune on the triangular trade between France, Africa and the West Indies. The Age of Enlightenment was also the golden age of Bordeaux, marked by its quay facade, places and courtyards 'à la française' (like the Place de la Bourse) connecting riverbanks with the typical long and narrow wine cellars of the Chartrons district. All of these developments showcased its rich stone architecture[1] and led to the city centre's designation as a United Nations Educational, Scientific and Cultural Organization (UNESCO) World Heritage Site in 2007.

This 'stone city' is also characterised by a low skyline on the outskirts of the city centre,[2] made of one or two-storey buildings and *échoppes*,[3] typical ground-floor terraced houses built in large numbers in the nineteenth century for employees during the era of industrialisation (see Figure 5.1).

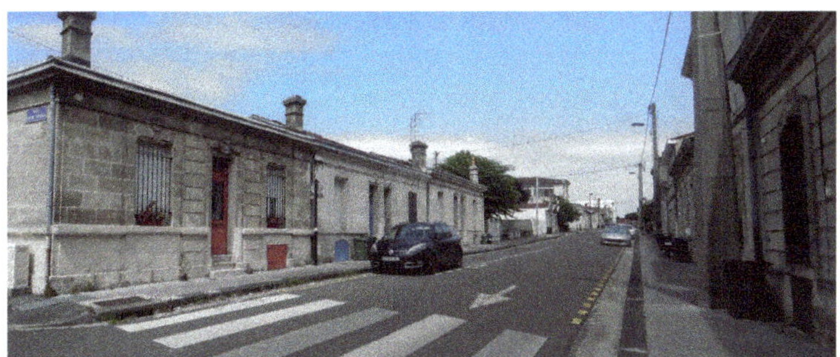

Fig. 5.1 Echoppe housing in Pannetier street, Bordeaux. Author's photograph, 2021, CC BY-NC-ND.

These archaeological typologies were shunned in the 1970s and 1980s as households pursued homeownership and modernity, moving to pavilions in the developing suburbs of the Urban Community of Bordeaux. A series of revitalisation and renovation projects began in 1995 under the mayorship of Alain Juppé. These projects emphasised delicate architectural details, enduring construction quality and density,

1 Robert Coustet and Marc Saboya, *Bordeaux : le temps de l'histoire, architecture et urbanisme au XIXe siècle, 1800–1914* (Bordeaux: Mollat, 1999).

2 Gwenaël Querrien, *Portrait de ville* (Paris: Cité de l'architecture et du patrimoine, IFA, 2006).

3 Chantal Callais, *L'échoppe de Bordeaux* (**La Crèche:** La Geste, 2018).

and several sustainability characteristics, such as green spaces and gardens, urban facilities and nearby transportation, which breathed new life into these areas. The stone buildings also represent a great heritage value, being both expandable and aesthetically pleasing.

This model of 'conservatory upgrading'[4] was opposed in the early twentieth century by the hygienists, who sought to eliminate substandard and unsanitary housing, such as existed in the old Mériadeck neighbourhood of Bordeaux. The Second World War and the influx of migrants arriving to help with the country's reconstruction exacerbated the housing crisis. In this immediate economic and demographic context, the state initiated new urban planning and housing solutions to alleviate the housing crisis, resulting in suburban urbanisation. Along with the country's modernisation and increased private vehicle ownership, transportation infrastructures, airports, car parks and commercial and tertiary areas were built. These developments were more or less inspired by the Modernist architectural experiments conducted since the 1920s, including the establishment of social housing estates in 1951 and Urbanisation Priority Areas (ZUP) in 1958.

After the war, slab neighbourhoods developed, influenced by Chicago's superimposed city concept, which incorporates networks and infrastructures both above and below ground. This urban form drew inspiration from utopian projects like Sant'Elia's *Città Nuova* (1914), Richard Neutra's Rush City (1923), Ludwig Hilberseimer's Hochhausstadt (1924) and Le Corbusier's *Plan Obus* for Algiers (1930). These slab neighbourhoods increased the number of floors to enhance density, efficiency and security by separating pedestrian and car traffic. Beyond the historical area, the slab represented a new level of reference, a 'concrete island' conducive to all manner of experiments. Modern architecture within a controlled environment formed the essential basis for the advent of a new era of humanity.

In this context and benefiting from the national prominence of Bordeaux Mayor Jacques Chaban-Delmas, the city underwent major transformations to secure its place as one of France's major metropolitan centres and to enhance its citizens' well-being in a modern world.[5] This modern urban environment embodied the progress and development

4 Patrice Godier, Claude Sorbets and Guy Tapie, *Bordeaux métropole, un futur sans rupture* (Marseille: Parenthèses, 2009).

5 Kent Fitzsimons and Fanny Gerbeaud, 'Mériadeck et les Aubiers à l'ère de la ville durable: vie et survie de deux quartiers modernistes à Bordeaux', in *Racines*

of the 'Trente Glorieuses'[6] and complemented the outdated yet majestic historic city centre in terms of functionality and mobility. Multifunctional slab neighbourhoods flourished on *tabula rasa* terrain (see Figure 5.2), while smaller, dense row-housing projects reflecting a 'reasoned modernity' took root in the first ring of the emerging metropolis (see Figure 5.3).

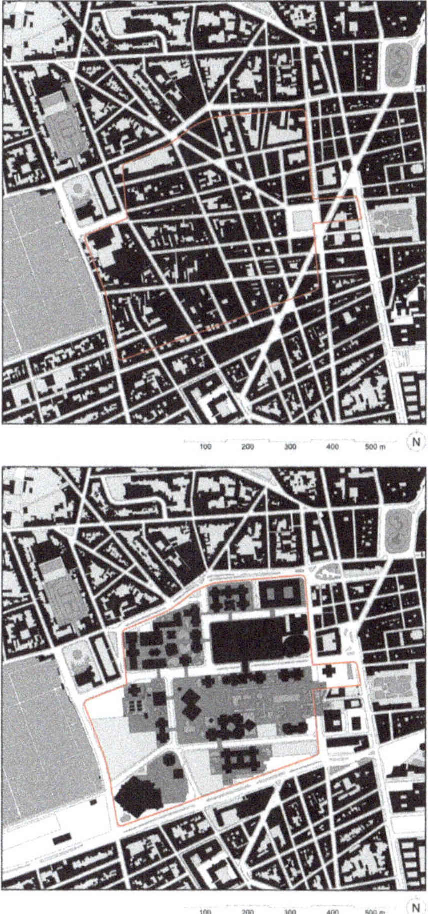

Fig. 5.2 Mériadeck before and after construction, respectively, in 1930 and 1984. Illustration by Louise Jammet, 2021, CC BY-NC-ND.

---

modernes de la ville contemporaine. Distances et formes de résilience, ed. by Panos Mantziaras and Paola Vigano (Geneva: Métis Presses, 2019), pp. 157–76.

6 The Mériadeck and Pontet-Lamartine settlements were developed in the context of the 'Trente Glorieuses', a term coined by economist Jean Fourastier to describe the period during which France sought to address the shortages of housing and amenities resulting from the war and the human consequences of decolonisation and globalisation.

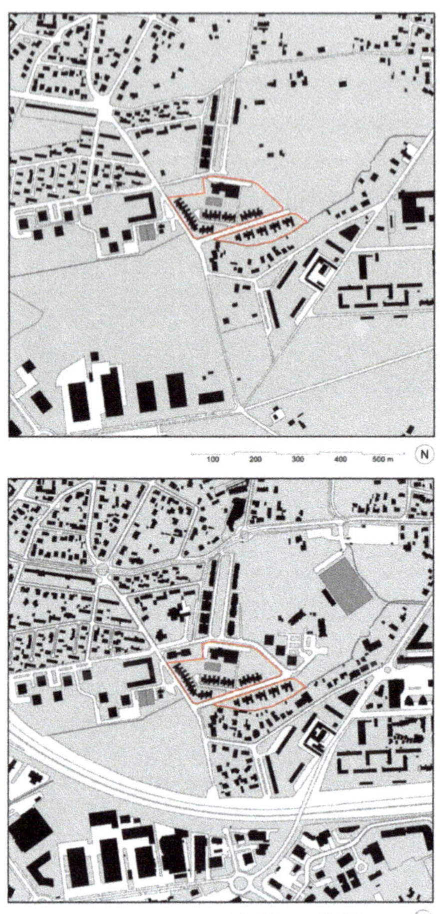

Fig. 5.3 Pontet-Lamartine in 1976 and in 2018. Illustration by Louise Jammet, 2021, CC BY-NC-ND.

These automobile-centric neighbourhoods subsequently witnessed the growth and densification of the Bordeaux metropolis. The areas are now generally regarded as cautionary examples while the elder housing districts of the stone city inspire designs for the sustainable city of the future. Indeed, Bordeaux has recently reclaimed its splendour with programmes for the renovation of ancient buildings, the return of the tramway and soft mobilities, the landscaping of the Garonne riverbanks and a strong ambition to promote high-density housing development. As a result, the modern housing neighbourhoods are commonly described as energy thieves, hampered by their brutalist architecture. As urban sustainability paradigms evolve, the traditional urban fabric has regained its prominence on account of its compact, multifunctional and picturesque old quarters. Nowadays, eco-neighbourhoods at the 'human scale' are developing on the city outskirts, based on the traditional urban design, with streets and lower buildings in smaller housing estates. Thus, the question naturally arises: does this indicate that modern urbanisation is now outdated and unsustainable?

Mériadeck and Pontet-Lamartine: Diverging with the Past to Create 'the City of the Modern Man'[7]

During the 'Trente Glorieuses', France embraced a policy asserting housing as a right for all. This marked a decisive shift, as little importance had been given to housing since the creation of *Habitation à Bon Marché* (inexpensive housing) (HBM) companies in 1889 and the adoption of the Loucheur law of 1928. To achieve this ideal, architects had at their disposal theoretical models developed by hygienists during the nineteenth century. Following Camillo Sitte and Ebenezer Howard, the culturalists referenced the irregular composition of medieval and small-scale garden cities. The progressists expanded on the scientific approach of Georges-Eugène Haussmann, Ildefons Cerdà and Tony Garnier, with large urban blocks and their abstract composition influenced by Neoplasticism.

In 1933, the Fourth Congress of International Modernist Architecture (CIAM IV) led to the Charter of Athens, which effectively banned traditional architecture and town planning in favour of regularity, geometry, separation of functions and flows, space, clean air and

7 The term 'modern man' is frequently used in reference to the artistic and avant-garde dimension of Bordeaux, with its urban space presented as particularly conducive to 'his' fulfilment. The excerpt below on Le Corbusier's architectural work is particularly eloquent: 'Between 1910 and 1960, by taking up the challenges of modern society, the modern movement aimed to stimulate an exceptional debate of ideas on a global scale, invent a new architectural language, modernise architectural techniques and respond to the social and human needs of modern man' (UNESCO, 'L'oeuvre architecturale de Le Corbusier, une contribution exceptionnelle au Mouvement Moderne' (2016), *UNESCO*, https://whc.unesco.org/en/list/1321/).

sunlight. The aim was to create functional cities and housing fully conducive to the development of modern life in this period of societal renewal.[8]

Technologies and amenities emerged that further influenced changes in housing designs. This included air-conditioning and mechanical ventilation set back from the facades, and large glazed panels which let more light into other rooms, ensuring a healthy environment.[9]

Few cities in France adhered to these principles strictly, with the exception of Firminy Vert, where Mayor Eugène Claudius-Petit, the Minister of Reconstruction and Town Planning (1948–1953), praised Le Corbusier's ideas. However, the influence of the Charter of Athens became a major reference point for architects and building owners, as attested to by the Mériadeck district, with the earliest sketches of Jean Royer and Jacques Willerval dating back to 1951. The mixed housing and tertiary and commercial esplanades, elevated on a high slab reserved for pedestrians, are detached from the historic city and the traffic. The master plan, divided into squares linked together by footbridges, comprises cruciform buildings based on a functionalist approach and solar and thermal considerations. Mériadeck, comprising 800 flats and 1300 inhabitants, faces one of France's first safeguarded historical districts. This clear break from the classical city reinforces the insular character of this new district, although both have been included within the UNESCO perimeter since 2007.[10]

In addition to this large urban and architectural complex, criticised for its extreme density and disproportionate aesthetics, detached housing extends to the periphery, contributing to urban sprawl. Mixed housing settlements with small collective and individual units are seen as an alternative. The Pontet-Lamartine neighbourhood in Pessac, designed by Pierre Calmon (architect, AUA studio), addresses this concern for urban development on a human scale with small terraced residential buildings

8 Ignacio Requena-Ruiz, 'Thermal Comfort in Twentieth-century Architectural Heritage: Two Houses of Le Corbusier and André Wogenscky', *Frontiers of Architectural Research*, 5.2 (2016), 157–70, https://doi.org/10.1016/j.foar.2016.02.001

9 Ignacio Requena-Ruiz, 'Building Artificial Climates. Thermal Control and Comfort in Modern Architecture (1930–1960)', *Ambiances*, 2 (2016), https://doi.org/10.4000/ambiances.801

10 UNESCO, 'Bordeaux, Port of the Moon' (2007), *UNESCO*, https://whc.unesco.org/en/list/1256

and row houses with patios centred around green recreational areas. This layout contributes to the experiments of the period by combining intimacy and density while adopting modern architecture characterised by flat roofs and purist designs.

Initially, these modern creations garnered more criticism than praise, but over time, their functional quality and heritage value have become evident. While the majority of Bordeaux citizens consider them second-class heritage, this research reveals that the inhabitants of these neighbourhoods, constructed between the 1960s and 1980s, are, on the contrary, keen to promote their Modernist environment.

Mériadeck's central location is all the more noteworthy in today's expanded Bordeaux. Surrounded by shops, services and cultural life, its tree-lined slab offers a unique urban promenade devoid of streets, avenues or squares. In the truest sense, it has the city at its feet. The typology of the towers, with their vast balconies, enables residents to stay connected with the park's green canopy and enjoy a splendid view of Bordeaux's traditional districts (see Figure 5.4).

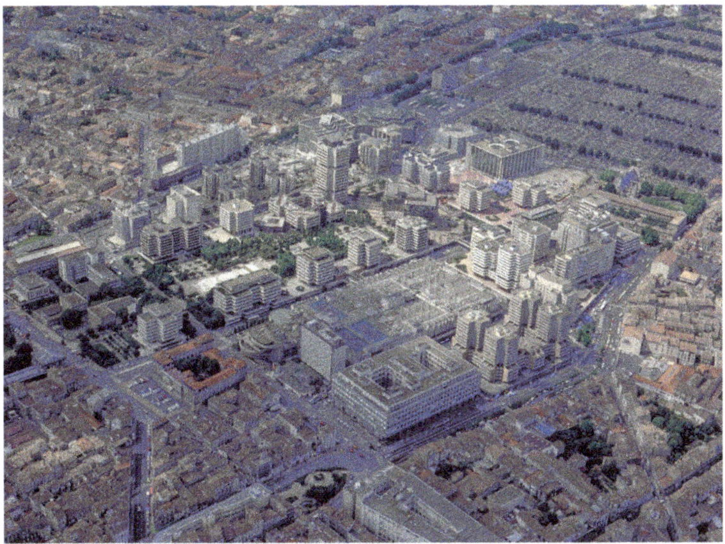

Fig. 5.4 Mériadeck, J. Royer, J. Willerval and P. Lagarde, architects 1951–1980 (2007), Bordeaux (France). Photograph by Denys Carrère, 2019, A'urba, CC BY-NC-ND.

Despite the encroachment of urbanisation over time, Pontet-Lamartine has managed to preserve its outdoor collective spaces, thanks to its *non-ædificandi* buffer zones. These unbuilt and intimate areas, though less expansive in recent developments, foster social interactions among inhabitants, while the spacious halls and patios facilitate transitions between public and private life and opportunities for personalisation.

Using an assembly and offset arrangement akin to a checkerboard pattern, the urban layout ensures the houses' privacy while bringing sunlight and openness to the landscape, in line with the architects' persistent hygienic concerns. Based on a few typical housing units, repetition has become a means of integrating diversity and uniformity.

The abundant housing typologies and functionality proposed by the Modernism movement appeal to different profiles, including families with young children, disabled or older people, and students. This represents a first step towards social diversity and inclusion, in contrast to other typologies and locations which unintentionally exclude these profiles.[11] Moreover, the adaptability of these neighbourhoods to new users and functions, with the capacity to transition between residential and commercial activities, adds to their sustainable qualities. Modern housing districts generally offer open areas, natural light and expansive views of the surroundings. The partition between day and night spaces and the numerous storage areas, cellars or garages are also distinctive features of this period's architecture that are still considered valuable by residents. The structural flexibility of the beam and column design is amenable to modern needs and desires, such as open kitchens, wide living rooms and large bedrooms. Compared to the eco-neighbourhoods currently being built in Bordeaux, Mériadeck and Pontet-Lamartine are more easily modified and expanded due to these elements. The material quality and strong concrete structures align these two modern districts with Bordeaux's historic sustainable neighbourhoods.

Recently, city councils have taken an interest in how inhabitants adapt their modern neighbourhoods, especially since some are gaining recognition as examples of 'Remarkable Contemporary Architecture'. These post-war districts are thus joining the ranks of traditional *échoppes* and stone buildings in the sustainable design database, enriching the future of housing developments and better preparing for climatic and social changes in the years to come.

---

11 Guy Tapie, *Habitat, vieillissement et filières de production, vers des innovations sociales ?* (Research Report for the Nouvelle-Aquitaine Region, 2020).

A Sustainable Living Environment for Residents

The conceptualised modernity challenges the daily activities of inhabitants, encompassing their roles as neighbours and citizens but also addressing issues that were unimaginable at the time of their construction, like energy transition, the era of soft mobility and urban densification. Nevertheless, the living environments in Mériadeck and Pontet-Lamartine continue to exhibit quality in terms of mobility, amenities and atmosphere.

In Mériadeck, property prices have long remained lower than in the historic centre due to the neighbourhood's architecture, which is considered brutal and outdated in design. However, the district benefits from its larger flats and access to numerous amenities, making its modern architecture an appealing opportunity for living. With its covered car parks, convenient pedestrian access and multiple public transportation options in the congested city, residents experience urban life without the usual inconveniences. The automobile slab and urban layout in general effectively complement the historic centre.

In Pontet-Lamartine, the inhabitants' satisfaction is related to the amenities and numerous transportation options more than the location of the neighbourhood itself. The metropolitan ring road, tram system and cycle paths contribute to its sustainability.

Modern post-war districts have found different ways to manage parking without eliminating it. In Mériadeck, underground car parks are used by residents, shoppers and local businesses with company vehicles. Pontet-Lamartine offers garages and street parking options, easing city traffic and complementing evolving family lifestyles. In contrast, parking in traditional districts is challenging and expensive. Current urban policies tend to encourage public transportation and pedestrian areas over personal vehicles. However, not all citizens are ready—or able—to transition away from cars in favour of soft transportation (non-motorised means) like walking, cycling, roller-skating, etc.

Modernist architecture is characterised by expansive-built spaces and highly structured unbuilt surroundings, which prove complementary. These areas offer commercial or recreational facilities that enhance the residents' quality of life. The open spaces facilitate the emergence of innovative uses: green islands, slab ends and planted alleyways create transitions between private and public spaces, conducive to gatherings and individual use. One Mériadeck resident expressed appreciation for being able to find 'everything you need: car parks, much larger apartments than you wanted, a caretaker, elevators, a garden... the most extraordinary effect here is that you enter via a garden'. The fully built-up old districts and trendy neighbourhoods rarely offer such green public spaces, accessible to passers-by or even inhabitants. While many private planted areas can be found in traditional *échoppe* lots and new housing estates, only residents are able to enjoy these enclosed green areas. In Pontet-Lamartine, people enjoy the best of both worlds, as the resident noted: 'coming from a farming background [...] we like to stay in a green setting, to be at home while having close neighbours'.

The amenities, spatial and structural flexibility and high-quality urban atmosphere are favourable for local life and proved highly efficient during the isolation measures imposed in 2020 due to the COVID-19 crisis. Free from the usual drawbacks of urban life like noise and heat, the location of these districts near or in the heart of the city centre makes them a resource. Bordeaux is known for its urban landscape dominated by stone and concrete, a characteristic that modern districts seek to balance—both in the old centre and its suburban districts—by preserving extensive green spaces within these neighbourhoods. The dense buildings of the 1970s and the abundance of vegetation limit the heat island effect, a concern not foreseen when these Modernist districts were conceived. Mériadeck and Pontet-Lamartine, with their summer comfort, are ideal for outdoor activities, even in periods of high heat. Studies conducted by the Bordeaux metropolis show that the stone compounds in the old city centre contribute to a heat island effect, particularly due to the materials used, the solar orientation of the streets and the lack of vegetation.

Moreover, the centres of the modern districts offer very quiet environments, protected from one of the main sources of urban noise—traffic (see Figure 5.5). As one flat owner in Mériadeck observed, 'the slab urbanism concept concerning the street is very clear: no cars, no noise, that's for sure; it's a real comfort'.

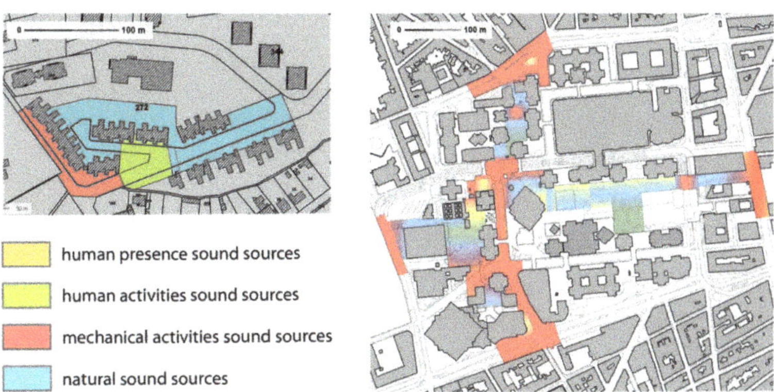

Fig. 5.5 Characterisation of sound sources at Pontet-Lamartine and Mériadeck. Author's illustration, CC BY-NC-ND.

This sound level can be found in certain parts of the traditional city, especially where the urban fabric is particularly tight, characterised by narrow streets with little traffic, or in the heart of a city block. In other ancient housing lots, the sound environment is strongly marked by traffic noise, increased by the sound reverberations on the stone facades.

Bordeaux comprises diverse parts—the picturesque stone city and the contemporary ecological settlements—where the Modernist districts' architectural and urban land reserve contribute to the city's sustainability, fluidity and functionality. On the architectural level, the patio-house typology, gardens, free-plan layouts and modular designs offer flexibility, allowing, for example, the concrete skeleton and slab of a tower in Mériadeck to be recycled for new office space or flats (see Figure 5.6).

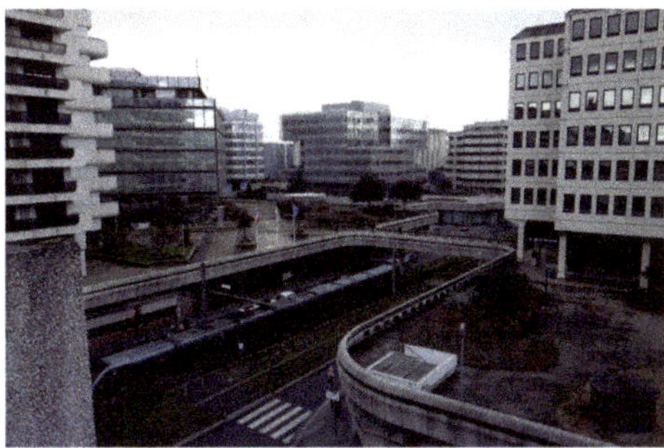

Fig. 5.6 A view of a cross-shaped building in Mériadeck renovated into a bioclimatic office block (2017), Bordeaux. Photograph by Louise Jammet, 2021, CC BY-NC-ND.

When considering comfort at the scale of housing, there is a noticeable contrast between objective data obtained from onsite measurements and the inhabitants' perceptions and discourses. These constructions are often subject to thermal problems, such as overheating and humidity in summer and uncomfortably low temperatures in winter, mainly resulting from defects or deteriorating insulation systems. Moreover, while many dwellings lack sufficient natural light, this is mitigated by the level of visual comfort achieved through the treatment of openings (such as large glazed facades), which establish a strong relationship to the outdoors, and the clarity of the walls (often in white concrete). In short, the hygrothermal or visual discomforts measured in some dwellings are offset by the appreciated architecture and the overall sense of well-being among the inhabitants. Therefore, it can be inferred that the comfort and atmosphere perceived by inhabitants are more related to heritage aspects—such as market value, attachment to place or cultural significance—and a sensitive approach that considers the feeling of space and openness, rather than strictly measurable physical living conditions, which often do not correspond to sustainability issues.

At the same time and contrary to popular belief, the overall energy consumption of the modern dwellings studied is very close to that of more recent dwellings of comparable size and meeting current requirements. Mériadeck and Pontet-Lamartine, thanks to their urban organisation (including vegetation) and their architectural details and typologies, limit thermal exchanges. This prevents houses from overheating in summer, shields against the 'cold glass effect' in winter and reduces energy consumption (see Tables 5.1 and 5.2).

Table 5.1 Dwelling measures in eight Pontet-Lamartine houses.

Summer measures	1	2	3	4	5	6	7	8
Temperature (°C)	25-25.5	22.3-22.8	23.3-24.7	23-24	24.8-28	24.1-25.6	23.5-24	22.1-22.6
Humidity (%)	60-72	60-71.9	51-62	74-84	61-74.7	70-89	59.4-69	51-73
Sound level (dB)	26-38	23-41	25-47	36-54	34-36	32-50	30-38	24-38
Lighting (lx)	30-990	120-1500	85-850	20-552	60-1040	21-450	47-1200	30-1000
CO_2 (ppm)	874-1052	580-874	597-880	568-874	940-1139	780-1158	545-619	529-811

Winter measures	1	2	3	4	5	6	7	8
Temperature (°C)	18.8-21.2	18.3-20.9	18.8-20.3	18.8-20.4	19.8-22.5	16.5-19.1	18.3-19.9	21-24.5
Humidity (%)	26-62	53.7-63.5	30.4-49	52.6-56	32.2-43.2	48.6-60	37-48	31.5-44.8
Sound level (dB)	27-45	27-43	30-47	36-53	28-44	28-40	32-44	33-40
Lighting (lx)	34-800	40-1380	10-1780	40-1750	15-440	0-12	3-1120	12-2160
CO2 (ppm)	936-1250	719-908	798-877	714-1083	747-864	787-977	869-974	655-859

Table 5.2 Dwelling measures in ten Mériadeck flats.

Summer measures	1	2	3	4	5	6	7	8	9	10
Temperature (°C)	26.3-27	22.3-23.6	26.1-26.4	25.7-26.9	23.8-24.5	21.9-22.9	28.2-29	23.4-25.2		23.7-24.2
Humidity (%)	48-52	63-71	46.3-48.1	54.8-63.6	51.5-56	71-74.9	45-49	49.2-58.9		54-63
Sound level (dB)	52	32-42	37-43	34-37	33-39	33-53	35	34-48		34-47
Lighting (lx)	1-2630	0-422	150-1400	60-1890	62-568	4-834	42-1453	47-2090		36-2180
CO2 (ppm)	547-692	925-1347	527-580	1081-1381	936-1295	1054-1259	1199	904-1125		966-1189

Winter measures	1	2	3	4	5	6	7	8	9	10
Temperature (°C)	20.2-22.7	17.9-20.3	17.4-18.7	20.5-21.5	19.1-20.1	18.3-19.2	19.3-20.9	17.3-22.4	16.6-18.5	18.3-20.7
Humidity (%)	45-56	31.2-37.4	47.7-58.9	31-42.5	31.5-45	42.1-54	39.4-50.9	22.9-31.6	45.9-59	46.7-52.6
Sound level (dB)	32-42	37-41	29	37-38	34-45	36-37	30-41	32-51	33-45	38-52
Lighting (lx)	18-400	0-212	--	144-2100	20-647	--	1.5-80	9-540	9-1116	1-467
CO2 (ppm)	532-1482	680-917	688-789	861-1027	713-952	1025-1474	691-977	719-1022	1114-1223	859-1040

In the case of traditional buildings, thermal and visual discomforts, notably due to urban density and stone-bearing walls, add to the discomforts associated with urban noise. However, it is often difficult for inhabitants to offset these discomforts given the constraints of the architecture and its environment. The choice to live in such buildings is influenced by their central location in the city rather than an attachment to the architectural style. Although these dwellings share similar typologies and insulation problems, they exhibit significantly higher energy consumption than the aforementioned average for modern housing estates. Summer comfort in these dwellings is much more challenging due to the heavy mineral composition of the traditional urban fabric.

Our study shows that for inhabitants, 'sustainability' does not refer to strictly measurable criteria but encompasses qualitative issues like appropriation potential, the housing experience and unique architectural features that can contribute to sustainability on a broader scale. Mériadeck and Pontet-Lamartine are appreciated for these urban and architectural features, which serve as a safeguard against the obsolescence seen in many modern districts. These features are rare in contemporary constructions and not widely recognised by urban services. Nevertheless, residents generally maintain the urban and architectural homogeneity and details. Renovations are carried out, for the most part, in keeping with original designs that are perceived as genuinely high-quality. How this post-war heritage is viewed and understood is essential to the potential sustainability of the modern legacy.

Inhabitants as Guardians of Sustainable Modern Heritage

Modern town planning is increasingly mobilising inhabitants not only through its physical spaces but also through its cultural and social value. While the unconventional architecture and urban design may have initially been the default choice for many, our interviews demonstrate that people discover the qualities of modern urban planning and ideas over time through their own experiences. Depending on their culture, interest in architecture, life choices and residential trajectories, residents maintain and adapt their housing by respecting and optimising the existing architecture and urban plan. Our interviews allowed us to identify four attitudes towards sustainability and architectural heritage among inhabitants, from the less interested 'consumer' to the more engaged 'evolutionist' and 'conservative'. Although archetypal, these attitudes highlight a tendency to rehabilitate these often-overlooked areas. These attitudes can change according to the opportunities provided for residents to actively engage in heritage or urban matters, such as public participation processes, architectural mediation and shared management regulations. They reveal how inhabitants progressively become proactive agents in heritage preservation, through both passive and active methods.

The 'consumer', or the materialistic inhabitant, is particularly appreciative of the comfort and practical location of their modern home. They take no real interest in architecture but value the functionality and accessibility of their trendy neighbourhoods, making these post-war areas desirable places to live and reside.

> Old buildings are beautiful, the facades and stone walls... but it is really poorly arranged inside [...] For me, Mériadeck was probably Bordeaux's ugliest district, but it has inner use qualities, a good price/surface ratio, and these specific urban and functional facilities. What I find here, on the slab, it's all the services! I am an urban person; I want all the services without being annoyed by cars. So, all in all, there's a real quality of life. (Flat renter—social housing building, Mériadeck)

As inhabitants are 'awakened' to architecture through life in their modern districts, some endeavour to maintain and optimise the amenities, staying true to the original design and concept embedded in these modern urban elements. These 'awakened' inhabitants appreciate original spaces and perspectives but are also concerned about sustainability issues in housing. Buying a modern house or flat represents a commitment to respecting and preserving the specific features of this post-war architectural production. While these inhabitants may not have precise knowledge about architectural movements and trends, their sensitive approach reflects careful consideration when adapting existing buildings, be they modern or older constructions. The period of lockdown experienced during the pandemic heightened their awareness of the inherent qualities of the mixed modern neighbourhoods. In the words of one 'awakened' homeowner in Pontet-Lamartine, 'we were all the happier to live in Pontet-Lamartine when confined. And many inhabitants from the surroundings came to walk the dog or relax outside, in the park, as there are no other open green spaces around'.

Finally, the 'conservative' (or 'heritage ambassador') and the 'evolutionist' (or 'eco-modern') inhabitants are part of the same group of 'engaged inhabitants'. The former aims to strictly preserve the original modern architecture and layout as a cultural and societal testament to what was considered progress at that time. Both the 'conservative' and the 'evolutionist' residents view the climatic features of their 1970–1980s buildings as appropriate for addressing the energy transition issue. However, while the former prefers to adapt their needs to preserve the architecture, the latter is inclined to transform the built environment to improve the house's energy efficiency.

> Whether you like the result or not, the first thing is to recognise the quality of this neighbourhood. The architectural quality, the architects' design precision, its homogeneity [...] This really is the Charter of Athens. It's not too bad, especially when you look at the new districts, like Ginko [a new sustainable neighbourhood in Bordeaux].' (A 'conservative' flat owner—Mériadeck)

> Houses must evolve, though we have to keep the architectural unity. Thermal insulation from the outside and photovoltaic panels or solar panels are good as long as they cannot be seen from the street. (An 'evolutionist' house owner—Pontet-Lamartine)

They nonetheless unite to promote the 'quality of life and construction' of these neighbourhoods, a defining feature of sustainability in modern heritage. Moreover, the intangible modern heritage inspires inhabitants to maintain and expand the generous open and accessible spaces to a larger scale. They vitalise these neighbourhoods, sometimes challenging experts or urban professionals, to draw attention to the moral and physical imperative of rehabilitating the modern districts in order to anchor them more securely in the metropolis.[12] Some residents are co-organising a debate on sustainability and modern housing with

12 Fanny Gerbeaud, *Living Modern Architectural Heritage in the Age of Sustainability. Ambiances and Use Quality* (International Workshop Synthesis, 2018), https://pave.hypotheses.org/files/2017/10/LIVRET-VERSION-FINALE-compress%C3%A9e.pdf

our research team to reach a wider audience and share experiences pertaining to these districts' specific management issues.

Beyond maintaining these neighbourhoods, the purpose of mobilising residents is to initiate collective projects focused on heritage or sustainable development, directly related to the modern conception of space. These social, cultural or ecological projects are led by the most committed inhabitants of the modern districts, such as representatives of district co-owners and experts in the urban history of Bordeaux. For instance, some projects launched by the residents' association 'Safeguarding Mériadeck' promote modern heritage as a model and source of inspiration for building the appealing city of tomorrow. The organisation's founder, a Bordeaux UNESCO council member, even registered Mériadeck's heritage features to help the district's identification in the DOCOMOMO database (an organisation dedicated to twentieth-century Modern district and building preservation).

Other projects aim to optimise the sustainability assets of modern heritage in an 'evolutionist' manner, even if it entails incorporating contemporary technologies or practices that harness modern potential. These initiatives include creating a fifth facade for renewable energies, establishing planted areas on the slab to grow community vegetable gardens and organising activities for the surroundings. Defenders of modern urban planning highlight the original collective dimension of energy management (geothermal energy, waste collection) and the generosity of the current project, which continues to operate, although undermined by a strict regulatory framework and the perceived disinvestment of public authorities concerning this urban planning. As articulated by a flat owner in Mériadeck, 'when they made Mériadeck, they thought of collective management of energy, waste, traffic and parking. That's what's interesting: today, what's left of that?'

Indeed, in a context where city stakeholders are often perceived as reluctant to make greater use of modern urban planning, our research underscores inhabitants' pivotal role in recognising these complexes. Their detailed knowledge of what makes modern districts interesting and their commitment to action in and around these neighbourhoods make residents indispensable resources for propelling these areas and the city itself towards greater sustainability. Most of the inhabitants we interviewed have previously resided in a traditional urban setting (such as the stone buildings of the city centre, the *échoppes* or suburban cottages or pavilions) and are now getting involved in modern heritage preservation precisely because they believe its contribution to sustainability is 'vastly under-exploited', in the words of one Mériadeck inhabitant.

Raising awareness and supporting these inhabitants in managing their neighbourhoods are essential if they are to effectively lead these areas towards a brighter future. Although recognising the value of this tangible and intangible heritage, they are ill-equipped to carry out large-scale projects focused on cultural and energy-related aspects, like building insulation or renovation, or social issues, such as mediation or neighbourhood development. This results in decisions to close down these districts—as in the case of the closure of the Mériadeck's 'esplanades'—or in the fragmentation of responsibilities for maintaining common spaces, as it is difficult to identify the leading authority on these matters. Without a consensus on which aspects should be preserved or the methodologies to utilise in these operations, post-war modern housing neighbourhoods are threatened, regardless of their recognition or the commitment of their inhabitants. Like the historical *échoppes* neighbourhoods that are now protected and appreciated, modern districts are at risk of losing elements integral to their sustainability and heritage value in the eyes of their inhabitants, notably the concrete slab, the buildings' design and the spacious open parks. Raising awareness without ensuring that all stakeholders can engage in discussions together may prove futile, as indicated by one flat owner in Mériadeck: 'this is the third year that we are fighting, [that] we are working with the organisations to restore this water basin. And there's no question of turning it into a grassy area again!'

Conclusion: Towards Several Expressions of Sustainability

Like most European cities, Bordeaux has experienced several urban and architectural paradigms, comprising disparate historical elements that have avoided the neglect or erasure of past heritage to make way for new eras and ideas. However, over time and through daily practices, what was once considered outdated is gradually being rehabilitated.

The energy transition is at the heart of contemporary concerns, inviting us to rediscover the unique contributions of two major components of Bordeaux's skyline and heritage: traditional stone residential districts and emblematic post-war modern districts.

While traditional neighbourhoods tend to inspire today's eco-housing estates, characterised by streets, densely built lower-scale houses and equipments as well as private green spaces, there is growing interest in restoring post-war modern housing neighbourhoods, which also offer operable features for the sustainable city. This chapter demonstrates that while the modern project certainly did not materialise as originally imagined, it has brought specific amenities that enhance the well-being of today's citizens. With its densification and environmental preservation issues, the contemporary city has caught up with these modern districts, which must now prove their worth and qualities to endure and exist within the urban fabric.

This research has shown that the values of modern districts are appreciated by their primary stakeholders—the inhabitants and users. With their accessibility and functionality, they appeal to specific populations that the metropolis might otherwise struggle to maintain, including families with young children, people with disabilities and the elderly. These post-war neighbourhoods thus embody a quality of life and specific sustainability that require a re-evaluation of the quantitative and normative criteria used to renovate and optimise the existing housing stock, regardless of preconceived notions about modern or older architecture. Like the *échoppes* neighbourhoods, Mériadeck and Pontet-Lamartine are examples of modern districts worthy of preservation to enhance the resilience of the metropolis. Leveraging the characteristics of each piece of the urban fabric has the potential to create what Chaban-Delmas once envisioned when describing Mériadeck: a functional complement to the old and majestic city centre that would bring Bordeaux into the twenty-first century.

Constructing a sustainable city requires considering the contributions and advantages of architecture and urban planning models resulting from design practices, be they traditional, vernacular or modern. Achieving this complementarity between all the disparate urban patches demands better integration of inhabitants' work and expertise, acknowledging their legacy in the city of tomorrow. In this sense, the modern project continues beyond the avant-garde: Mériadeck and

Pontet-Lamartine serve as a starting point for new uses that can revive the Modern movement's spirit. They also help us reconsider what 'sustainability' could mean if defined on a broader scale, with a more environmentally conscious and holistic conceptualisation of progress.

Bibliography

Callais, Chantal, *L'échoppe de Bordeaux* (La Crèche: La Geste, 2020).

Coustet, Robert and Saboya, Marc, *Bordeaux : le temps de l'histoire, architecture et urbanisme au XIXe siècle, 1800–1914* (Bordeaux: Mollat, 1999).

Fitzsimons, Kent, *et al.*, *Les mouvements modernes rattrapés par la marche du durable : Leçons, adaptations et inventions des lieux du quotidien* (Redivivus Research Report for the French Ministry of Culture, Programme Interministériel de recherche 2016–20, 2019).

Fitzsimons, Kent and Gerbeaud, Fanny, 'Mériadeck et Les Aubiers à l'ère de la ville durable : vie et survie de deux quartiers modernistes à Bordeaux', in *Racines modernes de la ville contemporaine. Distances et formes de résilience*, ed. by Panos Mantziaras and Paola Vigano (Geneva: Métis Presses, 2019), pp. 157–76.

Gerbeaud, Fanny, '*Living Modern Architectural Heritage in the Age of Sustainability. Ambiances and Use Quality* (International Workshop Synthesis, 2018), https://pave.hypotheses.org/files/2017/10/LIVRET-VERSION-FINALE-compress%C3%A9e.pdf

Godier, Patrice and Tapie, Guy, *Un futur sans rupture* (Marseille: Parenthèses, 2009).

Querrien, Gwenaël, *Portrait de ville* (Paris: Cité de l'architecture et du patrimoine, IFA, 2006).

Requena-Ruiz, Ignacio, 'Thermal Comfort in Twentieth-century Architectural Heritage: Two Houses of Le Corbusier and André Wogenscky', *Frontiers of Architectural Research*, 5.2 (2016), 157–70, https://doi.org/10.1016/j.foar.2016.02.001

Requena-Ruiz, Ignacio, 'Building Artificial Climates. Thermal control and comfort in Modern Architecture (1930–1960)', *Ambiances*, 2 (2016), https://doi.org/10.4000/ambiances.801

Tapie, Guy, *Habitat, vieillissement et filières de production, vers des innovations sociales ?* (Research Report for the Nouvelle-Aquitaine Region, 2020).

UNESCO, 'Bordeaux, Port of the Moon' (2007), *UNESCO*, https://whc.unesco.org/en/list/1256

UNESCO, 'L'oeuvre architecturale de Le Corbusier, une contribution exceptionnelle au Mouvement Moderne' (2016), *UNESCO*, https://whc.unesco.org/en/list/1321/

6. Sustainable Urban Conservation of Historical Cities: The Case of Fez Medina, Morocco

Khalid El Harrouni

Introduction

The historic urban area of the medina is the oldest section and historical heart of several Moroccan cities. Various international bodies have bolstered efforts to preserve such historical monuments, and even entire cities, with initiatives such as the Global Charter of Historic Cities adopted by the International Council on Monuments and Sites (ICOMOS) in 1987 and the 1972 United Nations Educational, Scientific and Cultural Organization (UNESCO) convention to protect built and natural heritage, both of which include Morocco's medinas in their scope of preservation. In the 1980s, UNESCO acknowledged the cultural significance of several old towns in Morocco by including them on their World Heritage List. These medinas are not only physical environments and places of activities; they are also social spaces characterized by historical, cultural and spiritual values. They are reflections of a civilization's way of life and social traditions, which is evident in their design, construction and spatial organization.

The Fez medina, founded in the ninth century, is one such environment. Reaching its peak first in the fourteenth century under the Marinides and again in the seventeenth century, it serves as an example of pre-colonial urban planning. Moreover, its spatial

 https://doi.org/10.11647/OBP.0412.06

organisation resulted from the slow and 'integrative' evolution of urban and architectural production, adapted to the community's needs and lifestyle in its principal components: habitat, equipment and activities.

The World Heritage City of Fez is Morocco's spiritual, scientific and cultural capital. The significance of its medina lies in several factors, including its vast geographical area of 300 hectares and its population density of 800 to 1200 people per hectare. It boasts a substantial number of historic buildings—14000 in total, of which fifty percent are in good condition, thity-four percent have degraded, fourteen percent risk ruin or collapse and two percent lie in ruin.[1] It is also the site of many historical monuments, numbering around 3000. These include 11 *madrasas* [schools], 43 Quranic schools, 176 mosques, 83 *zaouias* [religious edifices associated with Sufi Islam] and mausoleums and 117 *fondouks* [hotels] or caravansaries. Notably, it houses the historic Al Qarawiyine University, considered one of the oldest in the Islamic world.

Several years ago, Fez medina offered a striking contrast between areas of thriving economic activity and over-densified residential quarters with steadily deteriorating buildings, a juxtaposition of rich cultural and monumental heritage and a degraded historical built environment. Today, the medina is a major economic centre for the whole urban agglomerate of Fez,[2] with prosperous artisanal and tourism sectors. However, this wealth does not seem to reach its population. Of the city's nearly 160000 inhabitants, thirty-six percent are living below the poverty level.

The most serious problems facing Fez medina included deteriorating residential zones, infrastructural decay, the transformation of traditional handicrafts into partially mechanized small-scale manufacturing, a significant number of low-income households, complex property ownership and occupancy patterns and environmental pollution. Recognising these issues, the Moroccan public authorities, supported by international momentum and solidarity, have made safeguarding Fez medina a national priority.

1 ADER-Fès, *Bâti menaçant ruine à Fès-Médina, Rapport de suivi* (Fez: ADER-Fès, 2006).

2 Jelidi Charlotte, Fès, la Fabrication d'une Ville Nouvelle (1912–1956) (Lyon: Sociétés, Espaces, Temps, ENS Éditions, 2012).

The Fez medina was subject to an extensive rehabilitation programme that began in 1981 and has continued for over thirty years. The programme aims to restore and preserve the old city's economy, cultural value and social heritage.

This chapter uses observation and a system dynamics approach to describe and analyse the urban heritage safeguarding process over the last thirty-five years in order to identify the best practices, constraints and difficulties faced in the sustainable conservation of the Fez medina.

Safeguarding the Fez Medina: Principal Stages and Components

The overall rehabilitation strategy for the Fez medina focuses on alleviating the aforementioned constraints through a conservation programme. The implementation of this programme has depended on securing the appropriate tools, including institutional, financial and technical support. The safeguarding process began with the drafting of the first urban document, the *Schéma Directeur d'Urbanisme de Fès, SDUF* [urban planning orientation scheme of Fez], which underlined the importance of the medina in the development of the entire Fez agglomeration.[3] The first period of the safeguarding process, from 1980 to 2005, can be divided into three principal stages.

First Stage (1980–1989): Launching the Safeguarding of Fez

In 1981, the medina was officially classified by UNESCO. Subsequently, in 1985, the Moroccan government and UNESCO jointly launched the international campaign for the safeguarding of the Fez medina. In 1989, the government established the Agency for the De-densification and Rehabilitation of the Fez medina (ADER-Fez), creating a new institutional framework for the implementation of strategic projects within the medina. Today, ADER-Fez specialises in conserving and rehabilitating the World Heritage City of Fez. Through various local and international initiatives, ADER-Fez has accumulated extensive

3 Royaume du Maroc, Ministère de l'Habitat et de l'Aménagement du Territoire, Délégation Régionale de Fès, *Schéma directeur d'urbanisme de la ville de Fès* (Fez: Royaume du Maroc, 1980).

and valuable experience in intervening in the historic fabric of the Fez medina.

Table 6.1 Stage 1 (1980–1989) of the safeguarding process: objectives, approach, tools and actions.

STAGE 1 (1980–1989)	Launching the safeguarding of Fez medina
Objectives	Safeguard the medina including the historical monuments in the entire city
References	UNESCO Recommendation 1976 ICOMOS Charter 1987 Venice Charter 1964
Tools	SDUF Law (22–80): historical monuments and sites conservation Classification of the monuments UNESCO world heritage (Fez in 1981 and Marrakesh in 1985)
Actors	Government Local Authorities ADER-Fez

Second Stage (1990–1998): Expansion and Experimentation

During this period, every aspect of the safeguarding effort was examined, including the technical, institutional, legal and financial components. Simultaneously, experimental operations were undertaken such as monument restoration and the rehabilitation of housing and urban facilities. Local capacities to plan and carry out the various project components were strengthened through the development of a master plan, improvements in the field of restoration and urban rehabilitation, and implementation of certain management tools like a comprehensive Geographic Information System (GIS) linked with planning and cost estimate tools, which facilitated the supervision of the rehabilitation project.

Table 6.2 Stage 2 (1990–1998) of the safeguarding process: objectives, approach, tools and actions.

STAGE 2 (1990–1998)	Integrated rehabilitation and safeguarding: expansion and examination of legal, technical and financial components
Objectives	Integrated rehabilitation and safeguarding of the medina The medina is an entity of physical, social and economic structure
References	ICOMOS Charter 1987
Tools	Experimental operations: restoration of the monuments, rehabilitation of the houses, urban facilities, etc. Reinforcement of the regulation framework (master plan) and management tools implementation: GIS, improvement in the field of the restoration and urban rehabilitation
Actors	Public authorities Civil society Private sector

Third Stage (1999–2005): Collaboration with International Financial Institutions and Launch of the Major Structuring Programmes

ADER-Fez was the main liaison with the World Bank team[4] in charge of the 'Rehabilitation Project of the Medina of Fez'. The project's development objective was the 'conservation of the Fez medina by mobilizing its inhabitants and local institutions' and, more precisely, '(a) to support the efforts of conservation in progress; (b) to consolidate the partnerships between public and private and (c) to use the process of

4 Royaume du Maroc, Banque Mondiale, *Projet de réhabilitation de la médina de Fès: rapport de synthèse* (Fez: Agence de Dédensification et de Réhabilitation de la médina de Fès, 1998).

rehabilitation to eradicate poverty'. These global development objectives encompassed the following: developing rehabilitation programmes for historic buildings; improving accessibility and emergency vehicle access; enhancing the medina environment; exploring the potential of the rehabilitation process to eradicate poverty; strengthening institutions and capacity building.

All of these components were achieved by 2005, and the project had a positive impact on the development of the Fez medina.[5] Although financial indicators do not always fully capture the scope of a project of this size, it generated many partnerships among actors and investors, aligning with the articulated components. This established a model for development practices in conservation zones.

Table 6.3 Stage 3 (1999–2005) of the safeguarding process: objectives, approach, tools and actions.

STAGE 3 (1999–2005)	Urban requalification of historic cities
Objectives	Rehabilitation and development of the medina The medina is a part of the physical, social and economic structure in permanent transition through urban development.
References	Royal Letters to the participants of the 23rd session of the World Heritage Committee (29 November 1999)[6] The Vienna *Memorandum*, 2005[7]
Tools	Strategic and action plans for rehabilitation and development Social animation and participation in housing restoration/rehabilitation Institutional strengthening and capacity building

5 Radoine Hassan, 'Urban Conservation of Fez-Medina: A Post-Impact Appraisal', *Global Urban Development Magazine*, 4.1 (2008), https://www.globalurban.org/GUDMag08Vol4Iss1/Radoine.htm

6 See https://whc.unesco.org/archive/repcomx99.htm

7 UNESCO, *The Vienna Memorandum on 'World Heritage and Contemporary Architecture —Managing the Historic Urban Landscape'* (Paris: UNESCO, 2005).

Actors	Public authorities
	Civil society
	Private sector
	Funds for development

In addition to the World Bank, other financial entities such as FADES (Arab Fund for Social and Economic Development) engaged in these efforts. FADES has been heavily involved in rehabilitating Fez's monuments, housing and infrastructure. Private national and international donors also supported the restoration of many monuments in the city. Additionally, the Moroccan government was a main source of financing for ADER-Fez's operations. Various ministries, particularly the Ministry of Housing and Urban Planning, the Ministry of Cultural Affairs, and the Ministry of Islamic Affairs and Waqf provided substantial financial backing for different programmes based on their respective mandates. The financial structure of the conservation programme reflects the active participation of local authorities, municipal councils, NGOs, national and international donors and financial institutions.

The many rehabilitation projects realised in the Fez medina distinguish it as a successful case study, particularly concerning fundraising and financial investment in the heritage sector. Although a historic city of 160,000 inhabitants cannot be fully preserved from all potential threats, Fez has made significant advances in realising its conservation vision compared to other historic cities in Morocco. Analysis of the investments in Fez's conservation made between 1981 and 2005 shows that infrastructure was the most substantial, constituting fifty-three percent of the budget. The second largest investment was in the rehabilitation of buildings, at twenty-two percent. The restoration of monuments ranked third, with eleven percent of the funding. Some monuments have been restored by the holding company Al Omrane[8] under an agreement between the Ministry of Culture and the Ministry of Housing and Urbanism.

8 Groupe Al Omrane, *Médina de Fès, Réhabilitation du Triangle Historique* (Rabat: Groupe Al Omrane, 2009).

Housing and Development

The housing and development component includes the following sub-components.

Social Mobilisation and Participation in Housing Rehabilitation

Early on in the project's development, social scientists were recruited from the university in Fez to undertake a participatory and social assessment, which began with data collection and consultations with various stakeholders. Government officials, religious and civic leaders, merchants, artisans, homeowners, renters and many others shared ideas for the potential expansion of project components. The aim was to arrive at a consensus on interventions and strategies based on an understanding of the city's social dynamics and to ensure the alignment of plans, aspirations and local capacities.

Participation was high owing to the involvement of several local NGOs in project development, facilitating collaboration between ADER-Fez and the local population and stakeholders in the implementation of the social assessment. This engagement had a significant impact on the project design. The objectives were to achieve the direct involvement of the population in the rehabilitation process, thereby improving living conditions and combating poverty through job creation. ADER-Fez contributed to this participatory process and community development in two forms: financial aid, evaluated at thirty percent of the operational costs, and support in building materials and technical assistance. The inhabitants' contribution amounted to roughly seventy percent of the operational costs.

Emergency Intervention on Housing Units at Risk of Collapse

Housing in Fez's historic district presents a high risk due to the threat of structural collapse. In 1991, ADER-Fez launched an innovative emergency action programme intended to protect the inhabitants from this mortal threat. The programme consisted of an emergency team comprised of builders, architects and engineers, who worked to prevent the collapse of these buildings.

Addressing buildings at risk of collapse requires emergency action from both the public and private sectors. Beyond consolidation and critical repairs, building codes emerged as a significant issue, with municipalities often lacking the necessary technical capacities and political influence for their enforcement. ADER-Fez prioritised emergency repairs for at-risk housing units situated along improved roads and tourist routes. Reducing the exceptionally high population density within the historic urban fabric constituted one the most crucial tasks, as this factor was contributing to the rapid degradation of historical and traditional structures.

Various programmes related to emergency intervention in at-risk housing units have been implemented and a restoration and rehabilitation laboratory was established to oversee the stability of physical structures, monitor the rate of degradation and conduct diagnosis and material quality analysis. The structural laboratory is assisted by the survey and spatial analysis group, a team of skilled technicians whose main task is to gather data and survey the medina's various buildings and structures. In addition to scientific data, the laboratory also explores the technical expertise of master builders through the interaction of engineers with traditional techniques.

Upon the completion of the 1980–2005 stage of the project, improvements in the overall state of the medina's housing stock were negligible, except for specific interventions and private investments to transform historic houses and palaces into Riads and guest houses.[9] Indeed, the collapse of housing units due to deterioration and lack of maintenance has continued. However, this has not resulted in any loss of human life, thanks to a wooden buttressing initiative financed by the Ministry of Housing and Urban Planning and carried out by ADER-Fez.

Infrastructure and Facilities

The successful revival of the medina is closely linked to improvements in its infrastructure and facilities, including the following:

9 Bianca Stephano, 'Conservation and Rehabilitation Projects for the Old City of Fez', in *Adaptive Reuse: Integrating Traditional Areas into the Modern Urban Fabric*, ed. by M. Bently Sevcenko (Cambridge, MA: MIT Laboratory of Architecture and Planning, 1983), pp. 47–59.

- Emergency vehicular access: these networks have a noticeably positive impact on the communication and transportation networks in the medina.
- Traffic organization: the traffic network has been improved, especially around the historic walls and monumental gateways.
- Accesses and parking: improved access points have facilitated parking outside the pedestrian zones. This accessibility also contributes to economic growth and enhances real estate values in many parts of the medina.
- Water and sewage system: ensuring a reliable water supply and efficient sanitation services are critical to the quality of life and productivity of the medina's residents. Urban local bodies, including the municipal council, RADEEF (Régie Autonome de Distribution d'Eau et d'Electricité de Fès—Water Supply and Electricity Public Utility of Fez), and ADER-Fez, are the main actors engaged in improving traditional water channels and modern sewage systems.
- Electricity: the municipality and RADEEF have played a major role in the electrification of the entire medina. Public lighting, electricity and telephone networks have increased business activities and tourism.
- Urban facilities: adapting their equipment standards to fit historical building capacities, the Ministries of National Education and Public Health have constructed numerous schools and nurseries within the medina. This infrastructure is an example of the efforts made by many actors to improve the living conditions in the medina.

Fourth Stage (2005–2018): Continuation of the Safeguarding Process and New Development Programmes

The safeguarding process continued from 2005 until 2018 (Table 6.4) with the integration of development plans and programmes at central and local levels. During the first phase of this fourth stage (2005–2013), the historical space was able to incorporate new territorial development approaches launched by the National Initiative for Human Development (INDH), the Regional Development Programs of Tourism and Crafts, and the Millennium Challenge Corporation.

The next phase (2013–2018) of the new development activities focused on the restoration and rehabilitation of historical monuments and addressing buildings at risk of collapse, guided by conservation and sustainability strategies.

After 2018

The period following 2018 was characterized by the signing of conventions at the Royal Palace in Rabat, presided over by presidency of the King of Morocco. These agreements pertained to programmes to enhance the old medinas of Marrakech and Rabat, the complementary programme for the enhancement of the old medina of Fez and the third phase of the programme for at-risk housing. The latter is an integral part of the rehabilitation programme for the old medina of Casablanca and the complementary programme for the requalification and upgrading of the medina of Essaouira.

Table 6.4 Stage 4 (from 2005) of the safeguarding process: objectives, approach, tools and actions.

STAGE 4 (2005–2018)	Requalification and protection of built heritage against natural disasters
Objectives	Develop sustainable strategies for the preservation, conservation and management of heritage
References	Kyoto Declaration ICORP-ICOMOS 2005 on Protection of Cultural Properties, Historic Areas and their Settings from Loss in Disasters ICOMOS Declaration 2005: Monuments and sites in their settings; Conserving cultural heritage in changing townscapes and landscapes ICOMOS Charter 2003: Principles for the analysis, conservation, and Structural Restoration of Architectural Heritage

Tools	Tools, planning and development practices of conservation and sustainable management of the urban environment Effective measures to control the impact of incremental or rapid change on the context
Actors	Public authorities Civil society Private sector Funds for development

A new generation of stakeholders emerged and became involved in this stage of historic city conservation (see Table 6.5).

Table 6.5 List of Stakeholders involved in this stage of historic city conservation.

- The Ministry of the Interior
- The Ministry of Islamic Affairs
- The Ministry of National Land Use Planning, Town Planning, Housing and Urban Policy
- The Ministry of Tourism, Air Transport, Handicrafts, and Social Economy
- The Ministry of Youth and Sports
- The Ministry of Culture and Communication
- Hassan II Fund for Economic and Social Development
- The *Wilaya* (administrative division of each region)
- The Council of each region
- The Communal Council of each city
- Al Omrane Group
- The National Agency for Urban Renovation and Rehabilitation of Buildings Threatened with Ruin

The sustainable urban conservation of historical cities is not only a concern of the cultural actors seeking to prevent the loss of historical values; it has also become a concern shared by a broader array of institutional and social actors interested in economic and social values.

In the context of conservation and sustainability in the historic city of Fez,[10] a system dynamics approach has been employed to examine the involvement of the key actors and the interconnections between them.[11] This analysis explored the interactions of various actors with the medina, including ADER-Fez, public authorities, civil society, private sector entities, and financial institutions. Based on a causal loop diagram, the research revealed the relationships among different variables in the Fez medina's rehabilitation system, including institutional investment, environmental quality, housing restoration, monument and site restoration, infrastructure rehabilitation, solid waste management, emergency intervention and accessibility improvement.

Promotion of Tangible and Intangible Cultural Heritage: The Case of Fez Medina

This analysis of the safeguarding of Fez medina has illuminated the evolution of its phases over time, its objectives, the approaches and tools used and the key actors. An important epistemological and semantic observation lies in the evolving terminology used in heritage conservation, expanding to encompass socio-terminology within the heritage domain. In addition, regarding social, environmental and integrated sustainability, the safeguarding the Fez medina has focused on local participation and integration in the rehabilitation and conservation project, continuing to benefit the community. The quality

---

10 Dennis Rodwells, 'The Coincidence Between Conservation and Sustainability', in Rodwells, *Conservation and Sustainability in Historic Cities* (Oxford: Wiley-Blackwell, 2007), pp. 183–203.

11 Belyazid Salim, Haraldson Hördur, Kalen Christer and Koca Deniz, 'A Sustainability Assessment of the Urban Rehabilitation Project of the Medina of Fez, Morocco', in Proceedings of the *21st International Conference of the System Dynamics Society*, ed. by Robert L. Eberlein, Vedat G. Diker, Robin S. Langer and Jennifer I. Rowe (New York: Publisher System Dynamics Society, 2003), n.p.

of the environment has been improved thanks to public investments in solid waste management, sanitation and sewerage networks, infrastructure and urban facilities.

The sustainable urban conservation of Fez as a historical city was based on coordinating diverse stakeholder perspectives. ADER-Fez, traditional artisans (*maalems* or master craftsmen) and local NGOs have participated in developing tools and disseminating best practices in restoration, rehabilitation and urban heritage conservation. Professional training has also contributed to developing scientific and experimental advances related to sustainable urban heritage conservation.

Conclusion and Lessons Learned

This chapter contributes to the literature on urban heritage and sustainability by providing insights into traditional Moroccan neighbourhoods, with a specific focus on the Fez rehabilitation project. It has outlined the basic principles of the sustainable urban conservation of the Fez medina, identifying the strengthening of local institutions, primarily through funding mechanisms, as an important pillar of the rehabilitation process. Positive outcomes of the Fez conservation programme include social participation, which is essential for successfully rehabilitating the historic housing stock. The project has demonstrated the feasibility of reconciling urban conservation objectives with the housing needs of underprivileged residents, facilitated through consultation and social participation in the design and implementation of interventions in historic housing.

However, certain challenges persist. Tenure of land and buildings is a critical obstacle in historic city rehabilitation, and municipalities should consider delegating urban rehabilitation operations to competent agencies. Additionally, urban rehabilitation projects should be straightforward in their objectives and design. Given the complexities of historic cities, interventions should adopt a programmatic approach, focusing on specific needs and opportunities rather than attempting to address all aspects within a single operation.

Bibliography

ADER-Fès, *Bâti menaçant ruine à Fès-Médina, Rapport de suivi* (Fez: ADER-Fès, 2006).

Belyazid, Salim, Hördur, Haraldson, Christer, Kalen and Deniz, Koca, 'A Sustainability Assessment of the Urban Rehabilitation Project of the Medina of Fez, Morocco', in *Proceedings of the 21st International Conference of the System Dynamics Society*, ed. by Robert L. Eberlein, Vedat G. Diker, Robin S. Langer and Jennifer I. Rowe (New York: Publisher System Dynamics Society, 2003), n.p.

Bianca, Stephano, 'Conservation and Rehabilitation Projects for the Old City of Fez', in *Adaptive Reuse: Integrating Traditional Areas into the Modern Urban Fabric*, ed. by M. Bently Sevcenko (Cambridge, MA: MIT Laboratory of Architecture and Planning, 1983), pp. 47–59.

Groupe Al Omrane, *Médina de Fès, Réhabilitation du Triangle Historique* (Rabat: Groupe Al Omrane, 2009).

Jelidi, Charlotte, *Fès, la Fabrication d'une Ville Nouvelle (1912–1956)* (Lyon: Sociétés, Espaces, Temps, ENS Éditions, 2012).

Radoine, Hassan, 'Urban Conservation of Fez-Medina: A Post-Impact Appraisal', *Global Urban Development Magazine*, 4.1 (2008), https://www.globalurban.org/GUDMag08Vol4Iss1/Radoine.htm

Rodwell, Dennis, 'Conservation and Sustainability in Historic Cities', in Rodwells, *Conservation and Sustainability in Historic Cities* (Oxford: Wiley-Blackwell, 2007), pp. 183–203.

Royaume du Maroc, Ministère de l'Habitat et de l'Aménagement du Territoire, Délégation Régionale de Fès, *Schéma directeur d'urbanisme de la ville de Fès* (Fez: Royaume du Maroc, 1980).

Royaume du Maroc, Banque Mondiale, *Projet de réhabilitation de la médina de Fès : rapport de synthèse* (Fez: Agence de Dédensification et de Réhabilitation de la médina de Fès, 1998).

UNESCO, *The Vienna Memorandum on 'World Heritage and Contemporary Architecture —Managing the Historic Urban Landscape'* (Paris: UNESCO, 2005).

III. SUSTAINABLE HERITAGE: CLIMATE, THERMAL COMFORT AND DESIGN

7. The Medina of Tunis, a Heritage Model for Urban Sustainability: Urban Morphology and Outdoor Thermal Comfort

Safa Achour

Introduction

Humans have always sought to protect themselves from environmental factors, such as bad weather and intense sunlight, giving rise to the concept of the 'living space'. From simple inhabited caves and huts to modern dwellings, living spaces remain a main human priority. We continuously seek to improve these spaces over time in order to maximise comfort. Among various concerns, thermal comfort is paramount, with a substantial impact on the well-being of users. Early humans were skilled in acclimatisation and designing structures according to their immediate environment. A prime example is the traditional architecture of the medina of Tunis, designed with respect to the specific parameter of thermal comfort. In addition to being well-adapted for ventilation and natural cooling, the construction materials and spatial configurations of patio houses are tailored to the climate of Tunis.[1]

1 Azeddine Belakehal, 'Ambiances patrimoniales : problèmes et méthodes', in *Ambiances in action/Ambiances en acte(s)—International Congress on Ambiances* (Montréal: International Congress on Ambiances, 2012), pp. 505–10, https://shs.hal.science/halshs-00745537/document

 https://doi.org/10.11647/OBP.0412.07

However, recent decades have witnessed evolving lifestyle patterns and urban transformations of considerable magnitude. The socio-economic changes induced by globalisation have led to an upheaval in urban spatial organisation, posing new challenges to development.[2] This chapter aims to evaluate outdoor thermal comfort conditions and their close relationship with urban morphology. This is done through the analysis of the medina of Tunis in comparison with more contemporary fabrics which are governed by urban planning regulations. The objective is to highlight the thermal qualities of the old fabric in terms of external thermal comfort, and consequently to draw lessons for improving the urban design of future cities.

Urban Changes and the Quality of Outdoor Spaces

In Tunis, new spatial configurations have adapted to modern needs such as vehicular traffic, as the narrow, winding streets of the medina were insufficient. Additionally, new forms of housing have emerged, including apartment buildings and standalone homes. Innovative construction techniques have enabled architects to create interior spaces that meet thermal comfort requirements, giving users greater control. Thus, heating systems provide a comfortable thermal atmosphere during the winter, while air conditioning systems allow for interior insulation during periods of intense heat.

However, these climate-adaptive solutions are not without consequences for the environment. Firstly, they lead to high levels of energy consumption, which is concerning in an era where the depletion of non-renewable energy sources is increasingly palpable. It should be noted that the building sector is among the world's largest energy consumers. In Tunisia, it is responsible for twenty-seven percent of national energy consumption.[3] Secondly, thermal control systems release anthropogenic energy that directly influences external air temperatures, altering outdoor thermal comfort and necessitating further regulation of interior conditions. This sets in motion a dangerous cycle of energy consumption.

2 Albert Lévy, 'Urban Forms and Significations: Revisiting Urban Morphology', *Spaces and Societies*, 122.3 (2005), 25–48 (p. 26), https://doi.org/10.3917/esp.122.0025

3 Mounir Bahri, *La nouvelle réglementation thermique en Tunisie et le programme de soutien* (Tunis: Consultation Nationale sur les technologies et le financement de la maîtrise de l'énergie dans le bâtiment, 2008).

Urban Heat Island Effect

Urbanisation leads to an 'artificial' climate[4] that has given rise to the phenomenon known as the Urban Heat Island Effect. This refers to 'the temperature difference observed between urban areas and the surrounding rural areas'.[5] These variations in the microclimate are attributable to several factors such as changes in natural land cover (deforestation, urban sprawl, etc.), reduced wind speed due to building construction, and the heat absorption capacity of building materials like glass, asphalt and concrete.[6]

As urbanisation expands to meet socio-economic demands, it constitutes a significant risk factor in the context of global warming. Thus, in the twenty-first century, there is no longer any viable approach to urban planning that does not take sustainability into account. Drawing insights from the proven success of the old city fabric of Tunis over centuries, this study proposes valuable lessons for sustainable urban systems.

While traditional architecture is widely acknowledged for the quality of its interior spaces, its urban planning elements continue to merit analysis. This research seeks to demonstrate the sustainability of traditional urban planning and investigates the impact of urban morphology on outdoor thermal comfort.

Outdoor Thermal Comfort

Outdoor thermal comfort is an area of increasing interest. Following the noticeable surge in studies of indoor thermal comfort, scientists are increasingly coming to understand the significance of external thermal factors. This growing interest is well-founded, given the complexity of the concept, its multitude of factors and their diverse interactions.

4 Pierre Carrega, 'Topoclimatologie et habitat' (PhD thesis, Université Sophia Antipolis, Nice, 1994).

5 Mélissa Guiguère, *Mesures de lutte aux îlots de chaleur urbains* (Quebec: Institut National de Santé Publique, 2009), https://www.inspq.qc.ca/publications/988

6 Neil Debbage and Shepherd J. Marshall, 'The Urban Heat Island Effect and City Contiguity', *Computers, Environment and Urban Systems*, 54 (2015), 181–94, https://doi.org/10.1016/j.compenvurbsys.2015.08.002

The effective study of outdoor thermal comfort must consider its various physical, physiological and psychological aspects.[7] The physical approach regards human beings as thermal machines, focusing on their interactions in terms of heat exchange with the environment. The physiological approach focuses on self-regulatory mechanisms like sweating and shivering, while the psychological approach attempts to assess the thermal sensations of users.

Outdoor thermal comfort thus emerges as a complex system of interactions between people and their environments, encompassing heat flow and sensory preferences. Research has classified the factors that affect this system into three main categories:[8] climatic factors (air temperature, mean radiant temperature, relative humidity and air speed); personal factors (metabolism and clothing); and contributing factors (acclimatisation, age, gender, etc.). Several studies have contributed to the 'standardisation' of comfort assessments, resulting in the development of thermal comfort indices for outdoor environments, including the Predicted Mean Vote (PMV), the Physiological Equivalent Temperature (PET), and the Universal Thermal Climate Index (UTCI).

Moreover, additional research has focused on factors influencing comfort which can be controlled through urban design.[9] With the relationship between urban morphology and outdoor thermal comfort established, scientists have sought to determine the most influential morphological factors.[10]

---

7 Ken Parsons, *Human Thermal Environments*, 2nd ed. (London: Taylor and Francis, 2003).

8 Andris Auciliems and Steven V. Szokolay, *Thermal Comfort: PLEA (Passive and Low Energy Architecture) Notes*, PLEA Note 3 (Brisbane: PLEA and Aepartment of Architecture, the University of Queensland, 1997).

9 Ahmed Memon Rizwan, Leung Y. C. Dennis, Chunho Liu, 'A Review on the Generation, Determination and Mitigation of Urban Heat Island', *Journal of Environmental Sciences*, 20.1 (2008), 120–28, https://doi.org/10.1016/S1001-0742(08)60019-4

10 Luc Adolphe, 'Modelling the Link between Built Environment and Urban Climate: Towards Simplified Indicators of the City Environment', in *Proceedings of IBPSA (International Building Performance Simulation Association)* (Rio de Janeiro: Actes IBPSA, 2001), pp. 679–84. Karima Ait-Ameur, 'Characterization of the Microclimate in Urban Public Spaces through the Validation of a « Morpho-climatic » Indicator System', in *Proceedings of PLEA 2002—The 19th Conference on Passive and Low Energy Architecture* (Toulouse: PLEA, 2002), pp. 305–11.

Research Framework

This study complements the author's previous comparative research on summer thermal comfort in the outdoor spaces of Tunis' main historical and contemporary fabrics.[11] In addition to demonstrating the outdoor thermal comfort of the Tunis medina during the summer, the research highlighted the most influential morphological indicators of exterior thermal comfort. The present chapter incorporates subsequent research pertaining to the winter season, assessing outdoor thermal comfort during both summer and winter. The analysis encompasses two distinct scales. The district scale evaluates the morphological indicators of built density (Ds) and urban roughness (Rm). This factor (Rm) refers to the urban fabric's slowing effect on the average wind speed.[12] The street scale focuses on the height-to-width ratio (H/W) and the Sky View Factor (SVF).[13]

These two scales are significant for several reasons. At the urban scale, the ongoing expansion of urban sprawl is leading to the emergence of energy-intensive megacities. The street scale serves as the interface between the architectural and urban scales, representing the common surface between buildings and their external environment.[14] Given that streets are heavily used public spaces, the comfort of their design is of considerable importance. As streets are a major factor influencing not only the outdoor microclimate but also the interior atmosphere, their design impacts the thermal sensations of users and the energy consumption of buildings.

---

11 Safa Achour-Younsi, 'Evaluation des conditions de confort thermique d'été en espaces extérieurs à Tunis: Des tissus historiques aux nouveaux quartiers' (PhD thesis, National School of Architecture and Urbanism in Tunis, 2015).

12 Ait-Ameur, 'Characterization of the Microclimate'.

13 Yupeng Wang and Hashem Akbari, 'Effect of Sky View Factor on Outdoor Temperature and Comfort in Montreal', *Environmental Engineering Science*, 31.6 (2014), 272–87, https://doi.org/10.1089/ees.2013.0430

14 Faiza Ali-Toudert and Helmut Mayer, 'Numerical Study on the Effects of Aspect Ratio and Orientation of an Urban Street Canyon on Outdoor Thermal Comfort in Hot and Dry Climate', *Building and Environment*, 41.2 (2006), 94–108, https://doi.org/10.1016/j.buildenv.2005.01.013

Area of Study

Climate

Tunisia, the smallest of the Maghreb states, is located in North Africa (36.48 ° N, 10.10 ° E). Its capital, Tunis, situated in the northern part of the country at the base of the Gulf of Tunis, extends over a coastal plain and the surrounding hills. The climate is classified as subtropical Mediterranean, characterised by an alternation of two highly contrasting seasons, namely a hot, dry summer and a cool, rainy winter. The average annual temperature in Tunis is approximately 20 °C, reaching an average of 28.8 °C in August and 12.9 °C in February. However, winter temperatures can drop to 7.6 °C, while summer temperatures can rise to 35.5 °C. Humidity levels are quite high, averaging sixty-six percent with a maximum value of up to ninety-five percent in winter and a minimum value of up to twenty-seven percent in summer. The winds in Tunis are predominantly north and northeast with an average speed of 3.7 m/s, which can reach 14.5 m/s in winter.

Urban Morphology of the City of Tunis

The historic heart and birthplace of Tunis is its medina, which is recognised as a United Nations Educational, Scientific and Cultural Organization (UNESCO) World Heritage Site. The urban planning of the medina is renowned for the patio house, a basic architectural unit used by all social groups. Whether a common dwelling, bourgeois house, large residence or palace, all units are constructed around a patio, with dimensions varying based on the category. These architectural units are then clustered together[15] back-to-back to form the fabric of the medina. The arrangement of the medina is based upon an introverted urban layout, leaving little room for outdoor public spaces. The narrow, winding streets have very small openings, catering to the needs of households and providing privacy. Public space is not designed by the delineation of subdivisions, avenues and streets, but rather emerges from the residual gaps between housing constructions.

The city later expanded into surrounding areas with the development of the European city adjoining the medina. It presents a stark contrast

15 Jalel Abdelkefi, *La Médina de Tunis : espace historique* (Paris: Editions CNRS, 1989).

with the medina itself, with its regular grid layout and distinct building typologies, previously unknown in the medina's landscape. Later, new neighbourhoods emerged on the outskirts of the city, governed by town planning regulations and standardised specifications. This development has transformed Tunis into an agglomeration with significant urban sprawl and population density.

In order to demonstrate the superior outdoor thermal comfort conditions of the traditional urban fabric, this study draws a comparison with a district of the 'new city' governed by the existing urban planning regulations. In selecting a plot within the medina to optimally represent the traditional heritage fabric, we focused on the central medina, excluding its suburbs and the souks district. At the urban scale, we ultimately chose the Place du Tribunal district, a small plot which offers a microcosm of the diverse morphologies found within the medina's fabric. At the street scale, six reference points representing different street prospects were chosen in order to detect variations.

Within the regulated fabric, we similarly selected a district representative of the most prevalent residential units, with a variety of standalone and collective housing, as well as identified six reference points (see Figure 7.1).

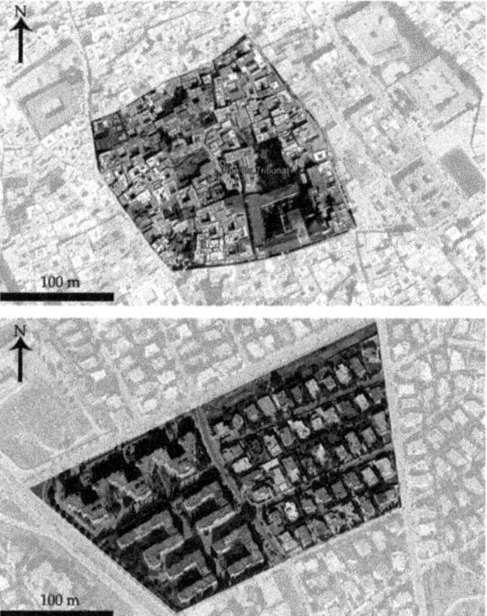

Fig. 7.1 Site map for the old city (top) and the new one (bottom). Author's illustration, based on Google Earth (2021), CC BY-NC-ND.

Methodology

A three-step investigative methodology was devised in order to demonstrate the high level of outdoor thermal comfort inherent in the town planning of the medina. This approach aims to illustrate the impact of urban morphology on the microclimatic conditions of outdoor space, which in turn influences the level of outdoor thermal comfort. The comparison between the old town and the new city confirms the efficiency of the medina's town planning and reveals the correlations between urban morphology and outdoor thermal comfort.

Urban Morphology Analysis

For the typo-morphological analysis of the medina of Tunis, influential morphological indicators identified in previous research were utilised.

At the neighbourhood scale, built density (Ds) is calculated as the total built-up area over the total plot area using the formula where *Ap* is the building floor area, and *As* is the total surface.

Next, urban roughness (Rm) is measured as the average height of the urban canopy, determined by the product of the building height by the area, divided by the total of built-up and non-built areas. This factor is calculated using the formula where *Ai* is the floor occupancy of buildings, *Hi* is the building height, *Aj* is the unbuilt area and *i* is the number of buildings.

At the street scale, two highly dependent indicators are studied. First is the H/W ratio, which represents the ratio of average building height to the shortest distance between streets.

Next is the Sky View Factor (SVF), defined as the solid angle at which the sky is viewed from space. The assessment of this indicator requires an equidistant image, produced using a fisheye lens photograph. An SVF of 1 means that there is no obstacle to the view of the sky, such as from isolated terrain. In this case, we can estimate that the temperatures recorded on this same site will be practically equal to those given by the meteorological stations. On the other hand, an SVF of 0 indicates a completely obstructed space. In this case, temperatures will be strongly influenced by the immediate urban environment.

Urban Microclimate Analysis

Microclimatic conditions in outdoor spaces are analysed through four key parameters impacting outdoor thermal comfort: air temperature, mean radiant temperature, relative humidity and wind speed. A measurement campaign was conducted, followed by numerical simulations using the Envi-met model (version 4.0) by Michael Bruse[16] from the Institute of Geography at the University of Bochum in Germany. This software has been tested and applied in a variety of research related to urban climatology and thus to the evaluation of external thermal comfort.[17]

Table 7.1 Configuration of the simulations and characteristics of the fabrics.

Characteristics of the simulated plots		
	Old City	New City
Tissue location	36.48° N/10.10° E	36.51° N/10.9° E
Fabric size (m)	210 x 198	477 x 246
Plot size (cells)	70 x 66 x 15	159 x 82 x 20
Rotation of the model with respect to the North	65°	-24°
Maximum building height (m)	15	24
Climatic parameters for simulation configuration		
	Winter season	Summer season
Date of the simulation	10/02/2020	20/08/2020
Duration of the simulation	24h00	24h00
Simulation beginning	06h00	06h00
Air temperature	283.15°K (10° C)	299.15°K (26° C)
Relative humidity	67%	61%
Wind speed at 10m on the ground	12.91 m/s	3.1 m/s
Wind direction	N-NE	N-NE

16 Michael Bruse, 'Simulating Microscale Climate Interactions in Complex Terrain with a High-resolution Numerical Model: A Case Study for the Sydney CBD (Model Description)', in *Proceedings of International Conference on Urban Climatology and International Congress of Biometeorology* (Sydney: n.p., 1999), https://www.envi-met.net/documents/papers/CBDSimu1999.PDF

17 Ferdinando Salata, Iacopo Golasi, Roberto De Lieto Vollaro and Andrea de Lieto Vollaro, 'Urban Microclimate and Outdoor Thermal Comfort. A Proper Procedure to Fit ENVI-met Simulation Outputs to Experimental Data', *Sustainable Cities and Society*, 26 (2016), 318–43, https://doi.org/10.1016/j.scs.2016.07.005

To achieve this, both fabrics were modelled to reflect reality, considering building locations and characteristics (height, materials, vegetation, soil type, etc.) as outlined in Table 7.1. Simulation results were compared with measured values to validate the accuracy of the simulations.

Outdoor Thermal Comfort Analysis

In order to assess the complex concept of outdoor thermal comfort, we employed several tools. First, for the physical dimension of comfort, our evaluation is grounded in the Universal Thermal Climate Index (UTCI) scale. The latest in thermal comfort indices, it was developed for evaluating outdoor thermal comfort in various fields such as bioclimatic mapping, urban planning and climate impact research.[18] Utilizing a simplified regression function,[19] we calculate this index and generate comfort zone diagrams, along with daily averages in summer and winter.

Subsequently, to evaluate comfort from a physio-psychological perspective, an in-situ survey was administered to the users of the space during both the summer and winter seasons. The survey involved forty-five people in each season, questioning them about their perceived thermal sensations and preferences using the following model:

- Scale of perceptual judgments:
    - Temperature (perceived as very cold/cold/slightly cold/ neutral/slightly hot/hot/very hot).
    - Wind (estimated as too much/neutral/not enough).
    - Humidity (found to be damp/neutral/dry).
- Scale of evaluative judgments:
    - Thermal ambiance (judged as unacceptable/acceptable/ good).

18 Gerd Jendritzky, Richard de Dear and George Havenith, 'UTCI—Why Another Thermal Index?', *International Journal of biometrology*, 56.3 (2011), 421–28, https://doi.org/10.1007/s00484-011-0513-7

19 Peter Bröde, Dusan Fiala, Krzysztof Błażejczyk, Ingvar Holmér, Gerd Jendritzky, Bernhard Kampmann, Birger Tinz and George Havenith, 'Deriving the Operational Procedure for the Universal Thermal Climate Index (utci)', *International Journal of Biometrology*, 56.3 (2012), 481–94, https://doi.org/10.1007/s00484-011-0454-1

- Scale of thermal preference:
    - Sun preference (desired more/neutral/less).

Results

Morphological characterisation of the studied fabrics

Beginning with the neighbourhood scale, the indicators Ds and Rm (see Table 7.2) reveal significant differences between the old town and new district. The fabric of the old town is very dense, roughly four times denser than that of the new district. Likewise, the roughness of the old fabric is considerably higher, nearly three times that of the new fabric.

Table 7.2 Built density and urban roughness of the two fabrics.

	Built density	Urban roughness
Old city	Ds = 0.71	Rm = 6.87 m
New city	Ds = 0.17	Rm = 2.48 m

Table 7.3 H/W ratio and SVF of references points.

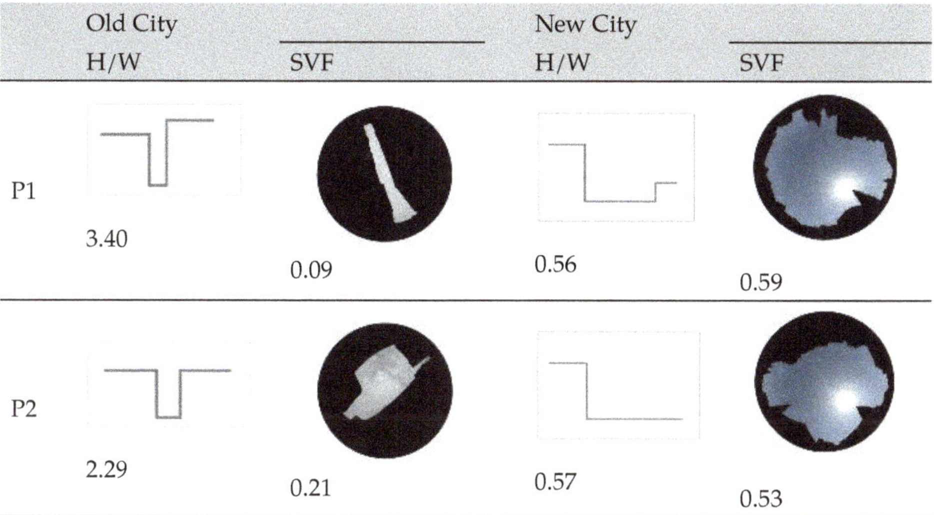

	Old City		New City	
	H/W	SVF	H/W	SVF
P1	3.40	0.09	0.56	0.59
P2	2.29	0.21	0.57	0.53

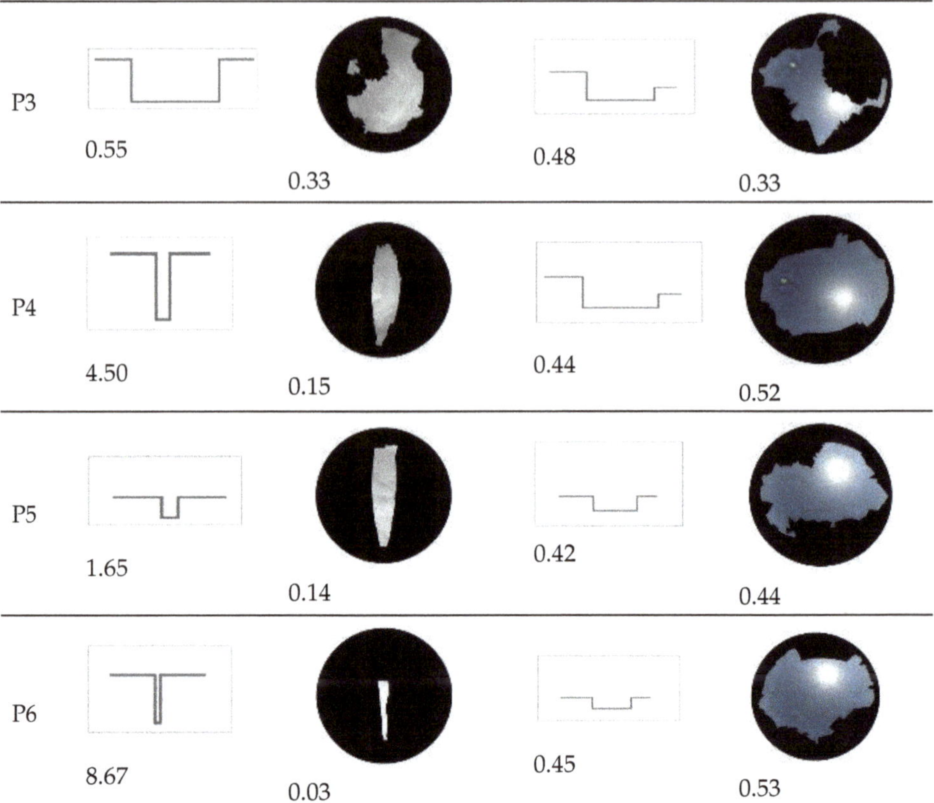

At the street scale, the results of the H/W ratios and the SVF presented in Table 7.3 indicate that the old town fabric mainly consists of canyon-type streets, with fairly high H/W ratio values, averaging at 3.51 and reaching up to 8.67. The new town has an average H/W ratio of 0.48, representing a fabric with more open dihedral spaces. Thus, it is evident that the two fabrics are vastly different from a morphological perspective, although it should be noted that one reference point in the old fabric has an H/W ratio close to that of the new fabric, with a value of 0.55.

Microclimate Analysis

Daily variations of the microclimatic parameters (air temperature, mean radiant temperature, relative humidity and wind speed) were calculated in the selected urban fabrics at the various reference points previously set. This was followed by the calculation of tissue means to compare the two fabrics.

According to the observed results (Figure 7.2), the wind speed of the old fabric appears fairly constant in both summer and winter. Notably, the difference in wind speed between the old and new fabrics is approximately 2.46 m/s in winter and 0.75 m/s in summer. As for air temperature, the curves of both fabrics are similar in both seasons, although there is an average difference of 2.31 °C in winter, doubling in summer to reach 4.48 °C.

Regarding relative humidity, the difference between the old and the new city is around 6.33% in summer and 17.23% in winter. Finally, concerning mean radiant temperature, the disparity between the two fabrics can reach up to 16 °C in summer.

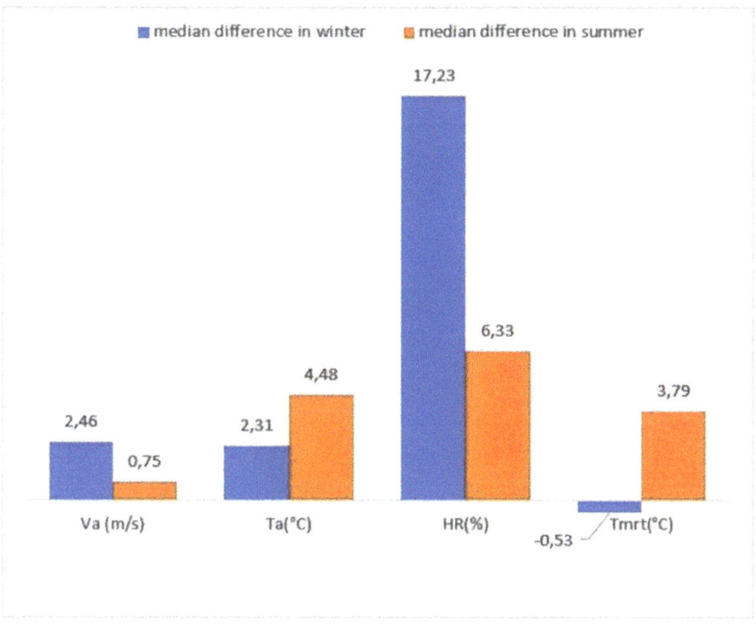

Fig. 7.2 Median differences between old and new cities. Author's graph, CC BY-NC-ND.

Assessment of Outdoor Thermal Comfort

Physical Aspect

The physical aspect of comfort is evaluated based on the UTCI thermal comfort index. UTCI values were calculated for both seasons on full days, followed by the daily average for each season. Figure 7.3 illustrates that the daily average in winter situates the old fabric in the 'slight cold stress' zone and very close to the 'no thermal stress' zone, while the new fabric falls within the 'moderate cold stress' zone. In summer, the old fabric is positioned in the 'no thermal stress' zone while the new fabric is in the 'moderate heat stress' zone.

Table 7.4 UTC ranges and related stress categories.

UTCI (°C) range	Stress category	UTCI (°C) range	Stress category
above +46	extreme heat stress	+9 to 0	slight cold stress
+38 to +46	very strong heat stress	0 to -13	moderate cold stress
+32 to +38	strong heat stress	-13 to -27	strong cold stress
+26 to +32	moderate heat stress	-27 to -40	very strong cold stress
+9 to +26	no thermal stress	below -40	extreme cold stress

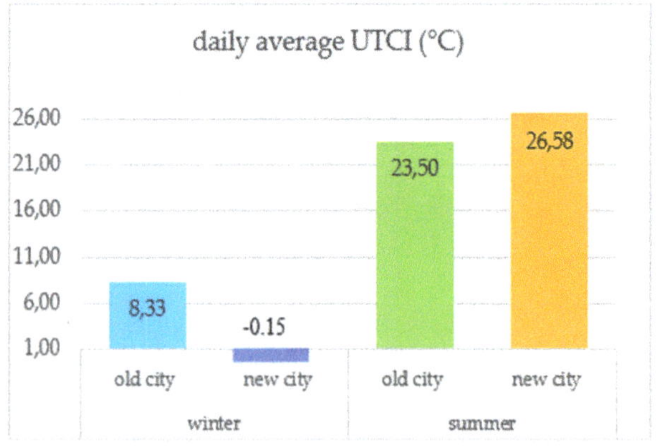

Fig. 7.3 Daily average of UTCI and Stress categories. Author's graph, CC BY-NC-ND.

Analysing the comfort zones diagram (Figure 7.4) reveals that in winter, the old fabric has 37.5% of comfort zones compared to 25% for the new fabric. Moreover, the new fabric has 66% of its areas in moderate cold stress, while the old fabric has none. For the summer season, the fabric of the old city offers 62.5% of comfort zones with 33% of strong heat stress zones, in contrast to 58% of comfort zones for the new fabric and 37.5% of strong heat zones.

In both summer and winter, the fabric of the old city performs better with regard to outdoor thermal comfort. Indeed, according to the UTCI rating scale, the old fabric is within the thermal comfort zone in summer and is very close to it in winter. On the other hand, the fabric of the new neighbourhoods is in moderate cold stress in winter and moderate heat stress in summer.

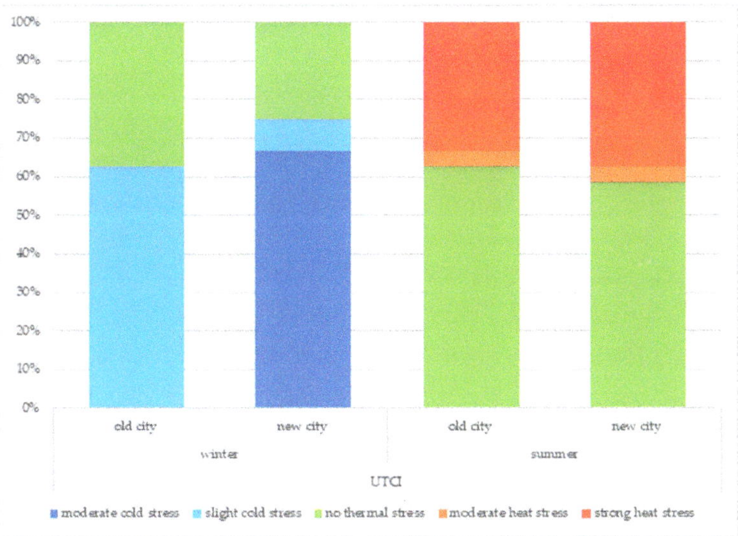

Fig. 7.4 Comfort zones percentages. Author's graph, CC BY-NC-ND.

Physio-psychological Aspect

Following the summer and winter surveys, encompassing a total of ninety participants, the data was coded and the results analysed in order to identify user opinions and perceptions regarding thermal sensation. On the perceptual judgments scale, the survey responses indicate that the old fabric satisfies a greater number of people in terms of temperature and humidity. Conversely, the modern fabric provides more satisfaction concerning wind. On the evaluative judgments scale, the old fabric exhibits overwhelming satisfaction compared to the new fabric. Finally, on the thermal preference scale, the old fabric registers thirty-five percent satisfaction whereas the new fabric registers only five percent. In addition, the dissatisfaction rate is around forty-six percent for the new city in contrast to only five percent for old fabric. It is evident from this research that the notion of thermal comfort must be evaluated in its entirety and cannot be assessed based on individual factors. Nonetheless, the survey results support the findings of the physical aspect analysis, showing that the old fabric is more comfortable than the new fabric.

Discussion and Conclusion

This analysis demonstrates the superior outdoor thermal comfort of the medina fabric as compared to that of the new town. The results of the physical aspect, based on the UTCI index, align with the survey responses relating to the physio-psychological aspect, reinforcing this conclusion.

The study revealed that, for a subtropical Mediterranean climate like that of Tunisia, a high H/W ratio may contribute to creating acceptable thermal comfort conditions in both the summer and winter seasons. The results show that a higher H/W ratio correlates with increased comfort. In summer, the new fabric heats up more than the old fabric, and in the winter, the new fabric cools much more than the old one. For the old fabric, with an average H/W ratio of 3.51, the average UTCI in the winter season is 8.36 °C, a value very close to the neutral comfort zone (9 °C), and the UTCI average in summer is 23.43 °C, which falls within the comfort zone. Meanwhile, the modern fabric, with an average H/W ratio of 0.49 and average UTCI in winter of 2.15 °C, falls within the slightly cold zone, while the summer average of 26.61 °C indicates the moderate stress zone.

This difference is primarily due to the shading effect of the old fabric's urban morphology, reducing surface sun exposure and ambient temperatures. Moreover, this configuration diminishes solar radiation's penetration into public space preventing radiative trapping.

Notably, the factors of built density and urban roughness play a significant role in the evaluation of outdoor thermal comfort, with considerable disparities apparent between the old and new fabrics. The old fabric is four times denser than the modern one and its urban roughness is 2.77 times greater. Nevertheless, two reference points within the two fabrics were found to possess similar H/W ratios but different UTCI values (see Table 7.5). This demonstrates that urban morphology cannot be considered at the street scale alone but must also be evaluated at the neighbourhood scale.

Table 7.5 Difference between same H/W ratio in the two fabrics.

		Old city	New city
Neighbourhood scale	Ds	0,71	0,17
	Rm (m)	6,87	2,48
Street scale	Reference point	P3	P1
	H/W	0,55	0,56
	SVF	0,33	0,59
Winter	UTCI min (°C)	-0,50	-3,80
	UTCI max (°C)	20,30	14,90
	UTCI mean (°C)	6,88	1,45
Summer	UTCI min (°C)	12,60	18,00
	UTCI max (°C)	34,20	39,00
	UTCI mean (°C)	22,39	27,11

The ancient fabric of the medina proves to be an exemplary model of outdoor thermal comfort. Its urban organisation, both at the neighbourhood and street scales, presents several advantages for sustainable urban planning given the relative comfort of its microclimate. Apart from its well-known sustainable characteristics, it offers additional advantages that warrant further study for recommendations in sustainable urban planning. Given the correlation between urban fabric density and a positive thermal environment, it is advisable to take measures to avoid the urban sprawl being witnessed in many modern cities as it contributes to the urban heat island effect, along with the deforestation and soil waterproofing that follows. Additionally, at the street scale, adapting street prospects to modern needs by widening streets while maintaining the same H/W ratio can mitigate radiative trapping phenomena, addressing the main causes of street-scale air heating.

Bibliography

Abdelkefi, Jalel, *La Médina de Tunis : espace historique* (Paris: Editions CNRS, 1989).

Achour-Younsi, Safa, 'Evaluation des conditions de confort thermique d'été en espaces extérieurs à Tunis : Des tissus historiques aux nouveaux quartiers' (PhD thesis, National School of Architecture and Urbanism in Tunis, 2015).

Adolphe, Luc, 'Modelling the Link between Built Environment and Urban Climate: Towards Simplified Indicators of the City Environment', in *Proceedings of IBPSA (International Building Performance Simulation Association)* (Rio de Janeiro: Actes IBPSA, 2001), pp. 679–84.

Ait-Ameur, Karima, 'Characterization of the Microclimate in Urban Public Spaces through the Validation of a « Morpho-climatic » Indicator System', in *Proceedings of PLEA 2002—The 19th Conference on Passive and Low Energy Architecture* (Toulouse: PLEA, 2002), pp. 305–11.

Ali-Toudert, Faiza and Mayer, Helmut, 'Numerical Study on the Effects of Aspect Ratio and Orientation of an Urban Street Canyon on Outdoor Thermal Comfort in Hot and Dry Climate', *Building and Environment*, 41.2 (2006), 94–108, https://doi.org/10.1016/j.buildenv.2005.01.013

Auciliems, Andris and Szokolay, Steven V., *Thermal Comfort: PLEA (Passive and Low Energy Architecture) Notes*, PLEA Note 3 (Brisbane: PLEA and Aepartment of Architecture, the University of Queensland, 1997).

Bahri, Mounir, *La nouvelle réglementation thermique en Tunisie et le programme de soutien* (Tunis: Consultation Nationale sur les technologies et le financement de la maîtrise de l'énergie dans le bâtiment, 2008).

Belakehal, Azeddine, 'Ambiances patrimoniales : problèmes et méthodes', in *Ambiances in action/Ambiances en acte(s)—International Congress on Ambiances* (Montréal: International Congress on Ambiances, 2012), pp. 505–10, https://shs.hal.science/halshs-00745537/document

Bröde, Peter, Fiala, Dusan, Błażejczyk, Krzysztof, Holmér, Ingvar, Jendritzky, Gerd, Kampmann, Bernhard, Tinz, Birger and Havenith, George, 'Deriving the Operational Procedure for the Universal Thermal Climate Index (utci)', *International Journal of Biometrology*, 56.3 (2012), 481–94, https://doi.org/10.1007/s00484-011-0454-1

Bruse, Michael, 'Simulating Microscale Climate Interactions in Complex Terrain with a High-resolution Numerical Model: A Case Study for the Sydney CBD (Model Description)', in *Proceedings of International Conference on Urban Climatology and International Congress of Biometeorology* (Sydney: n.p., 1999), https://www.envi-met.net/documents/papers/CBDSimu1999.PDF

Carrega, Pierre, 'Topoclimatologie et habitat' (PhD thesis, Université Sophia Antipolis, Nice, 1994).

Debbage, Neil and Shepherd, J. Marshall, 'The Urban Heat Island Effect and City Contiguity', *Computers, Environment and Urban Systems*, 54 (2015), 181–94, https://doi.org/10.1016/j.compenvurbsys.2015.08.002

Giguère, Mélissa, *Mesures de lutte aux îlots de chaleur urbains* (Quebec: Institut National de Santé Publique, 2009), https://www.inspq.qc.ca/publications/988

Jendritzky, Gerd, De Dear, Richard and Havenith, George, 'UTCI—Why Another Thermal Index?', *International Journal of biometrology*, 56.3 (2011), 421–28, https://doi.org/10.1007/s00484-011-0513-7

Lévy, Albert, 'Urban Forms and Significations: Revisiting Urban Morphology', *Spaces and Societies*, 122.3 (2005), 25–48, https://doi.org/10.3917/esp.122.0025

Parsons, Ken, *Human Thermal Environment*, 2nd ed. (London: Taylor and Francis, 2003).

Rizwan, Ahmed, Memon, Dennis, Leung Y. C. and Liu, Chunho, 'A Review on the Generation, Determination and Mitigation of Urban Heat Island', *Journal of Environmental Sciences*, 20.1 (2008), 120–28, https://doi.org/10.1016/S1001-0742(08)60019-4

Salata, Ferdinando, Golasi, Iacopo, De Lieto Vollaro, Roberto and De Lieto Vollaro, Andrea, 'Urban Microclimate and Outdoor Thermal Comfort. A Proper Procedure to Fit ENVI-met Simulation Outputs to Experimental Data', *Sustainable Cities and Society*, 26 (2016), 318–43, https://doi.org/10.1016/j.scs.2016.07.005

Wang, Yupeng and Akbari, Hashem, 'Effect of Sky View Factor on Outdoor Temperature and Comfort in Montreal', *Environmental Engineering Science*, 31.6 (2014), 272–87, https://doi.org/10.1089/ees.2013.0430

8. The Colonial Heritage of Tunis: Simple Collective Memory or an Environmental Resource?

Athar Chabchoub and Fakher Kharrat

Introduction

In less than a century, Tunisia has faced the two major challenges of colonisation and globalisation. As Paul Sebag writes:

> The year 1881, which was the year of the institution of the protectorate, marked a turning point in the history of Tunis. The city, which until then had known only slow changes of modest magnitude, has entered an era of rapid change which, in two or three decades, has profoundly transformed it.[1]

The period of colonisation from 1881 to 1956 affected several Tunisian cities, including Bizerte, Sousse and Sfax, among others. However, Tunis remains by far the most profound testament to the impact of colonisation on the country's architectural history. Far from the winding streets of the medina and traditional patio houses, colonisation enabled the advent of new architectural forms. Apartment buildings sprang up in Tunis in a checkerboard pattern, carving out an original urban and architectural landscape.[2]

1 Paul Sebag, *Tunis, Histoire d'une ville* (Paris: L'Harmattan, 1998), p. 336.

2 Chiraz Mosbah, 'L'héritage colonial de la ville de Tunis entre 1900 et 1930: étude architecturale et décorative des édifices de style néo-mauresque' (PhD thesis, Université Paris 1 Panthéon-Sorbonne, 2006); Catherine Coquery-Vidrovitch,

 https://doi.org/10.11647/OBP.0412.08

This European influence, which gave rise to colonial towns in different regions of Tunisia, has propelled the country toward a global perspective since the nineteenth century, shaping its future trajectory and opening the door to globalisation. Industrial and economic developments, coupled with technological advances driven by globalisation, are shifting societal norms. In the late 1990s, the far-reaching impact of these trends became tangible in urban space, as architecture began to break free from the restraints of the past and adopt new forms. The metamorphosis of the built environment introduced contemporary aesthetic elements, heralding the country's engagement in a process of universal modernity, far removed from traditional symbolic references.

Like most major world cities, Tunis has embraced a modern aspect, relegating colonial buildings, which no longer meet the requirements of contemporary life, to the background. In addition, with the development of modern commercial and residential centres, the city centre of Tunis has suffered depopulation due to persisting harmful activities, traffic and parking difficulties resulting in its depreciation and its tertiarization.[3] Buildings and even entire islets have been destroyed to make room for modern constructions. Other structures, neglected and abandoned, are now showing concerning signs of aging. Thus, colonial heritage is increasingly fading away and ceding ground to contemporary architecture.

This drastic transformation of downtown Tunis disrupts the urban landscape, creating a dual divide: first through the demolition, abandonment and neglect of colonial buildings and, second, through the emergence of new architecture devoid of character and uniform in appearance throughout different regions with diverse natural and human environments. Additionally, the excessive use of glazing in a country with intense sun exposure like Tunisia clearly demonstrates the

La ville européenne outre mers un modèle conquérant (XVe–XXe siècle), ed. by Odile Goerg (Paris: L'Harmattan, 1996); Mercedes Volait, 'Colonial Architecture', in *Abécédaire de la ville au Maghreb et au Moyen-Orient*, ed. by B. Florin, A. Madoeuf, O. Sanmartin, R. Stadnicki and F. Troin (Tours: Presses universitaires François-Rabelais, 2020), pp. 45–46; Isabelle Grangaud and M'hamed Oualdi, 'Tout est-il colonial dans le Maghreb ? Ce que les travaux des historiens modernistes peuvent apporter', *l'Année du Maghreb*, 10 (2014), 233–54; Serge Santelli, *Tunis, le creuset méditerranéen* (Paris: Éditions du CNRS, 1995).

3 Leila Ammar, *Histoire de l'architecture en Tunisie : de l'Antiquité à nos jours* (La Manouba: Centre de Publication Universitaire, 2005).

unsuitability of contemporary buildings for the local climate. Based on this observation as well as heritage and environmental concerns, this research undertakes a study of the environmental quality of colonial buildings within the urban fabric of Tunis.

Environmental Quality: From Indoor Thermal Comfort to its Energy Impact

The quality of life a building provides and its closely related architectural quality both define a building's environmental quality (QEB). Indeed, the architectural quality of a building, including its construction materials and architectural design, resides in its adaptation to the climate, thus offering users comfortable and energy efficient spaces conducive to residents' well-being. On the other hand, the decontextualisation of a building from its environment alters its quality of life, creating uncomfortable spaces with environmental repercussions, such as increased energy consumption from the use of air conditioning to mitigate discomfort. Additionally, it can adversely affect the health of the occupants.

Given current environmental concerns, there is a growing body of research focused on QEB.[4] From numerous studies, it is clear that QEB is associated with the thermal, acoustic, olfactory and visual aspects of comfort. However, the notion of 'comfort' has a multitude of dimensions, making its definition somewhat ambiguous.

Historically, the first form of comfort achieved by humanity was shelter as a form of protection from the elements. Over the years,

4 Nadège Chatagnon, 'Développement d'une méthode d'évaluation de la qualité environnementale des bâtiments au stade de la conception' (PhD thesis, Université de Savoie Mont Blanc, Chambéry, 1999); Alice Micolier, 'Développement d'une méthodologie d'évaluation cohérente et intégrée de l'impact des choix de conception sur la qualité de l'air intérieur et les performances énergétiques et environnementales des bâtiments résidentiels' (PhD thesis, Doctoral School of Physical Sciences and Engineering (Gironde) in partnership with the Institute of Mechanics and Engineering of Bordeaux, Bordeaux, 2019); Céline Mandallena, 'Elaboration et application d'une méthode d'évaluation et d'amélioration de la qualité environnementale de bâtiments tertiaires en exploitation' (PhD thesis, Université Bordeaux 1, 2006); Endrit Hoxha, 'Amélioration de la fiabilité des évaluations environnementales des bâtiments' (PhD thesis, Université Paris-Est, 2015); Philippe Madec, 'Architecture et qualité environnementale', *Les Annales de la Recherche Urbaine* (2002), 140–42.

'comfort' has diverged from its most basic conceptualisation and adapted to changes in societies and lifestyles. The notion of domestic comfort initially signified simply having a 'home'. Between the seventeenth and the mid-nineteenth century, with houses not connected to a central power supply system, hygienic concerns led to the designing of houses with greater domestic comfort.

Since the late twentieth century, progress has been made in all areas of scientific knowledge, including architecture and construction. The installation of technical networks from streets to urban housing, as well as the electrification of homes, has reshaped the entire domestic environment. Coupled with the rationalisation of housing, the functional definition of comfort comes again to the fore.

Today, driven by continuous technological advances, the comfort of modern humans is assessed according to material standards. According to the National Centre of Textual and Lexical Resources (CNRTL), this results from the availability of equipment for making residences and other buildings comfortable according to present standards and requirements. Modern comfort in this context is none other than 'material comfort' as it is based on the search for enhanced performance through new technologies.[5] Some scholars criticise this dependence on the material, viewing comfort as a combination of both the material (technologies, objects, etc.) and immaterial (emotions, sensations, etc.).[6]

The evolution of the notion of 'comfort', according to the exponential progress of society, propels humans on a perpetual quest for greater comfort. Given its semantic scope, the concept of comfort remains vast. No matter the dimension under consideration, the common thread uniting its various aspects lies in the human effort to make their 'space' comfortable by all available means. In this sense, of all the 'comforts' studied so far, the majority of scholars agree on the immense significance of thermal comfort.

A variety of research has explored the topic of thermal comfort within interior spaces. From this body of scholarship, several definitions have emerged. For some researchers, a 'comfortable'

5 Jean-Pierre Goubert, *Du luxe au confort* (Paris: Edition Belin, 1988).

6 Grégoire Chelkoff, 'Problématique du confort et de l'inconfort dans l'espace construit', DEA Course (Architectural and Urban Ambiances), Grenoble National School of Architecture (ENSA) (2002).

environment is one in which the human organism can maintain a consistent body temperature without perceptibly engaging instinctive thermoregulatory mechanisms against heat or cold.[7] Other perspectives found in the literature define interior thermal comfort as a state of satisfaction with the thermal environment,[8] with emphasis placed on the absence of discomfort. This viewpoint implies that discomfort is the consequence of efforts to resist ambient conditions, and that comfort is determined by the body's reactions to these conditions rather than the physical parameters of the environment.[9]

It is thus understood that the essential parameters defining overall thermal comfort are not contingent on the environment but on the organism. These definitions view thermal comfort exclusively from a physiological angle. As individuals vary in their habits, moods, perceptions and behaviours, these differences modify the thermal sensations experienced by each person. This realisation illuminates the physical and psychological aspects of thermal comfort.

Thus, thermal comfort can readily be defined as a pleasant state of harmony between physiology, psychology and physics between a human being and the environment.[10] Proceeding from this conceptualisation, the thermal comfort of interior spaces can be assessed as a whole by taking into account its three different but complementary aspects: the physical, the physiological and the psychological.

Moreover, its association with quality of life renders thermal comfort essential to our well-being. A person occupying a thermally comfortable space will not need to adopt adaptive solutions or to resort to air conditioning adjustments. Conversely, the more uncomfortable the space, the more the user will use all available means to ensure their comfort, leading to heightened energy consumption and thus directly

---

7 Patrick Depecker et al., *Qualité thermique des ambiances* (Paris: AMFE, 1989). Baruch Givoni, *Climate Consideration in Building and Urban Design* (New York: John Wiley & Sons Inc., 1998).

8 ASHRAE, *Handbook of Fundamentals* (Atlanta, GA: SI Edition, 1997); AFNOR, *Ambiances thermiques modérées, détermination des indices PMV et PPD et spécification des conditions de confort thermique* (Paris: AFNOR, 1995); Ole Fanger, *Thermal Comfort* (Copenhagen: Danish Technical Press, 1970).

9 Jean-Baptiste Hoffmann, *Ambiances climatisées et confort thermique* (Paris: Presses des Ponts et Chaussées, 1994).

10 Keith Slater, *Human Comfort* (Springfield, IL: Charles. C. Thomas Pub Ltd, 1985).

affecting the environment. This demonstrates the impact of thermal comfort on energy consumption and the environment.

Research Context: The Colonial Fabric of Tunis

Tunis, the capital of Tunisia since 1159, is located in the northeast of the country. Of all Tunisian cities, the features of colonisation are most evident in Tunis due to its strategic location. Focusing on the colonial fabric of Tunis necessitates the identification of a specific research area. For the purposes of this study, Lafayette district, with an expanse of over five hundred hectares, has been selected as the designated intervention area.

Methodology

1. Selection of Sample Buildings

The colonial heritage of the Lafayette district, like the whole of the colonial fabric of Tunis, is gradually giving way to contemporaneity, as modern buildings continue to encroach on the colonial architecture. Thus, two representative buildings have been chosen for comparison in the present study: one colonial and one contemporary. Both are corner buildings, coexisting within the colonial fabric of Tunis' Lafayette district. Each of these structures was subject to an in-situ survey to collect the data necessary for the simulation, including their architectural design and construction materials.

The colonial building, built in 1947, consists of three floors and covers an area of 260.44 m^2 per floor. Its architectural design dates back to colonial times, with solid brick walls and vault floors made of hollow bricks and metal I-joists (IPN). Glazed surfaces constitute twenty-five percent of the facade and the windows are simple clear four-millimetre glazing. The contemporary building occupies 182.7 m^2 on the first three floors and 194.18 m^2 on the fourth floor. It features hollow brick double-partition walls and a hollow brick floor, with double-glazed Securit blue windows making up 49.48% of the facade.

2. Determination of the Study Period

Benefiting from a subtropical Mediterranean climate, the city of Tunis is characterised by two starkly contrasting seasons: a hot, dry summer and a cool, rainy winter. The study was carried out during the summer season in Tunis, in August, the hottest month of the year.

The choice of this study period was informed by the fact that summer temperatures in Tunis occasionally exceed 40 °C, with approximately eleven hours of sunshine per day. These factors have a significant impact on the thermal and energy performance of buildings.

3. Numerical Modelling on the Trnsys Model (Version 16)

As this is a comparative study between a colonial building and its contemporary counterpart within the same colonial fabric, the thermal behaviour and energy consumption of these structures is evaluated through simulation, based on version 16 of the Trnsys model.[11] The process of data collection, the most crucial phase and foundation of this research, is divided into two phases.

In accordance with the meticulous demands of thermodynamic simulation, the first phase involved gathering data related to the buildings themselves, including surveys, construction materials, and architectural design. This information was then systematically transcribed into Trnsys for both buildings.

The second phase concerns measurements taken in situ and the division of thermal zones. This short-term measurement campaign makes it possible to obtain the microclimatic data necessary for the evaluation of thermal comfort, including ambient temperature (Ta), relative humidity (RH), mean radiant temperature (Tmrt) and air velocity (Va). The measurement points were chosen to represent a variety of orientations and locations. The thermal zones were delineated on the basis of the positioning of the measurement points. The division of the zones is a critical step as Trnsys reconstitutes the model zone by zone (the geometric modelling of the the building on TRNBuild is done zone by zone).

11 *Trnsys*, http://www.trnsys.com/

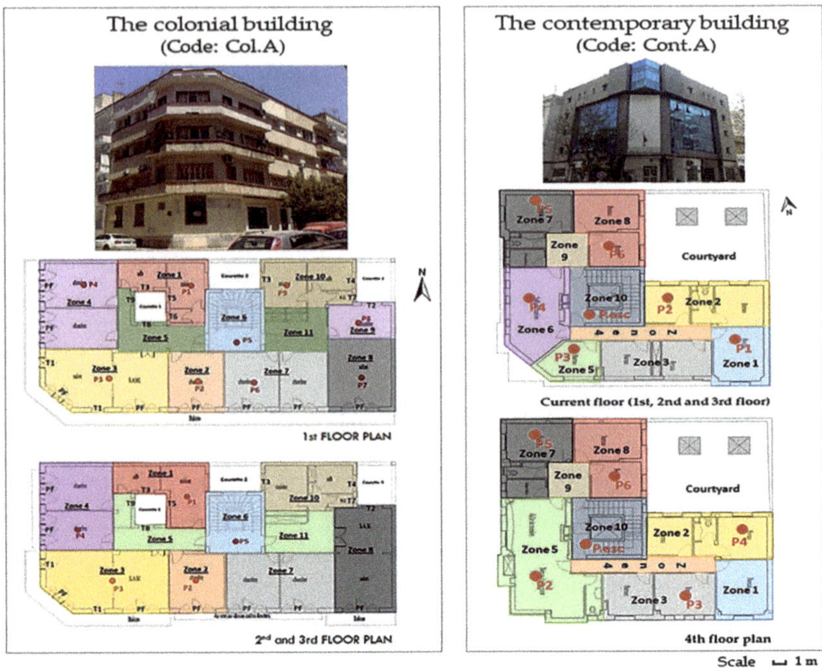

Fig. 8.1 Thermal cutting and positioning of measurement points (Plans scale: 1/500). Author's illustration, CC BY-NC-ND.

Next, optional equipment data and operating specifications, encompassing infiltration and various thermal gains (from people, electronic devices, artificial lighting, etc.), were entered for each zone, adhering to ISO 7730 regulations. This was followed by the simulation of daily variations on the same date of measurements in order to validate the simulation results. Validations made, Trnsys simulates surface microclimate interactions as well as thermal and energy behaviour through transient multizone modelling (type 56) with a time step of one hour.

4. Thermal and Energy Analysis

The analysis focused on the comparison of the two buildings with regard to thermal and energy properties. This began with the thermal assessment of the buildings under investigation, followed by an evaluation of the impact of the buildings' thermal conditions on their energy consumption. This required the adaptation of the analysis protocol through combining research methods and techniques in order to better achieve the predetermined research objectives.

The evaluation and analysis of the thermal environment of an interior space must take into account the physical, physiological and psychological aspects of comfort. To achieve this, appropriate analysis protocols were developed for each aspect of thermal comfort.

In approaching the physical aspect, humans are considered thermal machines that interact with the environment through heat exchange, allowing an objective assessment of comfort. The physical aspect of thermal comfort was evaluated based on the calculation of comfort indices: Predicted Mean Vote (PMV)[12] and Standard Effective Temperature (SET). PMV values were obtained through numerical simulation on Trnsys, while SET values were calculated from the numerical simulation (Ta, Tmrt and HR) entered into the ASHRAE-recommended CBE Thermal Comfort Tool.[13]

Approaches to the psychological and physiological aspects tend to define comfort as the absence of discomfort, using subjective indicators in its assessment. Thus, the study employed questionnaires to analyse occupants' well-being and perceptions of the thermal environment (the psychological aspect), and behavioural thermoregulation (the physiological aspect). During the measurement period, fifteen questionnaires were distributed to the occupants of each building.

Regarding the energy aspect, we simulated and compared the amounts of cooling energy consumed by each building.

Results

Comparison of Thermal Performance

The Physical Aspect of Indoor Thermal Comfort

Using both the PMV index and the SET index, the evaluation of interior thermal comfort began by analysing the variations throughout the day in all zones across the different floors. The daily average for each floor was then calculated, followed by the overall building averages for both structures.

12 ISO-7730, *Ergonomie des ambiances thermiques, Détermination analytique et interprétation du confort thermique par le calcul des indices PMV et PPD et par des critères de confort thermique local*, 3rd ed. (Geneva: ISO, 2005).

13 *CBE Comfort Tool*, https://comfort.cbe.berkeley.edu/

Evaluation of Thermal Comfort through the PMV Index

The PMV value for the entire colonial building is 1.45, while that of the contemporary building is 1.59. These values, which do not represent a large difference, indicate that the two buildings are in a *slightly warm* zone.

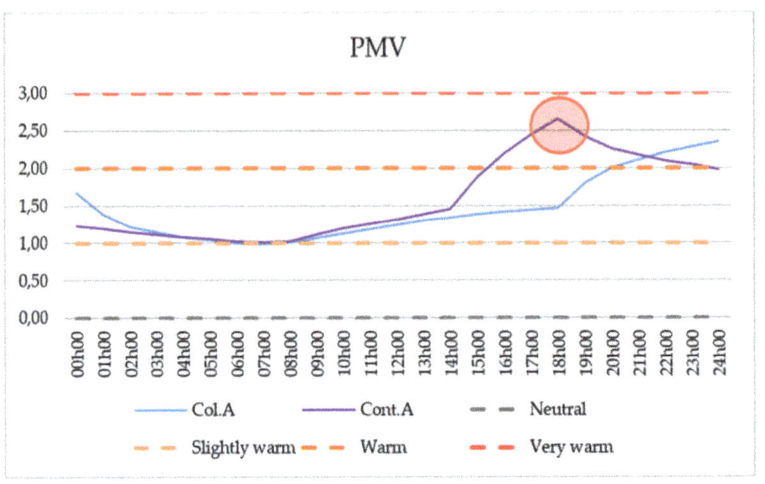

Fig. 8.2 Daily variations in PMV. Author's graph, CC BY-NC-ND.

However, referring to the graph of daily averages above, it is evident that the contemporary building (Cont.A) spends nine hours in the 'warm' zone, compared to the four hours spent in this zone by the colonial building (Col.A). Notably, Cont.A exhibits a peak at 6 p.m. when it reaches its maximum PMV value of 2.66.

Evaluation of thermal comfort through the SET index

With a SET value of 30.56° C for the colonial building and 30.79 °C for the contemporary building, the difference is minimal between the structures, positioning the two buildings in the 'warm, uncomfortable' zone. However, if we compare the results of the daily variations, we see that at 6 p.m., Cont.A reaches its maximum at 34.09 °C, exceeding Col.A by 3 °C.

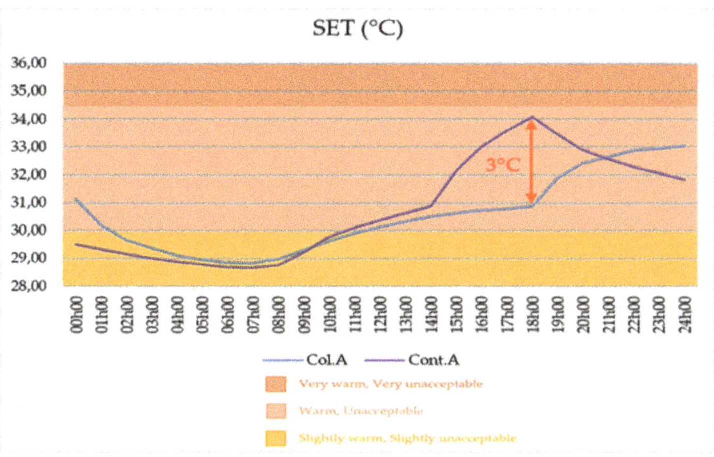

Fig. 8.3 Daily changes in SET. Author's graph, CC BY-NC-ND.

In addition, the analysis of the physical aspect shows that the two buildings are 'slightly warm'. However, when evaluating thermal comfort using the PMV index, the buildings fall into the 'warm, unacceptable' zone according to the SET index. This disparity is due to differences in the valuation levels adopted for the two indices. Whereas PMV represents thermal perception, SET describes the sensation. Consequently, indoor thermal comfort is not evaluated in the same way. In order to consolidate these results and compensate for this difference, the two indices for the two types of buildings have been subjected to comparative analysis.

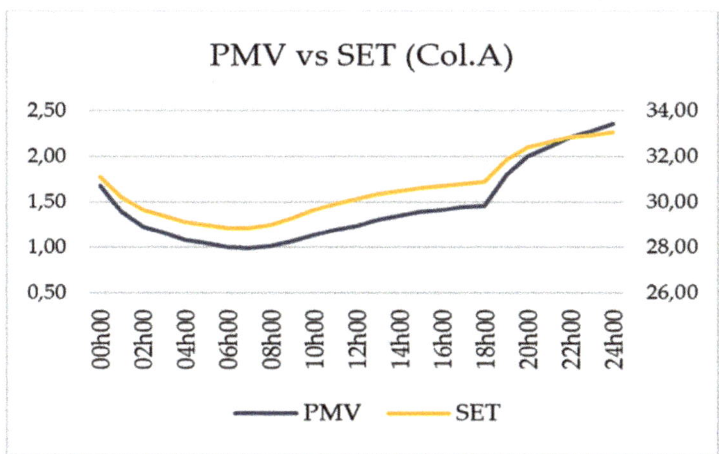

Fig. 8.4 Comparison of the results relating to the PMV and SET indices for the colonial building (Col.A). Author's graph, CC BY-NC-ND.

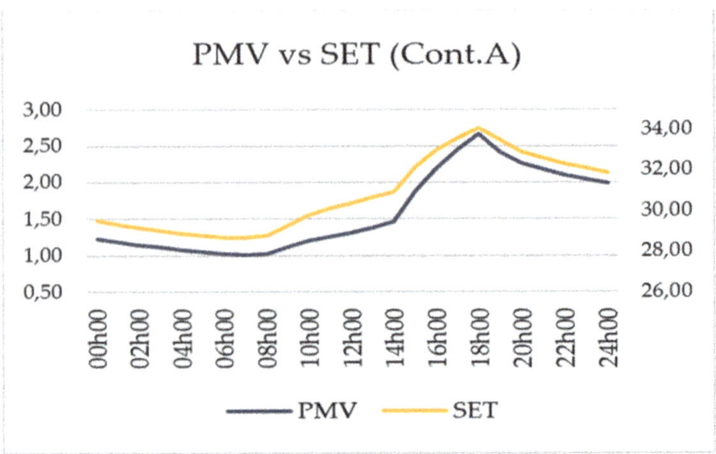

Fig. 8.5 Comparison of the results relating to the PMV and SET indices for the contemporary building (Cont.A). Author's graph, CC BY-NC-ND.

These graphs exhibit similar curves, indicating consistent trends for the two types of buildings.

The Psychological Aspect of Indoor Thermal Comfort

To assess the psychological aspect of interior thermal comfort, we compared the subjective perceptions of the buildings' occupants by means of their response to a structured questionnaire.

Temperature

Ambient temperature was evaluated according to the Feel, Perceive and Preference scale. This analysis revealed that Col.A is considered 'neutral' by 33.33% of its occupants, 'slightly warm' by 40% and 'warm' by 26.67%. On the other hand, no one regarded Cont.A as 'neutral', with 46.15% considering it 'warm' and 38.46% 'very warm'. Furthermore, whereas none of the Cont.A occupants rated the buildings as 'good', with 76.92% explicitly deeming it 'unacceptable', the temperature of Col.A was labelled 'good' by 26.67% of its residents.

Air Movement, Humidity and Sunshine

In Col.A, 86.67% of occupants were satisfied with the ventilation and air flow in their building and did not express the desire for any changes.

Alternately, 76.92% of Cont.A occupants reported insufficient ventilation and unanimously supported increased air flow.

Humidity satisfaction among Col.A residents was recorded as 86.67%, as compared to just 53.85% among inhabitants of Cont.A. Additionally, 30.77% of Cont.A occupants qualified the building as 'humid' and 15.38% as 'very humid'.

With regard to sunshine, 66.67% of Col.A respondents found the sunshine in the building adequate, while 20% described it as 'strongly sunny' and 13.33% as 'weakly sunny'. Meanwhile, only 15.38% of residents in Cont.A reported sunshine satisfaction, with 46.15% deeming it 'very or strongly sunny' and 38.46% finding it 'not at all sunny' to 'weakly sunny'.

Global Thermal Environment

The results show that opinions on the thermal environment of Col.A were divided, with 66.67% of its users qualifying it thermally as 'neutral' and/or 'comfortable', indicating a satisfaction percentage of 60%. On the other hand, 92.31% of Cont.A occupants found it 'uncomfortable' and were dissatisfied with its thermal environment.

The Physiological Aspect of Indoor Thermal Comfort

For this aspect, the comparison is made in relation to users' behavioural adjustments, classified into two categories: adjustments for natural ventilation and adjustments for air conditioning.

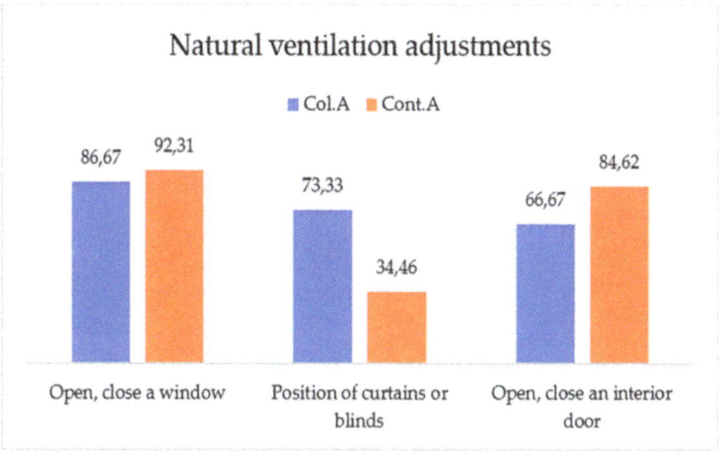

Fig. 8.6 Behavioural adjustments related to natural ventilation. Author's graph, CC BY-NC-ND.

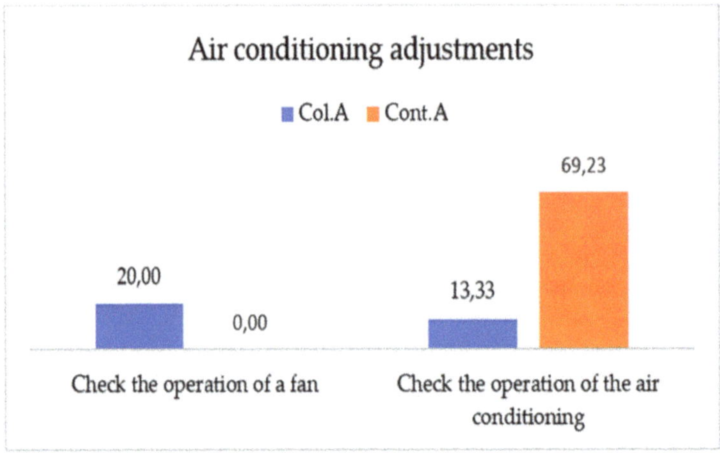

Fig. 8.7 Behavioural adjustments related to air conditioning. Author's graph, CC BY-NC-ND.

Based on the data collected from the questionnaire, it is evident that residents of the colonial building are content with natural ventilation as a means to improve the indoor thermal environment and use minimal air conditioning adjustments, unlike the occupants of the contemporary building.

Comparison of Energy Consumption

As the thermal comfort of indoor spaces influences energy consumption, the study also compared the energy performance of the two buildings to simulate the amount of energy in cooling. The results of the simulation show that the contemporary building consumes 2442.87 kWh while the colonial building consumes only 1867.07 kWh. However, these figures have been adjusted for differences in the structures' area and number of floors.

Table 8.1 Energy consumption of the two buildings studied.

	Energy consumption (kWh)	Area (m^2)	
Colonial building (Col.A)	1867.07	781.32	**2.39 kWh/m²**
Contemporary building (Cont.A)	2442.87	742.28	**3.29 kWh/m²**

Discussion

Referring to the physical aspect of thermal comfort, the results show that both buildings are 'slightly warm' based on the PMV index, and in the 'warm, unacceptable' zone according to the SET index. These results were deduced from the respective means of the two indices. Upon closer examination of the daily variations in PMV values, it is apparent that the colonial building spends only four hours in the 'warm' zone, while the contemporary building remains there for nine hours.

This supports the survey findings indicating that all of the responses favour the colonial building. Residents find this structure 'neutral' and 'slightly warm', well-ventilated (by the high ceilings and windows) and well-protected from direct sunlight (by means of solar protection, balconies and projections). Thus, the thermal environment of the colonial building is qualified as 'neutral' to 'comfortable' by 66.67% of occupants, expressing satisfaction. In contrast, the contemporary building is considered 'hot' or even 'very warm', not sufficiently ventilated, very sunny (due to excessive glazing without recourse to sun protection), according to the opinion of 92.31% of residents, who are dissatisfied with it and describe it as 'uncomfortable'.

The physiological findings also support the results for the other two aspects of thermal comfort. Only 44.45% of the occupants of the colonial building utilise behavioural adjustments, contenting themselves with natural ventilation. By contrast, 69.85% of contemporary building residents are more likely to use cooling systems to mitigate summer overheating.

Objective, subjective and evaluative assessments of the thermal environment of the two buildings show that the colonial building is more thermally comfortable than its contemporary counterpart.

Considering the impact of thermal conditions on energy consumption, the thermal discomfort of the contemporary building explains its higher rate of energy consumption as compared to the colonial structure.

Table 8.2 Summary of thermal and energy analysis results.

<table>
<tr><th colspan="4"></th><th>Colonial building (Col.A)</th><th>Contemporary building (Cont.A)</th></tr>
<tr><td rowspan="12">Indoor thermal comfort</td><td rowspan="3">Physical aspect</td><td rowspan="3">Analytical indices</td><td rowspan="2">PMV</td><td>1.45 (S-W)</td><td>1.59 (S-W)</td></tr>
<tr><td>4h in ‘warm’ zone</td><td>9h in ‘warm’ zone</td></tr>
<tr><td>SET</td><td>Avg: 30.56°C Warm, Unacceptable</td><td>Avg: 30.79°C Warm, Unacceptable</td></tr>
<tr><td rowspan="6">Psychological aspect</td><td rowspan="4">Subjective judgments</td><td>Ta</td><td>Neutral (33.33%)
Slightly warm (40%)</td><td>Warm (46.15%)
Very warm (38.46%)</td></tr>
<tr><td>Air Flow</td><td>Good (86.67%)</td><td>Insufficient (76.92%)</td></tr>
<tr><td>HR</td><td>Adequate (86.67%)</td><td>Adequate (53.85%)</td></tr>
<tr><td>Sunshine</td><td>Adequate (66.67%)</td><td>Strongly sunny (38.46%)
Slightly sunny (23.08%)</td></tr>
<tr><td rowspan="2">Evaluative judgments</td><td>Ambiance</td><td>Adequate (33.34%)
Comfortable (33.33%)</td><td>Uncomfortable (92.31%)</td></tr>
<tr><td>Satisfaction</td><td>Yes (60 %)</td><td>No (92.31 %)</td></tr>
<tr><td rowspan="2">Physiological aspect</td><td rowspan="2">Behavioural adjustments</td><td>Natural ventilation</td><td>75.56%</td><td>70.46%</td></tr>
<tr><td>Air conditioning</td><td>16.67%</td><td>34.62%</td></tr>
<tr><td colspan="4">Energy consumption (kWh/m²)</td><td>2.39</td><td>3.29</td></tr>
</table>

With: S-W = Slightly warm

Conclusion

Aside from their heritage, historical and cultural value, the architectural treasures of the colonial period hold significant environmental value. The results of this study underscore these conclusions in the context of the colonial heritage of Tunis.

In Tunisia, the price of belated awareness of the values of this heritage is compounded by current management strategies that remain largely focused on the needs of the present. Indeed, the national environmental standards in real estate cater to new and contemporary constructions at the exclusion of older buildings. The limited interventions undertaken on colonial buildings raise questions about the rightful place of this heritage in Tunisian society.

This study duly calls attention to the alarming state of colonial buildings as non-renewable and irreplaceable resources. Preserving these buildings not only safeguards heritage and a part of the city's history, but also preserves vanishing expertise, which also constitutes intangible heritage. Safeguarding, protecting, conserving and even adapting colonial buildings to contemporary needs offer environmental, social and economic benefits, aligning with the three pillars of sustainable development. Consequently, the safeguarding of this colonial-built heritage emerges as a lasting solution for shaping the future of the city of Tunis.

Moreover, given the dilapidated state of some buildings, authorities often have little choice but to demolish them. However, for the sake of sustainability, we recommend recycling the materials from demolished buildings for use in new constructions, especially in light of colonial buildings' strong thermal inertia which makes them thermally comfortable.

Regarding existing contemporary constructions, the Tunisian state has set up an energy renovation project for social housing (RELS) to mitigate the discomfort engendered by their thermal shortcomings. In this context, we advocate for an approach to energy renovation which incorporates the specificities of colonial heritage, considering envelope composition, thermal inertia and other elements.

Beyond its environmental utility, this research serves as a call to action, raising awareness of the urgency of saving colonial heritage and harnessing its potential to remedy the shortcomings of contemporary buildings.

Bibliography

AFNOR, *Ambiances thermiques modérées, détermination des indices PMV et PPD et spécification des conditions de confort thermique* (Paris: AFNOR, 1995).

Ammar, Leila, *Histoire de l'architecture en Tunisie : de l'Antiquité à nos jours* (La Manouba: Centre de Publication Universitaire, 2005).

ASHRAE, *Handbook of Fundamentals* (Atlanta, GA: SI Edition, 1997).

CBE Comfort Tool, https://comfort.cbe.berkeley.edu/

Chatagnon, Nadège, 'Développement d'une méthode d'évaluation de la qualité environnementale des bâtiments au stade de la conception' (PhD thesis, Université de Savoie Mont Blanc, Chambéry, 1999).

Chelkoff, Grégoire, 'Problématique du confort et de l'inconfort dans l'espace construit', DEA Course (Architectural and Urban Ambiances), Grenoble National School of Architecture (ENSA) (2002).

Coquery-Vidrovitch, Catherine, *La ville européenne outre mers un modèle conquérant (XVe–XXe siècle)*, ed. by Odile Goerg (Paris: L'Harmattan, 1996).

Depecker, Patrick et al., *Qualité thermique des ambiances* (Paris: AMFE, 1989).

Fanger, Ole, *Thermal Comfort* (Copenhagen: Danish Technical Press, 1970).

Givoni, Baruch, *Climate Consideration in Building and Urban Design* (New York: John Wiley & Sons Inc., 1998).

Goubert, Jean-Pierre, *Du luxe au confort* (Paris: Edition Belin, 1988).

Grangaud, Isabelle and Oualdi, M'hamed, 'Tout est-il colonial dans le Maghreb ? Ce que les travaux des historiens modernistes peuvent apporter', *L'Année du Maghreb*, 10 (2014), 233–54.

Hoffmann, Jean-Baptiste, *Ambiances climatisées et confort thermique* (Paris: Presses des Ponts et Chaussées, 1994).

Hoxha, Endrit, 'Amélioration de la fiabilité des évaluations environnementales des bâtiments' (PhD thesis, Université Paris-Est, 2015).

ISO-7730, *Ergonomie des ambiances thermiques, Détermination analytique et interprétation du confort thermique par le calcul des indices PMV et PPD et par des critères de confort thermique local*, 3rd ed. (Geneva: ISO, 2005).

Madec, Philippe, 'Architecture et qualité environnementale', *Les Annales de la Recherche Urbaine* (2002), 140–42.

Mandallena, Céline, 'Elaboration et application d'une méthode d'évaluation et d'amélioration de la qualité environnementale de bâtiments tertiaires en exploitation' (PhD thesis, Université Bordeaux 1, 2006).

Micolier, Alice, 'Développement d'une méthodologie d'évaluation cohérente et intégrée de l'impact des choix de conception sur la qualité de l'air intérieur et les performances énergétiques et environnementales des bâtiments résidentiels' (PhD thesis, Doctoral School of Physical Sciences and Engineering (Gironde) in partnership with the Institute of Mechanics and Engineering of Bordeaux, Bordeaux, 2019).

Mosbah, Chiraz, 'L'héritage colonial de la ville de Tunis entre 1900 et 1930: étude architecturale et décorative des édifices de style néo-mauresque' (PhD thesis, Université Paris 1 Panthéon-Sorbonne, 2006).

Santelli, Serge, *Tunis, le creuset méditerranéen* (Paris: Éditions du CNRS, 1995).

Sebag, Paul, *Tunis, Histoire d'une ville* (Paris: L'Harmattan, 1998).

Slater, Keith, *Human Comfort* (Springfield, IL: Charles. C. Thomas Pub Ltd, 1985).

Trnsys, http://www.trnsys.com/

Volait, Mercedes, 'Colonial Architecture', in *Abécédaire de la ville au Maghreb et au Moyen-Orient*, ed. by B. Florin, A. Madoeuf, O. Sanmartin, R. Stadnicki and F. Troin (Tours: Presses universitaires François-Rabelais, 2020), pp. 45–46.

9. The Evaluation of Passive Cooling Strategies in the Persian Garden Pavilion as a Model of Sustainable Heritage

Honey Fadaie[1]

Introduction

Persian gardens have a historical legacy dating back millennia. Their physical structure consists of three systems: irrigation, planting and construction,[2] all of which are based on specific geometric principles. This geometric structure is the main feature distinguishing Persian gardens from other gardens worldwide.[3] Persian gardens comprise both natural and built elements, the latter including walls, pavilions and service spaces such as stables and baths. Among these, pavilions stand out as one of the most significant structures, rooted in thousands of years of history. Archaeological findings have shown that Cyrus the Great built the first pavilions in the garden of Pasargadae,[4] whereafter pavilions of various shapes were constructed along the main axes of Persian gardens (see Table 9.2).

1 The author began her studies on Persian gardens in 2008 at the Department of Architecture, Roudehen Branch, Islamic Azad University (RIAU), Roudehen, Iran.

2 Azadeh Sahcheraghi, *Paradigm of Paradise: Recognition and Re-creation of Persian Garden* (Tehran: JahadDaneshgahi, 2010), p. 65.

3 Mostafa Mostafazadeh and Mojtaba Ansari, *Pari De Aza: A Survey of Persian Gardening Traditions* (Tehran: Gostareh Press, 2015), p. 5.

4 David Strinach, *Pasargadae. A Report on the Excavations Conducted by British Institute of Persian Studies from 1961–1963* (Oxford: Clarendon Press, 1978).

 https://doi.org/10.11647/OBP.0412.09

Royal families often used pavilions as temporary residences or ceremonial venues. Pavilions, like other elements in Persian gardens, adhere to sustainable design principles like optimal irrigation, effective planting, solar orientation and high-thermal-capacity materials to ensure residents' comfort. Furthermore, the design of living spaces, whether mansions or pavilions, is based on environmental sustainability parameters and capitalising on fresh garden air.

The present chapter analyses climatic parameters in the design and spatial arrangement of these garden pavilions in hot and arid regions, excluding other influential factors. Due to the diversity of pavilion shapes, the study focuses on a single shape category selected on the basis of prevalent samples in each climatic zone, analysing each pavilion separately. The chapter begins by delineating weather conditions and passive design strategies in hot-arid climates, before analysing and evaluating the passive cooling strategies within these pavilions.

Identification of Hot and Arid Climate (B) and Design Strategies

According to the Köppen classification system, nearly two-thirds of Iran possesses a hot-arid climate. This area experiences virtually no rain for at least six months per year, leading to exceptionally dry and hot conditions. The hot-arid climate is further categorised into two subtypes: desert biome-dry tropical climate (BW) and steppe-dry mid-latitude climate (BS). Within these categories, there are four distinct microclimates: BWhs, BWks, BShs and BSks.[5] Climatic characteristics in arid regions include irregular and unreliable rainfall, the highest percentage of sunshine of any climate, a large diurnal temperature range, the highest daytime temperature of any climate and annual precipitation of less than half the annual potential evapotranspiration.[6] Thus, the climatic design objectives in this area include solar protection, natural ventilation, increased humidity and dusty wind control. Table 9.1 summarises the common design strategies according to climatic objectives in these regions.

---

5 Farzaneh Soflaei, Mehdi Shokouhian and Seyed Majid Mofidi Shemirani, 'Investigation of Iranian Traditional Courtyard as Passive Cooling Strategy (a Field Study on BS climate)', *International Journal of Sustainable Built Environment*, 5 (2016), 99–113, https://doi.org/10.1016/j.ijsbe.2015.12.001

6 Farzaneh Soflaei, Mehdi Shokouhian and Amir Soflae; 'Traditional Courtyard Houses as a Model for Sustainable Design: A Case Study on Bwhs Mesoliamte of Iran', *Frontiers Architectural Research*, 6 (2017), 329–45 (pp. 332–33), http://dx.doi.org/10.1016/j.foar.2017.04.004

Table 9.1 Design Strategies in Hot-arid Climates

Design principles		**Sustainability and climatic objectives**
Form and orientation		– Optimal orientation of rectangular structure along the east-west axis to minimise solar radiation exposure,[7] reducing heat in the summer while maximising solar impact in winter[8] – Wind aware placement to align the building with wind directions[9]
Building elements	**Entrance**	– Deflection of dusty wind and heat from the interior with an entry space that acts as a buffer zone between the main entrance and the building[10]
	Floor	– Stabilisation of day and night temperatures through basement floor design to leverage the earth's thermal properties[11] – Strategic placement of water elements such as ponds to provide evaporative cooling inside the building
	Wall	– Daytime heat reduction by minimising wall area on eastern and western sides[12] – Horizontal and vertical shading according to wall orientation[13]
	Opening	– Openings of various sizes and at different heights on walls and roofs for stack effect ventilation
	Roof	– Double shell dome roof partially shaded during the day, acting as thermos on the physical basis[14] – Wind catchers and other elements on top of buildings for natural ventilation
Colour and materials		– Light-coloured walls and ceilings to reflect solar radiation and minimise absorption[15] – Utilisation of renewable local materials in light of their thermo-physical properties in the arid region[16]

7 Donald Watson and Kenneth Labs, *Climatic Design: Effective Building Principles and Practices*, trans. by Vahid Ghobadian and Mohammad Feizmahdavi (Tehran: Tehran University press, 1997), p. 214.

8 Honey Fadaie, *Iranian Gardens in Arid Regions from Sustainable View* (PhD thesis, Islamic Azad University (RIAU), Roudehen, Iran, 2016), p. 135.

9 Watson and Labs, *Climatic Design*, p. 214.

10 Ibid.

11 Fadaie, *Iranian Gardens*, p. 154.

12 Watson and Labs, *Climatic Design*, p. 214.

13 Holger Koch Nielson, *Stay Cool: A Design for the Built Environment in Hot Climates* (London: James and James, 2002), p. 78, https://doi.org/10.4324/9781315074429

14 Ibid., p. 72.

15 Soflaei, Shokouhian and Soflae, 'Traditional Courtyard Houses as a Model for Sustainable Design', 333.

16 Ibid.

Pavilion Description: Location, Shape and Constituent Spaces and Elements

In most Persian gardens, pavilions served as one of the main spaces for temporary accommodation, celebrations and official ceremonies. The essential components of Pavilion design are their location and orientation in the garden, as well as their architectural form, materials and constituent elements.

Pavilion Location and its Connection to the Environment

In Persian gardens, pavilions are mainly positioned along the central axis, between the centre and furthest end of the garden (Table 9.2). There are several factors that influence pavilion placement, including the garden's size, the slope of the land, the view of the garden and climatic conditions like solar exposure and local wind direction.[17] Pavilions are directly connected to other elements in the garden. For instance, water flows from inside the pavilion out through the garden, irrigating the plants. This connection and spatial continuity between the pavilion and the natural environment are classic features of Persian gardens, blurring the distinction between pavilion and garden space.

Table 9.2 Examples of pavilion placement in various Persian gardens.

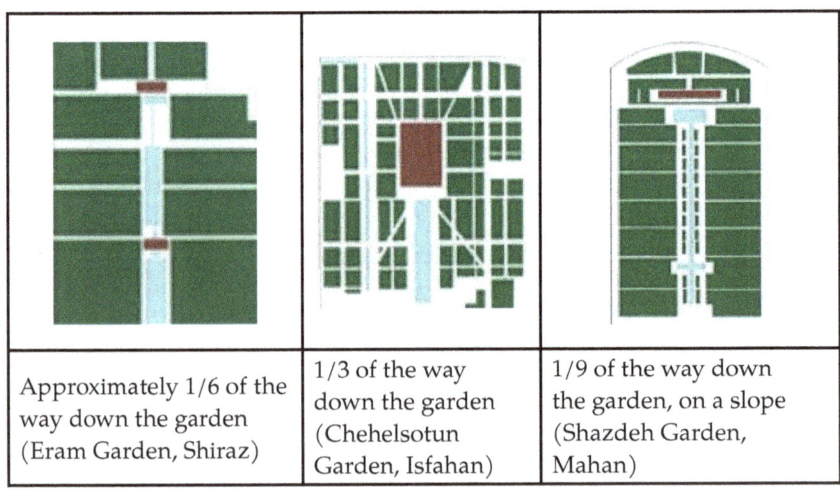

Approximately 1/6 of the way down the garden (Eram Garden, Shiraz)	1/3 of the way down the garden (Chehelsotun Garden, Isfahan)	1/9 of the way down the garden, on a slope (Shazdeh Garden, Mahan)

17 Fadaie, *Iranian Gardens*, p. 135.

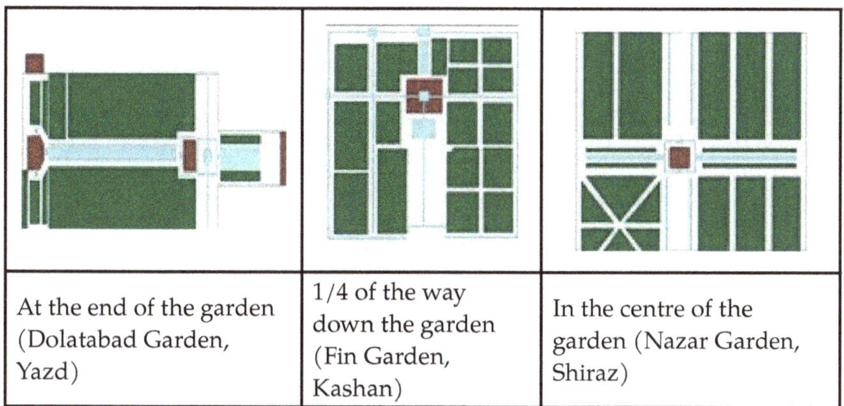

At the end of the garden (Dolatabad Garden, Yazd)	1/4 of the way down the garden (Fin Garden, Kashan)	In the centre of the garden (Nazar Garden, Shiraz)

Pavilion Shapes and Materials

Based on historical documents and existing examples of Persian garden pavilions, their designs can be classified into five types: square, rectangular, octagonal, semi-octagonal and nine-part shapes. The height of these buildings is typically two stories, although in some cases it may reach three stories. While it is difficult to find a specific rule governing pavilion height, we can conclude that most of these buildings have two stories with balconies offering uninterrupted views.[18]

Table 9.3 Types of Persian garden pavilions and their existing examples.

Shape	**Name**	**Plan**	**Other similar examples**
Square	Fin (Kashan)		**Hasht-Behesht (Isfahan)**
Rectangle	Chehelsotoun (Isfahan)		**Shazdeh (Mahan), Eram (Shiraz), Afifabad (Shiraz), Pahlevanpour (Mehriz)**

18 Mohammad Gharipour, *Pavilion Structure in Persianate Gardens Reflection in the Textual and Visual Media* (PhD thesis, School of Architecture, Georgia Institute Technology, Athlanta, USA, 2009), p. 135, http://hdl.handle.net/1853/33831

Octagon	Nazar (Shiraz)	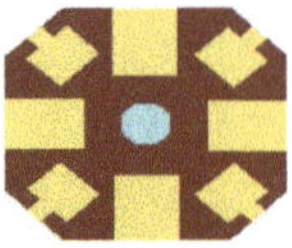	**Ghadamgah (Nishabour), Mosala (Naeen)**
Semi-Octagon	Dolatabad (Yazd)	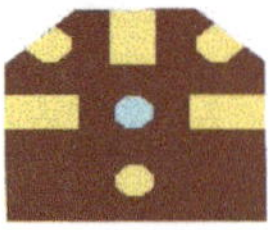	**Jahan Nama (Shiraz)**
Nine-Part (crossed-shape)	Delgosha (Shiraz)	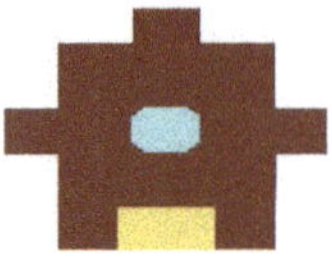	**Pasargadae (Shiraz)– Khan (Yazd)**
■**Closed space**		**Semi-open space**	**Water elements (pond)**

Most pavilions share uniform physical properties on their four primary facades. The main facade is chosen on the bases of factors such as climatic orientation, sight and perspective, location, and other physical characteristics.[19] In some cases, such as Hahst-Behesht in Isfahan, the porches are open to the garden. Among the materials used in pavilion construction are clay, brick, tile and sometimes wood. These local materials have different advantages such as thermal insulation, cost-effectiveness, ease of preparation, renewability and high permeability.

Constituent Elements and Spaces of Pavilions

The following spaces and elements existed in nearly all Persian pavilions, influenced by the climatic conditions of their cities.

Porch (Iwan)

The porch, or Iwan, is an outward-facing arched space that serves as an entrance, connecting the pavilion to the garden. One or three doors usually connect the porch and internal spaces.[20] A more precise definition

19 Heshmatollah Motedayen and Reza Motedayen, 'Pavilion in Persian Gardens; A Review on Nine-part Pavilions', *Manzar: The Iranian Scientific Open Access Journal of Landscape*, 7.33 (2016), 38–45 (p. 41).

20 Gharipour, *Pavilion Structure*, p. 138.

describes the porch as a 'double-height hall, enclosed on three sides by supporting walls, and open on the fourth. This space is generally vaulted'.[21] The porch also balances between the interior and exterior spaces regarding lighting, thermal regulation and air conditioning.

Talar

In the Safavid period (seventeenth century), the addition of the columned porch, known as a Talar, expanded the pavilion outward. The Talar consists of a spacious full-height porch opening on three sides, with a protruding roof supported by wooden columns (see Figure 9.1). The combination of porch and Talar is the dominant design element in a series of Safavid era pavilions in Isfahan, like Chehelsotoun.[22]

Pond

Ponds constitute one of the main water elements in Persian gardens, located within the porches and main halls of the pavilions. They increase evaporative cooling, especially during hot seasons. In many Persian garden pavilions, like the Fin pavilion, water canals connect the pond inside the building to other water features in the garden. Water elements take the form of ponds, fountains and canals inside the building (see Figure 9.2 and Figure 9.4).

Selection of Gardens and their Pavilions

Given the inextricable connection between Persian pavilions and the gardens for which they are constructed, this section explores Iran's historical gardens which have been formally recognised as cultural heritage.

Selection of Gardens According to Climatic Conditions

Iran has had numerous gardens over the millennia, many of which have been demolished. In accordance with the purpose of this research, which

21 Mahvash Alemi, 'The Royal Gardens of Safavid Period: Types and Models', in *Gardens in the Time of Great Muslim Empires, Theory and Design*, ed. by Attilio Petruccioli (Leiden: Brill, 1997), pp. 72–96 (pp. 76–77).

22 Ibid.

is to study the climatic parameters in pavilion design, the remaining gardens are classified first by the cities where they are located and then by the climate of these cities (Table 9.4). This research entailed a statistical analysis of local metrological data from several stations to classify different cities within Iran's hot-arid climate (B) based on the Köppen climate classification system.[23] As Table 9.4 indicates, there are thirteen Iranian cities located in a hot and arid climate, encompassing thirty-five historical gardens, ten of which have outward-facing residential pavilions. Among the microclimatic areas, there are no pavilion garden in BSks. The selected gardens in other microclimates are highlighted in Table 9.5.

Table 9.4 Historical gardens in arid climate cities.

Climate	City	Current gardens (no.)	Gardens with pavilions (no.)	Garden names	Date of construction	Garden shape	Pavilion shape
BWhs	Yazd	2	1	Dolatabad	1750	Two rectangles	Semi-octagon
	Taft	1	-	-	-	-	-
	Tabas	3	-	-	-	-	-
	Kashan	1	1	Fin	1571–1629	Square	Square
	Mehriz	1	-	-	-	-	-
	Naeen 1		-	-	-	-	-
	Birjand	7	-	-	-	-	-
BWks	Isfahan	2	2	Chehelsotoun	1544	Square	Rectangle
				Hasht-Behesht	17th century	Rectangle	Octagon
	Kerman	3	1	Fathabad	-	Rectangle	Rectangle
	Mahan	2	1	Shazdeh	1870	Rectangle	Rectangle
	Damghan	1	-	-		-	-

23 Soflaei, Shokouhian and Soflaei, 'Traditional Courtyard Houses as a Model for Sustainable Design', 332.

BShs	Shiraz	10	5	Eram	13th century	Rectangle	Rectangle
				Afifabad	1863	Rectangle	Rectangle
				Nazar	16th century	Square	Octagon
				Jahan Nama	13th century	Square	Octagon
				Delgosha	Pre Islamic era	Trapezoid	Cross-Shape
BSks	Neishabour	1	-	-	-	-	-

Final Pavilion Selection Based on Geometric Shapes

The next step in the research was to select samples from the ten chosen gardens on the basis of the shapes of both the gardens and their pavilions. Table 9.3 shows that these gardens can be classified into four shapes: rectangular, square, trapezoid and other. The data from Table 9.4 indicates that, with few exceptions, the geometric shapes of Persian gardens have been rectangular or square. Therefore, the initial criterion at this stage was to select gardens from each microclimate with square or rectangular layouts.

The pavilions in Persian gardens commonly assume shapes such as rectangles, squares, octagons and semi-octagons (Table 9.5). Thus, square or rectangular gardens with rectangular, square or octagonal pavilions were selected from among the identified gardens. Delgosha Garden has thus been excluded from the sample due to its cross-shaped pavilion. To facilitate the study's combination of the two primary garden shapes and three main pavilion shapes, the rectangular and square gardens are coded A and B, respectively, and pavilions with rectangular, square, octagonal (and semi-octagonal) shapes are designated by numbers 1, 2 and 3. After analysing the feasibility of different gardens and pavilions from each microclimate, pavilions were selected as case studies (Table 9.5).

According to the data in Table 9.4, two gardens in the BShs area have the A-1 code, located in the cities of Kerman and Mahan. Since these locations are in close proximity and share the same microclimate, only Shazdeh Garden has been selected for this study on the basis of its attributes and renown among Persian gardens. Between the Eram and Afifabad Gardens in Shiraz, Eram Garden was deemed more appropriate for study because of its originality and historical significance. In the microclimate between the two gardens identified by the B-2 code, Jahan Nama Garden was preferred as a case study, given the substantial loss of large parts of Nazar Garden over time. The seven pavilions selected as case studies are presented in Table 9.5.

Table 9.5 Gardens identified by climatic criteria and shape.

Code	Garden and Pavilion Shape	Gardens' Climates		
		BWhs	**BWks**	**BShs**
A-1		–	Shazdeh	Afifabad Eram
A-2		Dolatabad		–
A-3		–	–	–
B-1		–	Chehelsotoun	–
B-2		–	Hasht-Behesht	Jahan Nama Nazar
B-3		Fin	–	–

Sustainable Design Strategies in the Seven Selected Pavilions

Chehelsotoun Garden in Isfahan

In Chehelsotoun Garden, the pavilion is located at the western end of the main axis and has been developed gradually over several periods.

The location of the pavilion, coupled with the location of the main hall on its eastern side, capitalises on the cool air of the garden. The strategic orientation of the pavilion (northwest to southeast) protects the building from intense sunlight and heat. The pavilion's semi-open spaces such as halls and porches on the east, north and south sides, along with the ponds inside the hall and the water channels around the pavilion, are additional design strategies that provide shade and promote evaporative cooling.

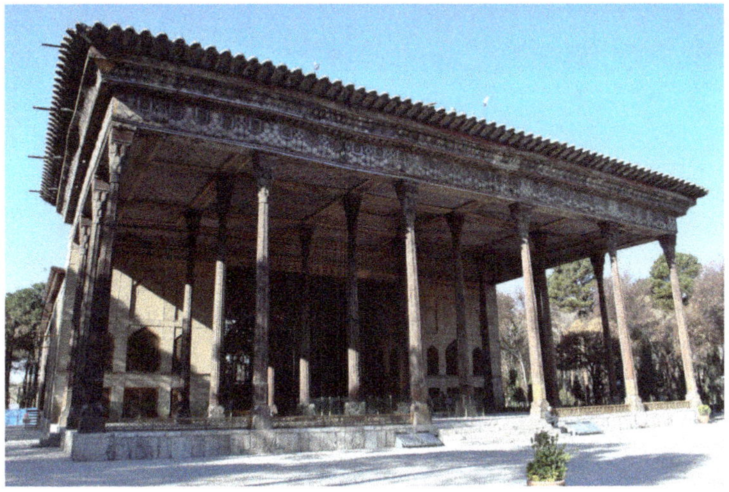

Fig. 9.1 Chehelsotoun pavilion. Photograph by Zenith210 (2010), Wikimedia, https://commons.wikimedia.org/wiki/File:Chehelsotun2.JPG, CC BY-SA 3.0.

Hasht-Behesht Garden in Isfahan

The pavilion in Hasht-Behesht Garden is located along the main axis in the southern part of the garden to maximise the benefit of the garden's cool air. Another climatic design strategy is the four porch spaces on each of the main sides,. which allows for cross ventilation inside the building. The north porch, located in front of the wider garden area, is larger and higher, drawing in air that cools as it passes over the porch's pond. The smaller south porch suctions the air through the pavilion, acting as a ventilation outlet. Furthermore, water from the pond on the upper floor cascades down the southern porch's wall, flowing into the pool in the centre of the pavilion.[24]

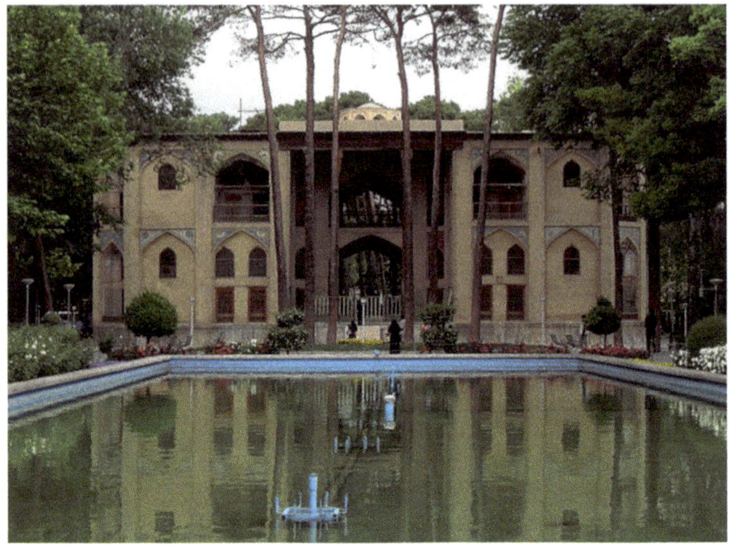

Fig. 9.2 Hasht-Behesht Garden and its pavilion. The natural ventilation is carried out through the porches. Photograph by David Stanley (2013), Wikimedia, https://commons.wikimedia.org/wiki/File:Hasht-Behesh_ (9214641903).jpg, CC BY 2.0.

The semi-open spaces, ponds, water cascades and surrounding water channels all contribute to evaporative cooling.

Shazdeh Garden in Mahan

In Shazdeh Garden, the pavilion is situated on a slope along the northern end of the main axis, approximately one-ninth of the way down the garden. This location provides cool air from the large portion of the garden, with pools and twelve cascades in front of the pavilion (Figure 9.3). The pavilion's elongated structure and east-west orientation, with several openings on these sides, are among the strategies that shield the building from intense sunlight, heat and dusty winds. Moreover,

24 Samira Tafazol and Armin Bahramian, 'Recognition the Garden and Pavilion Hashtbehesht as a Sustainable Environmental Architecture', in *Proceeding of 2nd National Conference on Climate, Building, and Energy Consumption Optimization* (Isfahan: n.p., 2013), pp. 6–7.

semi-open spaces like the main porch and canopies provide shade, which can moderate the hot summer air.

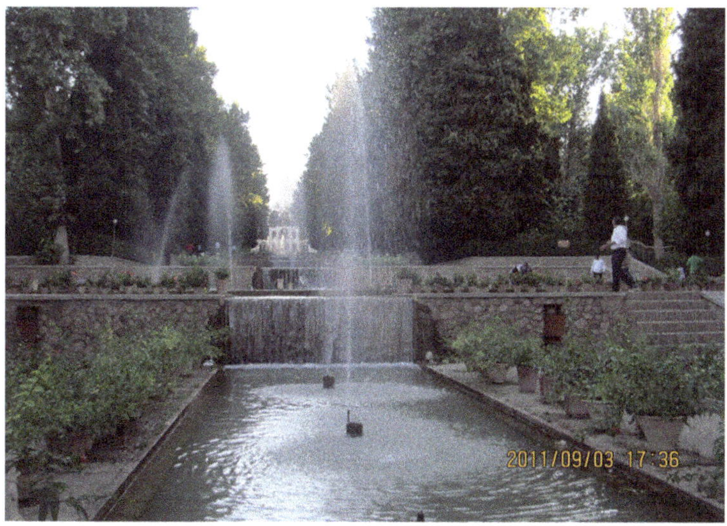

Fig. 9.3 The Pavilion of Shazdeh garden on the slope. Author's photograph, 2011, CC BY-NC-ND.

Fin Garden in Kashan

Fin Garden's main pavilion opens to the garden with four porches on each side. The pools on the north and south sides of the building and the central pond are connected to water supply canals throughout the garden. When the wind passes over these water features, it generates evaporative cooling inside the pavilion. In addition to the ponds and water canals in and around the pavilion, semi-open spaces like porches and vaulted canopies offer shade and mitigate the summer heat (Figure 9.4).

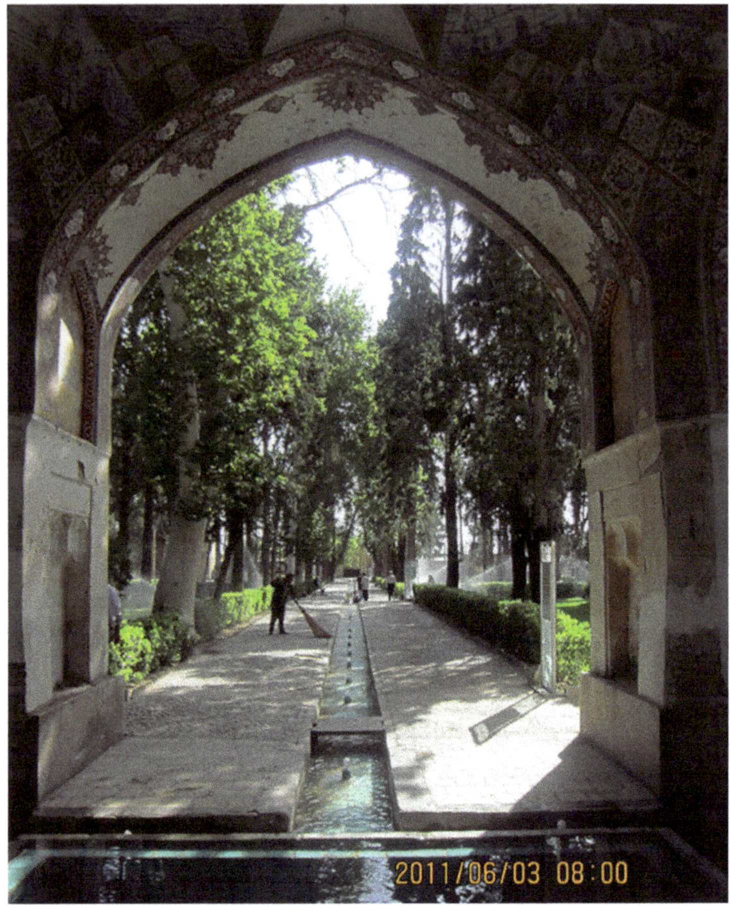

Fig. 9.4 Inside of Fin pavilions: water pond and canals. Author's photograph, 2011, CC BY-NC-ND.

Dolatabad Garden in Yazd

In Dolatabad Garden, the pavilion is a summer mansion at the garden's southern end, with windows facing the northwest and northeast, opening to the garden with small porches and balconies. Compared to the other cases considered in this study, the Dolatabad pavilion has relatively small openings due to the region's tempestuous winds, and lacks the semi-open spaces observed in other pavilions. The large pool on the main northwest axis of the garden and the three surrounding ponds, connected to water supply channels throughout the garden, increase evaporative cooling due to the airflow over the water. Furthermore, the pond inside the pavilion, situated beneath the world's tallest wind catcher, provides natural ventilation in the interior of the building.

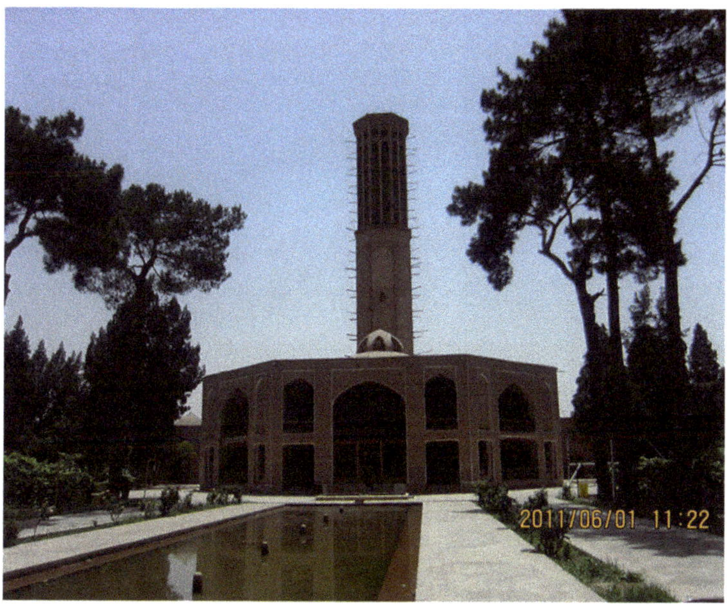

Fig. 9.5 Dolatabad pavilion: natural ventilation is carried out through the wind catcher. Yazd, Iran. Author's photograph, 2011, CC BY-NC-ND.

Eram Garden in Shiraz

Eram Garden's rectangular pavilion is located at the northern end, with a northwest to southeast longitudinal axis that effectively reduces the absorption of solar radiation. Like the Shazdeh Garden pavilion, wide porches are not present on all sides and the number of openings on its eastern and western sides is very few. Natural ventilation is facilitated by the building's narrow width and the windows opening onto porches to the north and south. Moreover, the main pool and the water channel in the southern and northern areas, the underground water supply channel and the interior pond increase evaporative cooling (see Figure 9.6). These elements create comfortable living conditions for residents during the hot seasons.

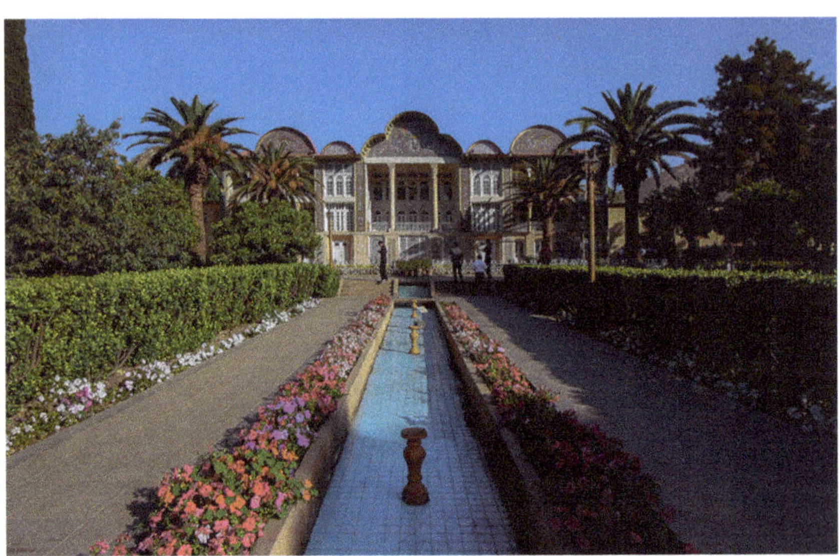

Fig. 9.6 Eram Garden and its pavilion. Shiraz, Iran. Photograph by Mostafameraji (2014), Wikimedia, https://commons.wikimedia.org/wiki/File:Eram_Garden_Shiraz_%D8%A8%D8%A7%D8%BA_%D8%A7%D8%B1%D9%85_%D8%B4%DB%8C%D8%B1%D8%A7%D8%B2_30.jpg, CC BY-SA 4.0.

Jahan Nama Garden in Shiraz

The octagonal pavilion in Jahan Nama Garden stands at a height of 120 centimetres (Figure 9.7). Semi-open spaces, including four entrance porches facing the garden's main axes and four side porches allow airflow into the pavilion. Breezes pass over the pavilion's central pond, contributing to the evaporative cooling of the space. The porches provide shade, serving as canopies across the openings on all sides.

In addition to the aforementioned features, the pavilions incorporate double-shell dome roofs for insulation, preventing excessive solar heat penetration. The use of local materials, such as bricks in most pavilions, tiles in the Fin pavilion, and adobe in the Dolatabad pavilion, reduces fluctuations in interior temperatures due to their high thermal capacity.

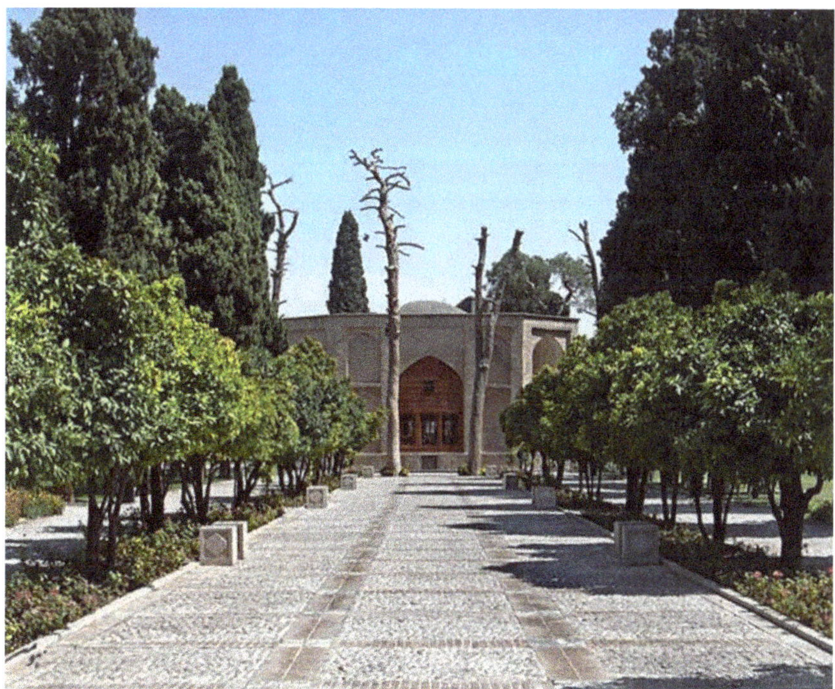

Fig. 9.7 Jahan Nama Garden, Shiraz, Iran. Author's photograph, 2011, CC BY-NC-ND.

Assessment of Climatic Strategies in Selected Pavilions

By analysing the climatic objectives of design strategies in arid regions (Table 9.1) and identifying the sustainable design strategies in selected pavilions, this study evaluates passive cooling strategies as crucial parameters of pavilion design. Tables 9.6 and 9.7 briefly outline the passive cooling strategies in pavilions and indicate their alignment with climatic objectives.

Table 9.6 Passive cooling strategies in Persian garden pavilions (Chehelsotun, Hahsht-Behesht, Shazdeh and Fin).

Climate objectives	Garden pavilions			
	Chehelsotoun	**Hashtbehesht**	**Shazdeh**	**Fin**
Solar preservation and decreasing heat	Positioning at the western end of the garden to capitalise on cool air	Positioning at the southern end of the garden to capitalise on cool air	Positioning at the northern one-sixth of the garden to capitalise on cool air	Positioning at the southern end of the garden to garden to capitalise on cool air from the north
	The east-west direction of building uses north and south daylight	Four porches on each facade provide shade	East-west direction	Arched porches on the four facades, as semi-open spaces, provide shade
	Northwest-southeast orientation for optimal use of the winter sun	Few openings on east and west facades	Large porch on the south facade, no porches on east and west facades	
	North and south porches and east Talar provide shade	No porch on the west facade, large porch on the north facade	Basement floor utilises earth's geothermal heat	Curved roof to modify heat absorption
	Minimal surface area on east and west sides		White stucco plaster covering	
	No porch on the west facade	Using a curved roof to modify heating absorption	Using a curved roof to modify heating absorption	Utilisation of local renewable materials (brick, tile, etc.)
	Utilisation of local renewable materials (brick, tile, etc.)	Utilisation of local renewable materials (brick, tile, etc.)	Utilisation of local renewable materials (brick, tile, etc.)	

<table>
<tr><td rowspan="5">Natural ventilation and increasing humidity</td><td>Surrounding walls preserve garden humidity</td><td>Surrounding walls preserve garden humidity</td><td>Surrounding walls preserve garden humidity</td><td>Surrounding walls preserve garden humidity</td></tr>
<tr><td>Water ponds inside the hall and Talar for evaporative cooling</td><td>Water ponds and fountains inside the hall and main porch for evaporative cooling</td><td>Openings on opposite sides provide interior cross ventilation</td><td>Four porches on opposite sides near pond provide interior cross ventilation</td></tr>
<tr><td>Surrounding water canals increase evaporative cooling</td><td>Water cascades from upstairs pond on the south porch</td><td rowspan="2">Positioning at the top of the slope near water pool in wind direction</td><td rowspan="2">Connection between pavilion and water ponds and canals increases evaporative cooling</td></tr>
<tr><td>Providing cross ventilation inside the pavilion by creating the porches on opposite sides</td><td>Placing water elements around the pavilion</td></tr>
<tr><td>Pool placement in front of main pavilion facade</td><td>Porches on opposite sides provide interior cross ventilation</td><td>Pools placement in front of pavilion facade</td><td>Placing the pond inside the pavilion</td></tr>
<tr><td rowspan="2">Dusty winds control</td><td>Surrounding water canals to mitigate dust</td><td>Surrounding ponds and water canals to mitigate dust</td><td>Minimal surface area on eastern and western sides</td><td>Connection between pavilion and water elements</td></tr>
<tr><td>Minimal surface area on eastern and western sides</td><td>Few openings on eastern and western sides</td><td>No openings on eastern and western sides</td><td>Porches on four sides to mitigate dust</td></tr>
</table>

Table 9.7 Passive cooling strategies in Persian garden pavilions (Dolatabad, Eram and Jahan Nama).

Climate objectives	Garden pavilions		
	Dolatabad	**Eram**	**Jahan Nama**
Solar preservation and decreasing heat	Positioning at the southern end of the garden to capitalise on cool air from the north	Positioning in the north-western sixth of the garden to capitalise on cool air	Central positioning in the garden to capitalise on cool air
	Openings on the northern facade, directed to the main garden space, allow the cool breeze of the garden to enter the pavilion	Northern and southern porches provide shade and protection from solar radiation	Eight porches on all facades provide shade
	Basement floor utilises earth's geothermal heat	East-west direction of building uses north and south daylight	Adobe walls around the garden provide shade
	Using small openings, balconies and vaulted canopies to control sunlight	Northwest-southeast orientation for optimal use of winter sun	
	Coloured windows that control sunlight	Basement floor utilises earth's geothermal heat	Coloured windows control sunlight
	Curved roof to modify heat absorption	Curved roof to modify heat absorption	Curved roof to modify heat absorption
	Adobe walls around the garden provide shade	A few openings on the east and west facades	Basement floor utilises earth's geothermal heat
	Utilisation of local renewable materials (brick, tile, etc.)	Utilisation of local renewable materials (brick, tile, etc.)	Utilisation of local renewable materials (brick, tile, etc.)

Natural ventilation and increasing humidity	Surrounding walls preserve garden humidity	Surrounding walls preserve garden humidity	Surrounding walls preserve garden humidity
	Wind catcher provides natural ventilation	Subterranean elements provide ventilation with interior water pond	Surrounding water elements (e.g., pond)
	Interior pond in the main hall and three ponds beneath wind catcher	Water canals on the main axis	Interior water pond
	Connection between interior and exterior pond		Cooling airflow over four cascades on four sides
		Porches on opposite sides provide interior cross ventilation	
Dusty winds control	Mitigating dust in wind direction	Minimal surface area and openings on eastern and western sides	Porches oriented in wind direction
	Water pond in front of main facade to mitigate dust	Water pond in front of main facade to mitigate dust	Surrounding water canals, ponds, and cascades

The evaluation criteria for the pavilion's climatic strategies the climatic objectives, which include solar preservation and heat reduction (S), natural ventilation and increasing humidity (N), and dusty winds control (C), are detailed in Table 9.8. Based on data from Tables 9.6 and 9.7, the criteria for assessing pavilions' climatic approach are presented in Table 9.8 and coded for ease of evaluation.

Table 9.8 Criteria evaluated in Persian garden pavilions.

Climatic objectives	Assessment code	Assessment criteria for climatic approaches in pavilion design
Solar preservation and decreasing heat (S)	SP1	Effective use of walls to control shading and sunlight exposure
	SP2	Positioning the main facade towards the garden to harness cool air
	SP3	Optimal orientation of pavilion
	SP4	Minimal surface area and openings on eastern and western sides
	SP5	Porches and canopies to manage sun exposure and provide shade
	SP6	Utilisation of geothermal heat with underground elements
	SP7	Two-shell dome roof design to reduce heat absorption
	SP8	Utilisation of local renewable materials
Natural ventilation and increasing h umidity (N)	NP1	Walled enclosure of the garden to retain internal moisture
	NP2	Opposite-facing windows to create cross ventilation
	NP3	Alignment of windows and porches with wind direction
	NP4	Proximity to water elements (pool, pond, etc.)
	NP5	Physical connection between pavilion and water elements
	NP6	Specific spaces and elements (porches, wind catchers, ponds, etc.) to promote passive cooling
Dusty winds control (C)	CP1	Minimal openings in wind direction
	CP2	Pre-spaces (porches) in front of the openings to manage dust infiltration
	CP3	Surrounding water elements (e.g., ponds, canals)

Table 9.9 illustrates the adherence of pavilion architecture in Persian gardens to the principles of passive cooling design in arid zones. Black and white squares are used to indicate compliance with the aforementioned assessment criteria distinguished by assessment

codes, according to climatic objectives. White squares indicate non-compliance with the criteria, while black squares indicate compliance. The percentage of each pavilion's adherence to climatic parameters can be gauged by tallying the white and black squares.

Table 9.9 Assessment of the compliance of selected pavilions with climatic objectives.

Climatic objectives	**Assessment code**	**Pavilion gardens**						
		Chehelsotoun	**Hashtbehesht**	**Shazdeh**	**Fin**	**Dolatabad**	**Eram**	**Jahannama**
Solar preservation and decreasing heat (S)	SP1	■	■	■	■	■	■	■
	SP2	■	□	■	■	■	■	■
	SP3	■	■	■	■	■	■	□
	SP4	■	□	■	■	□	■	■
	SP5	■	■	■	■	■	■	■
	SP6	□	□	■	■	■	■	■
	SP7	□	■	■	■	■	□	■
	SP8	□	■	■	■	■	■	■
Natural ventilation and increasing humidity (N)	NP1	■	■	■	□	■	■	■
	NP2	■	■	□	□	□	■	■
	NP3	■	■	■	■	□	□	■
	NP4	■	■	■	■	■	■	■
	NP5	■	□	□	□	■	□	■
	NP6	■	■	■	■	■	■	■
Dusty winds control (C)	CP1	■	□	■	■	■	■	■
	CP2	■	■	■	■	■	■	■
	CP3	■	■	□	□	□	□	■

Conclusion

This chapter has endeavoured to develop passive cooling criteria specific to the design of Persian garden pavilions, with a focus on arid climates. The research assessed selected pavilions according to climatic objectives and design parameters. Climatic factors within the elements of Persian garden pavilions in hot and arid regions were analysed, and passive design strategies were evaluated against established frameworks. The data from Table 9.9 revealed that all pavilions achieved a compliance rate of over seventy percent in meeting passive cooling standards. Specifically, the compliance percentages for Chehelsotoun, Hasht-Behesht, Shazdeh, Fin, Dolatabad, Eram, and Jahan Nama pavilions were 82.3%, 70.5%, 76.5%, 70.5%, 76.5%, 70.5%, and 94.1%, respectively.

Persian gardens, designed according to the environmental specificities of different regions in Iran, have various shapes and characteristics. Traditional Iranian buildings in arid regions have historically relied on indigenous construction systems to ensure internal comfort. However, pavilions, as outward-facing residential structures, leverage fresh garden air during hot seasons. Therefore, their design is inextricably linked to the geometrical shape of the garden.

The findings of this study underscore how environmental sustainability and climatic factors have influenced the design of pavilions in Persian gardens in arid regions. With diverse passive cooling strategies, the data indicates that the elements of Persian garden pavilions align with climatic objectives in arid regions such as solar protection, natural ventilation and dusty winds control. These aspects of sustainable heritage have acted as closed ecosystems for centuries, particularly in the arid regions of Iran.

The concepts and features discussed here represent various types of extroverted living spaces in hot and dry climates that embody the heritage of traditional Iranian architecture. These strategies can be generalised in the design of other structures located within green spaces in similar climates.

Bibliography

Alemi, Mahvash, 'The Royal Gardens of Safavid Period: Types and Models', in *Gardens in the Time of Great Muslim Empires, Theory and Design*, ed. by Attilio Petroccioli (Leiden: Brill, 1997), pp. 72–96.

Fadaie, Honey, *Iranian Gardens in Arid Regions from Sustainable View* (PhD thesis, Islamic Azad University (RIAU), Roudehen, Iran, 2016).

Gharipour, Mohammad, *Pavilion Structure in Persianate Gardens Reflection in the Textual and Visual Media* (PhD thesis, School of Architecture, Georgia Institute Technology, Athlanta, USA, 2009), http://hdl.handle.net/1853/33831

Mostafazadeh, Mostafa and Ansari, Mojtaba, *Pari De Aza: A Survey of Persian Gardening Traditions* (Tehran: Gostareh Press, 2015).

Motedayen, Heshmatollah and Motedayen, Reza, 'Pavilion in Persian Gardens; A Review on Nine-part Pavilions', *Manzar: The Iranian Scientific Open Access Journal of Landscape*, 7.33 (2016), 38–45.

Nielson, Holger Koch, *Stay Cool: A Design for the Built Environment in Hot Climates* (London: James and James, 2002), https://doi.org/10.4324/9781315074429

Shahcheraghi, Azadeh, *Paradigm of Paradise: Recognition and Re-creation of Persian Garden* (Tehran: Jahad Daneshgahi Publication).

Soflaei, Farzaneh, Shokouhian, Mehdi and Mofidi Shemirani, Seyed Majid, 'Investigation of Iranian Traditional Courtyard as Passive Cooling Strategy (a Field Study on BS Climate)', *International Journal of Sustainable Built Environment*, 5.1 (2016), 99–113, http://dx.doi.org/10.1016/j.ijsbe.2015.12.001

Soflae, Farzaneh, Shokouhian, Mehdi and Soflae, Amir, 'Traditional Courtyard Houses as a Model for Sustainable Design: A Case Study on Bwhs Mesoliamte of Iran', *Frontiers Architectural Research*, 6.3 (2017), 329–45, http://dx.doi.org/10.1016/j.foar.2017.04.004

Stronach, David, *Pasargadae. A Report on the Excavations Conducted by British Institute of Persian Studies from 1961–1963* (Oxford: Clarendon Press, 1978), https://doi.org/10.1017/S0003598X00042113

Tafazol, Samira and Bahramian, Armin, 'Recognition the Garden and Pavilion Hashtbehesht as a Sustainable Environmental Architecture', in *Proceeding of 2nd National Conference on Climate, Building, and Energy Consumption Optimization* (Isfahan: n.p., 2013), pp. 6–7.

Watson, Doland and Labs, Kenneth, *Climatic Design (Effective Building Principles and Practices)*, trans. by Ghobadian Vahid and Feizmahdavi, Mohammad (Tehran: Tehran University press, 1997).

IV. URBAN HERITAGE: RENEWAL OF LANDSCAPES AND ATMOSPHERES

10. Heritage as a Vector of Sustainable Urban Regeneration: The Case of North Shahjahanabad

Mrinalini Singh

Introduction

The city of Old Delhi, established in the seventeenth century by Mughal Emperor Shah Jahan, possessed a unique quality and culture. Originally designed as a residential city with winding roads, streets, waterways, nurseries and structures, today it stands as a bustling market centre and modern town, worn down by development.

However, amidst the crowded streets and masked buildings, there are still hints and glimpses of the town that existed in the seventeenth century. Centuries-old havelis,[1] with their intricate carvings and rich cultural heritage, endure amidst the commotion. These havelis were once the cultural centres around which cities evolved to meet the needs of affluent households. Bazaars, warehouses, gardens and religious and educational institutions surrounded these structures.[2]

Cities serve as arenas for cultural, social, physical and economic co-existence and conflict. Many traditional Indian cities, conceived according to the relative autonomy of the existing societal structure,

1 A haveli is a traditional townhouse or mansion, usually with historical and architectural significance.

2 DevikaSanah Rao, *Interactive Museum: Shahjahanabad Ki Haveli* (2017), https://www.behance.net/gallery/56221609/Interactive-Museum-Shahjahanabad-Ki-Haveli

 https://doi.org/10.11647/OBP.0412.10

were transformed into complex, fragmentary urban landscapes due to their failure to contend with relentless population pressures and new urbanisation trends. One of these cities is Shahjahanabad, commonly known as Old Delhi, which stands out as a prime example of this phenomenon. The walled city of Shahjahanabad was initially developed according to the formal geometries of axial planning and later devolved into a chaotic web of considerable complexity—first due to deliberate neglect under British colonialism and later as a result of the growing challenges of human migration.

Although the walled city is renowned for its historical significance due to its numerous architectural monuments, the indigenous settlement, known as Old Delhi, reflects the lasting socio-cultural patterns that isolate the city's traditional core from the rest of Delhi. The walled city of Shahjahanabad is characterised by the introverted nature of its public activities, bolstered by specialised markets (bazaars) and indigenous neighbourhoods (mohallas)[3] structured around religious sanctuaries. While this traditional core is known for its local economy, it grapples with the serious threats posed by internal traffic congestion and excessive commercialisation. Although various attempts have been made to decongest and revitalise the traditional core, these efforts have proven insufficient to address the root causes of these problems, which extend beyond the city peripheries to Delhi's broader urban and economic growth.[4]

Between Chandni Chawk and Kashmere Gate, the city's northern area has witnessed the bulk of the transformation. This part of the city remains one of the most vibrant and authentic areas of Delhi, surviving countless urban transformations, demolitions and reconstructions.

When the British first arrived in Delhi, they established this area as a hub of administrative power, constructing several new religious and institutional buildings and repurposing existing structures. This part of the walled city is a living example of diverse construction materials and architectural styles, encompassing Sultanate, Mughal and colonial influences as well as the fusion of these styles in unique combinations.

3 Mohallas are a sub-division spatially forming a pattern of quarters, divided and embedded with complex social inter-relations and primarily residential.

4 Ajit Singh, *Confrontation, Comparison and Reconstruction of the Walled City of Shahjahanabad* (Cambridge, MA: Massachusetts Institute of Technology, 2006).

Since the nineteenth century, North Shahjahanabad has been nationally recognised as a commercial hub for the automobile industry, leading to increased trade and job opportunities. Zone-1, sub-zone C-1 (North Shahjahanabad) stretches from Kashmere Gate to north of the Red Fort and east of Mori Gate to the Old Delhi Railway Station. The area is well connected and has nearly all essential amenities and facilities like schools and markets, fulfilling the daily needs of its residents.

Urban Regeneration

Cities emerge from the layering and intertwining of cultural and natural values over time, including the broader urban context and geographical setting.[5] India is home to one of the world's oldest civilisations and most Indian cities are enriched by multiple layers of history. Though India is progressing and evolving along with the rest of the world, the country's deep historical roots must not be forgotten. Thus, it is imperative to develop a framework that serves as a bridge between India's past and future.

Urban regeneration refers to a means of constructively addressing the problems faced by growing urban environments. Beyond infrastructural provisions like housing, sanitation, transport and basic amenities for populations, this constructive engagement also includes generating livelihoods and meeting the needs of society's most vulnerable.[6] Within this context, culture and heritage are often mistakenly perceived as expendable resources by administrators looking for ways to tighten budgets. However, these resources are far from expendable. Cultural and heritage initiatives often assume key roles in boosting local economies, renewing decaying urban areas and nurturing active citizens whose pride and self-esteem are assets to any community. Committing to these activities as an economic and social strategy constitutes a valuable investment for a nation-state. The rejuvenation of human settlements

---

5 Getty Conservation Institute, *Historic Urban Environment Conservation Challenges and Priorities for Action* (Los Angeles, CA Getty Conservation Institute, 2010), https://www.getty.edu/conservation/publications_resources/pdf_publications/historic_urban_environment.html

6 Rajeev Sethi, 'Art for the Sake of Urbanscape' (27 June 2014), *The Hindu*, https://www.thehindu.com/opinion/op-ed/Art-for-the-sake-of-urbanscape/article11640724.ece

stands at the core of India's future, integral to a long-term strategy where business, technology and heritage intersect.[7]

Over the years, the government has introduced various urban development and modernisation schemes, including the Jawaharlal Nehru National Urban Renewal Mission (JNNURM) between 2005 and 2012, the 2015 Smart City Mission and 2015 Pradhan Mantri Awas Yojana (PMAY) housing for all initiative. Although these schemes have shown progress, they have proven unable to swiftly transform the liveability standards of Indian cities. Important reforms visualised under JNNURM, like the enactment of a community participation law, water supply transfer, city planning functions and rent control reforms, have been implemented only sporadically by the country's states.[8]

Conservation can serve as a tool for integrating the past into modern functions. The urban regeneration approach aims to strike a balance between conservation and development, drawing upon heritage-led urban regeneration.[9] In recent years, as the regeneration and renewal of towns and city centres has gained momentum, the careful integration of historic buildings and areas has played an increasingly important role in major regeneration schemes, successfully generating noticeable benefits for local economies and communities. A heightened understanding of how places change and how historic buildings can enhance urban character and distinctiveness is now acknowledged as fundamental to successful and sustainable regeneration. Leveraging and reinvigorating the historic environment has become a cornerstone of the economic and social revival[10] of towns and cities. This chapter explores the use of urban regeneration as a tool, with heritage and culture as focal points.

---

7 Ibid.

8 Sanjay Das, 'Time to Re-imagine the Urbanscape' (12 June 2020), *Hindu Business Line*, https://www.thehindubusinessline.com/opinion/time-to-re-imagine-the urbanscape/article31805877.ece#

9 Ahmed Elseragy and Amira Elnokaly, 'Heritage-led Urban Regeneration as a Catalyst for Sustainable Urban Development', in *HERITAGE 2018*, ed. by R. Amoêda, S. Lira, C. Pinheiro, J. M. Santiago Zaragoza, J. Calvo Serrano and F. García Carrill (Granada: Editorial Universidad de Granada, 2018), https://core.ac.uk/download/pdf/163028369.pdf

10 Simon Thurley, Mark Walley and Liz Peace, 'Heritage Works: The Use of Historic Buildings in Regeneration. A Toolkit of Good Practice' (2013), *Academia*, https://www.academia.edu/30421656/The_use_of_historic_buildings_in_regeneration_A_toolkit_of_good_practice

Historical Background

Delhi, over its expansive history, has been an important Indian political centre as the capital of several empires. Its habitation was governed by certain natural advantages due to its geographical location, including a perennial river, hills rich with stones for construction, protection during times of war and a fertile agricultural hinterland to sustain its vast urban population engaged in non-agricultural pursuits. Over the years, various settlements emerged in the triangular area formed by the River Yamuna and the Ridge. The rulers of the successive dynasties that conquered Delhi developed portions of land in this triangular region, each with distinct walls, forts and supporting fabric, shaping the different forms of the city over time.[11]

Archaeological findings have revealed continuous cultural layers from the third to fourth centuries BC to the Mughal period, pottery fragments dating back to approximately 1000–500 BC and Lal Kot, the first city of Delhi, founded by the Tamar dynasty in AD 1060. The Chauhans succeeded the Tomars in the mid-twelfth century and extended Lal Kot to form Qila Rai Pithora. Delhi came to be the imperial capital in the time of the Delhi Sultanate, with the establishment of Siri, the second city of Delhi. Ghiyasuddin Tughlaq (r. 1320–1324), the first of the Tughlaq kings following the Khaljis, built Tughlaqabad, Delhi's third city. In AD 1326–1327, Muhammad-bin-Tughlaq linked the older cities of Lal Kot and Siri with two walls, creating the fourth city of Delhi, Jahanpanah. Firoz Shah Tughlaq (1351–1388) built Firozabad, the fifth city of Delhi, on the banks of River Yamuna. Unlike other dynasties, the Sayyid (fifteenth century) and Lodi dynasties (mid-fifteenth century) did not leave behind distinct cities during their rule. Delhi then served intermittently as the capital of the Mughal Empire, with a hiatus from the mid-sixteenth to mid-seventeenth centuries. Emperor Humayun, in 1533, built Dinpanah, the sixth city of Delhi. In 1639, Shahjahan shifted the Mughal Empire back to Delhi and the walled city of Shahjahanabad, Delhi's seventh city, was built. Delhi was taken over by the British in 1803, following their defeat of the Marathas. In 1911, they relocated their

11 Amit Mukherji and Indu Rawat, *Compilation on Heritage of Delhi* (New Delhi: Heritage Conservation Committee, 2012), https://hccdelhi.in/Upload/Link%20Page/Compilation%20of%20HCC/783144217514590.pdf

capital from Calcutta to Delhi, constructing New Delhi to the southwest of the walled city, Shahjahanabad.[12]

Today's historical core reflects a dramatic juncture between the imperial 'Traditionalism' and colonial 'Modernism' born from the architectural upheavals of industrial revolutions in the eighteenth and nineteenth centuries. This city, which was plundered, redefined and changed hands several times, still retains an overwhelming and enigmatic historical and symbolic character. This essence flourishes even today in the enduring socio-cultural patterns embedded in the lifestyles of its inhabitants.[13]

By the early nineteenth century, the British had effectively dominated the Indian subcontinent. In 1803, their control was further reinforced with the defeat of the Marathas under Mahadaji Scindia. They legitimised their rule by offering protection to the weakened Mughal Emperor, Shah Alam II, and ruling through him. However, their power was again challenged in 1857, when Indian soldiers in their employment, together with rebellious princes, rose up in an open revolt which came to be known as the Rebellion of 1857. However, this uprising was doomed from the start and brutally crushed by the British, marking the end of the Mughal Empire.

Soon after, the British embarked on a deliberate campaign of destruction, demolishing many of the buildings in the Red Fort, the seat of the recently extinguished Mughal Empire, and replacing them with towering but unremarkable barracks. This was the first step towards erasing the architectural legacy of the Mughals.

However, a distinct architectural tradition was necessary to usher in the new era of the British 'Raj'. Hence, they contemplated a fusion of existing Indian styles with styles imported from the West such as Gothic (with its sub-styles like French Gothic and Venetian-Moorish), Neo-Classical and Art Deco. Gothic architecture was particularly favoured because its design philosophy was inclined towards grand scale, exemplified by buildings like the Taj Hotel. By blending elements of British and European architecture with Indian characteristics and by

---

12 UNESCO, 'Tentative List: Delhi – A Heritage City' (22 May 2012), *UNESCO*, https://whc.unesco.org/en/tentativelists/5743/

13 Jyoti Hosagrahar, *Indigenous Modernities: Negotiating Architecture and Urbanism* (New York: Routledge, 2005), https://doi.org/10.4324/9780203022733

allowing some regional Indian princes to remain in power, the British attempted to make their presence more 'palatable' for the Indian populace. The British tried to encapsulate South Asia's past within their constructions, granting legitimacy to the British Raj while creating a modern network of railways, colleges and legal courts.

In the interim, various agencies have been established to preserve these elements of Indian heritage, with their historical, architectural and commemorative significance.

Table 10.1 Agencies responsible for managing tangible and intangible heritage in India.

Central agencies for the conservation of built heritage
Ministry of Urban Development
• Delhi Development Authority (DDA) Heritage Cell
• Delhi Urban Arts Commission
• Central Public Works Department
• Heritage Conservation Committee
• National Capital Region Planning Board
• Forest Department
Ministry of Culture
• Archaeological Survey of India (ASI)
• National Monuments Authority
Ministry of Home Affairs
• Municipal Corporation of Delhi (MCD)
Ministry of Defence
• Delhi Cantonment Board
Ministry of Tourism

State agencies for the conservation of built heritage
Government of National Capital Territory (GNTC) o ASI Delhi Circle o Delhi Tourism and Transportation Development Corporation (DTTDC) o State Department of Archaeology Delhi Development Authority Shahjahanabad Redevelopment Corporation (SRDC) North Delhi Municipal Corporation (NDMC)
Non-governmental organisations for the conservation of built heritage
• Indian National Trust for Art and Cultural Heritage (INTACH) • Aga Khan Trust for Culture (AKTC)
Agencies concerned with the protection of Delhi's built heritage
• Heritage Conservation Committee (HCC) • Archaeological Survey of India (ASI) • State Archaeological Department, Govt. of NCT of Delhi • Delhi Development Authority (DDA) • Municipal Corporation of Delhi (MCD) • Central Public Works Department (CPWD) • Cantonment Board, Delhi • Indian National Trust for Art and Cultural Heritage (INTACH) • Aga Khan Trust

The list of heritage sites, including buildings, precincts and natural features, is prepared by the NDMC, MCD and DDA, with the approval of the HCC and supplemented occasionally.[14] At present, 886 buildings in Delhi are on the official heritage list. Among these, 141 heritage

14 *HCC Heritage Conservation Committee*, https://hccdelhi.in/u/Default

buildings/precincts are under the jurisdiction of NDMC, and 745 are in areas managed by the Municipal Corporation, with information available on the HCC website.

Many structures have not been recognised on the lists of these established agencies. These unlisted and unprotected structures are thus overlooked amidst rapid urbanisation, with little to no effort invested in their protection. New laws and regulations are required to integrate this heritage into the growing Indian economy for the betterment of society.

The urban fabric of north Shahjahanabad diverges slightly from the rest of Old Delhi. Buildings in this area vary in height from G+1 to G+4, without setbacks.[15] The structures are compact, and even in the narrow alleys, the built environment offers ample light and ventilation. The facades of these structures are also of notable historical significance.

The larger plots serve primarily as storage spaces, while some are used for institutional purposes like banks and schools. Commercial zones with shops and warehouses are located near the cargo handling unit of the Old Delhi Railway Station.

A mixed-use pattern exists along the streets, as the ground floors of buildings are used as shops, followed by warehouses on the first floor and residences starting from the second floor. The residential area is used exclusively by local workers and shopkeepers. Wholesale trade is concentrated in the central area, attracting workers and traders and thus contributing to the deterioration of the city environment. The absence of developed land and infrastructure provisions results in haphazard growth patterns.

Analysis of North Shahjahanabad

Urban Network and Circulation

The location is easily accessible and commutable, situated at the centre of the auto repair market. It is well connected through various modes of transportation, including Interstate Bus Terminal-1 (Kashmere Gate),

15 G+ refers to the number of floors above ground level in a building. Setbacks are the minimum distance a building must be set back from property lines, streets of orther structures.

Metro Station-3 (Red, Yellow and Violet lines), Old Delhi Railway Station and arterial roads such as Ring Road and LalaHardev Marg (45 metres). It also features collector roads such as Shyam Lal Marg (30 metres), SP Mukherjee Marg (30 metres), Netaji Shubhas Marg (30 metres), Lothian and Hamilton (24 metres) and Nicholson Road (12 metres). The width of internal streets, also known as galis, varies from 6–9 metres to 2–4 metres.

Retail activities in the area contribute to traffic congestion, exacerbated by the parking of vehicles on the roads by shopkeepers and homeowners. Heavy vehicle traffic from the small- to medium-scale warehouses compounds this problem. Moreover, streets and public spaces are occupied by squatters and other illegal occupants, resulting in poor pedestrian infrastructure.

Table 10.2 Issues related to transportation and connectivity.

Issues	Hamilton Road	Nicholson Road
Public transport	Buses operate on the roads, but the lack of bus stops hinders connectivity. The encroachment of the right-of-way (ROW) also limits the space for buses	Due to inconsistent ROW, this road is devoid of public transport, resulting in a total disconnect from the Metro station
Paratransit system	Non-motorised vehicles operating in the area lack designated pick-up points and regulated parking spaces. Last-mile connectivity and subsequent services to Metro stations are absent due to a lack of connections	
Parking	Irregular on-street parking of both commercial and private vehicles due to non-demarcated spaces leads to heavy encroachment of ROW in this area	

Markets

This area predominantly functions as a wholesale market for spare automobile parts, electrical and electronic items and small-scale machinery. Warehouses have proliferated around these markets in residential buildings, leading to the deterioration of the infrastructure. The unprecedented illegal and unregulated constructions in the rehabilitation markets like Lajpat Rai has led to increased trade activity without adequate planning, causing further space-related problems. The wholesale trade of hazardous goods and chemicals in Tilak Bazar also continues without regulation. Moreover, the bulk trading of incompatible goods like food grains on Naya Bazar Road is leading to congestion, traffic jams and chaos in the city.

Despite the significant business potential of these medieval-era markets, their growth has been hampered by a lack of planning, sanitation, building maintenance, safety, traffic management and order. This unplanned and disorganised expansion of historically important markets results in economic losses to business communities and significant revenue loss for the government.

Festivals and Processional Paths

Three major processional parades take place in North Shahjahanabad:

- Janamasthmi (a celebration of the birth of Lord Krishna).
- Dussehra (a festival symbolising the triumph of good over evil).
- Muharram (a commemoration marking the anniversary of the battle of Karbala).[16]

These events attract large crowds to the area, making it difficult to manage the high concentration of foot traffic during the festivities.

Community Profile

Most residents of North Shahjahanabad are working class, as the area is a commercial hub for automobile parts. The community comprises people of diverse ethnic and religious backgrounds. In the seventeenth century, the area was divided into different quarters known as mohallas, generally organised according to occupational and ethnic groups.[17]

16 The Battle of Karbala (680 AD) took place in the city of Karbala, in present-day Iraq, and is one of the most significant battles in Shia Muslim history.

17 Uzma Azhar, Shahjahanabad: Physical vis-a-vis Socio-Cultural Space' (17 October 2018), *Sahapedia*, sahapedia.org/

Examples include Mohalla Dhobiwara (washerman's quarter) and Punjabi Mohalla (Punjabi quarter).

Different features can be found within the mohallas, including katras (gated building complexes enclosed by high walls, typically with ground floor commercial space and upper floor residences), kuchas (mohallas with one linear road), galis (residential lanes branching out from a main road) and chattas (upper stories of residential structures crossing over streets or lanes).[18]

Today, as per the Zonal Development Plan of 1999, the area is under sub-zone C for development works and maintenance. The MCD has further divided it into zones and wards, namely the Civil Lines Zone, the Kashmere Gate Area, and Ward 77.[19]

The area lacks tourism facilities, infrastructure to capitalise on economic opportunities and maintenance systems for basic amenities such as hospitals and schools.

Open Space

The unregulated encroachment on open spaces is disrupting the fabric of the historic city. The retail trade and warehouses draw commercial and private vehicles to the area, which has led to the emergence of parking areas as a new typology in open spaces, including neighbourhood public parks. Improper conservation and poor maintenance can be observed at Nicholson Cemetery, and illegal parking occurs inside Maharaja Agrasen Park. While streets and squares offer numerous interactive open spaces within the zone, there is an absence of public parks. Open garbage disposal in the nursery also adds to these challenges.

Built Typology

Most typologies in this zone are mixed-use structures combining shops and houses, followed by standalone shops, making it a highly commercial

---

shahjahanabad-physical-vis-vis-socio-cultural-space

18 Akhtar Badshah, *Interventions into Old Residential Quarters* (Cambridge, MA: Massachusetts Institute of Technology, 1983).

19 Delhi Urban Arts Commission, *Rejuvenation of Shahjahanabad* (New Delhi: DUAC, 2017), https://duac.org.in/Upload/City%20Level%20Studies/Site%20specific%20design%20for%20wards/653954173410426.pdf

zone. The zone has become a classic example of the repurposing of heritage buildings, such as the northern railway building, St. Stephen's College, the Chief Electoral Building, while retaining the heritage and functional value of these structures. Due to the extensive commercial activities in the zone, heritage structures are being used as shops and warehouses, resulting in their structural and aesthetic degradation.

Built Heritage

The zone has nine ASI-protected monuments: Nicholson Cemetery, Hathi Gate, Baradari, Qudsiya Mosque, Fortification Wall, Kashmere Gate, Magazine Gateway, Lothian Cemetery and Salimgarh Fort, as well as one state-protected monument, Dara Shikoh's Library.

For recognised heritage structures under ASI jurisdiction, a prohibited area of one hundred metres and a regulated area of two hundred metres must be designated around protected structures. The MCD prohibits intervention in Grade 1 buildings without permission, with some flexibility granted for Grade 3 structures.

INTACH has inventoried all heritage monuments, including in-use buildings and national, regional and local gateways. Several buildings with architectural value within the intervention area require preservation efforts in their present condition in order to maintain their essence and character.

Table 10.3 Strengths, Weaknesses, Opportunities and Threats (SWOT) analysis.

Strengths	**Weaknesses**
(1) Proximity to mass transit options to reach the centre of the old city (2) Importance as a centre of retail trade	(1) Lack of solid waste management facilities (for treatment and disposal), leading to the indiscriminate dumping of garbage and land pollution (2) Insufficient parking space and poor pedestrian infrastructure (3) Absence of tourism facilities, parks and open spaces (4) Inadequate public amenities (5) Ineffective integration of heritage concerns within planning processes

Opportunities	**Threats**
(1) Interest zones based on the different architectural styles of monuments can enhance the area's appeal as a tourist destination	(1) Continued neglect of heritage areas can reduce tourism revenues
(2) Developing heritage walks can educate people about the history, architecture and community	(2) Lack of repair and maintenance of heritage buildings can lead to rapid deterioration of the built fabric
(3) A time-based traffic management plan can reduce congestion	(3) Poor infrastructure like narrow streets, dilapidated buildings and outdated drainage systems pose a threat to residents' quality of life
(4) A disaster management plan can be formulated based on wider roadways	(4) The illegal occupancy of streets and public spaces occupied by squatters and other unauthorised occupants can have various negative impacts on the community

Issues and Strategies

Historical urban areas are integral to the collective memory of cities, encapsulating the distinctive essence of specific historical eras. Given their immense cultural and historical value, the preservation of these areas is imperative. This section highlights existing issues related to North Shahjahanabad and suggests various strategies for addressing them and thereby protecting and maintaining the integrity of this historical urban area.

1. Abandoned and Dilapidated Structures

Abandoned and dilapidated structures are a major issue in North Shahjahanabad. This is particularly evident in a heritage building under the ownership of the National Cadet Corps (NCC), the built fabric along Lothian Road, and the Art Deco and colonial architecture along Nicholson Road. The neglect and deterioration of these structures can be primarily attributed to insufficient building repair and maintenance compounded by a lack of public awareness about the commercialisation of heritage conservation.

Strategies to address this situation include the introduction of regulations and the creation of an informational guidebook for residents and business owners about safeguarding this urban heritage. Additionally, introducing heritage walks and a tourist information centre would contribute to raising awareness about the built heritage and conserving disintegrated structures on Nicholson and Lothian streets.

2. Obstruction of Facades

Another concern is the obstruction of building facades in this zone. High tension wires running parallel to the buildings are hazardous and diminish the aesthetics of the area. Similarly, the internal facades of heritage structures are entangled by electrical wires and cables, posing a serious safety threat. Furthermore, the haphazard placement of hoardings not only obstructs facades but also causes structural damage to buildings. Aesthetically pleasing architectural elements are being concealed by advertisements or shop hoarding boards.

Potential solutions for these challenges include advocating for underground wiring to avoid the clutter of wires on facades, while internal electrical wires could be hidden by false ceilings. Introducing guidelines for shop hoardings can also ensure harmony and aesthetic appeal for shops and residents. Facade improvements and heritage structure maintenance should also be implemented in collaboration with heritage-related authorities.

3. Signage and Heritage Interpretation

In many parts of North Shahjahanabad, there is inadequate signage and heritage interpretation, contributing to the neglect of this heritage and the loss of tourism interest. Nicholson Cemetery has no ASI protection signage, while the informative signage about the zone at Kashmere Gate Metro lacks basic details about the buildings highlighted by INTACH Delhi Chapter. Similarly, the signage at Kashmere Gate Metro is insufficient given the amount of tourist transit traffic at the location.

These oversights could be remedied by identifying effective locations for signage at the Metro Station and ASI-protected sites, and by posting both informative and directional signage at all tourist hotspots.

4. Open Spaces

There are also significant issues pertaining to the area's open spaces, such as the negligent maintenance of Nicholson Cemetery and the illegal parking of vehicles inside Maharaja Agrasen Park. In general, the zone lacks public parks, with streets and squares constituting the only interactive open spaces. Moreover, garbage is being improperly disposed of in the nursery and there is concerning encroachment along the bank of the Yamuna River.

Given that the relevant authorities are unable to maintain the zone's cemetery and parks, issuing private contracts for the upkeep of these spaces would be an effective strategy for their improvement, along with identifying open spaces in the zone for risk preparedness.

5. Infrastructure and Waste Management

North Shahjahanabad also faces considerable infrastructural challenges. Amenities like hand pumps are inappropriately located near heritage sites like the Fortified Wall, and public toilets are ineffectively allocated by local authorities. The dumping of waste near heritage sites, such as the portion of the wall not under ASI protection, as well as along the Nigambodh Ghat riverfront and Ganesh Ghat is unacceptable and contributes to the pollution of the Yamuna River. Overflowing waste encroaches on pedestrian paths and creates unhygienic conditions at roadside dumping areas. Additionally, dhalaos[20] are poorly designed, without adequate space for the sorting and separation of waste.

Various departments like the MCD and NDMC who are responsible for monitoring the zone's waste management system should be engaged in addressing these issues, including in the identification of suitable locations for dhalaos and adopting guidelines for waste management in and around heritage structures.

20 Dhalaos are large three-walled concrete structures meant for garbage collection from a locality or market.

6. Traffic Discipline

There are numerous traffic-related issues in the zone arising from a lack of discipline among drivers. Buses frequently stop near intersections, across lanes, and in the middle of the road to pick up and drop off passengers, without any consideration for the flow of traffic. Motorised vehicles park along roadsides, even where it is forbidden to do so. Drivers often fail to adhere to traffic rules, and are sometimes not even aware of them. This is attributable to poor driver training and a lax licensing system amenable to bribery.

Penalising bus and vehicle drivers for parking outside of designated areas and installing roadside bollards to prevent vehicle parking on streets would be major steps towards confronting these issues. Furthermore, strict traffic regulations must be applied consistently to all drivers.

7. Traffic Management

Compounding issues of traffic discipline are substantial shortcomings in roadway management. Road markings, including traffic lanes, are faded or non-existent, and very few road signs are installed even on the primary and secondary roads. Malfunctioning traffic signals are an additional problem, as are inefficient schedules for loading and unloading trailers, which add to roadway congestion.

To rectify these issues, traffic authorities should install proper road signage and markings and develop an appropriate time management plan for the loading and unloading of cargo. Additionally, the traffic department should be engaged to address traffic light issues.

8. Pedestrian Infrastructure

There is a notable deficiency in pedestrian infrastructure in North Shahjahanabad. Pedestrians are often forced to walk on roadways because the sidewalks are used by hawkers or for illegal vehicle parking. The lack of designated pedestrian crossings, even on wide and busy streets, creates safety risks. Moreover, there are no proper pick-up and drop-off points for paratransits, encroaching on the existing footpaths, and pathways are obstructed by various obstacles like garbage and construction materials.

To improve pedestrian infrastructure, a designated vendor zone should be established to eliminate encroachment on walking paths, alongside designated pick-up and drop-off points for paratransits. Furthermore, appropriately situating and marking garbage cans would reduce obstruction on these pathways.

Proposals

It is crucial to formulate a vision for positive urban development to improve the quality of space and affordability for local communities and other users. This must be achieved by integrating urban heritage conservation strategies to enhance the overall human environment. The objective is to tap into the potential of the existing built heritage and develop an urban landscape that supports this heritage. The focus should encompass the following heritage elements: built heritage, social practices, rituals and festive events, and trade and commerce. Thus, heritage, tourism and development emerge as three aspects that need to be interwoven to form effective strategies.

By prioritising heritage values, new intervention opportunities can be identified to capitalise on the historic environment as an asset and give it new life. This can serve as a cornerstone of the economic and social revival of North Shahjahanabad. Preserving and revitalising the essence of the heritage city to reflect its unique character can promote an aesthetically appealing, accessible, informative and secure environment. Furthermore, public-private partnerships offer an effective tool for adaptive urban rehabilitation. Identifying viable economic uses can support initial refurbishments, provide owners and developers with reasonable returns on their investments and generate sufficient income to ensure the long-term maintenance of the built fabric and associated public spaces. Moreover, the introduction and enhancement of basic services such as sanitation, public amenities, toilets, water taps and streetlights should incorporate the latest technologies to improve resident and visitor experience.

a) Interpretation Centre in Qudsiya Bagh

Providing a tourist information centre within the Baradari in Qudsiya Bagh would enable visitors to better understand the site's history. The centre should include an informative programme detailing the Rebellion of 1857 and the various historical layers of settlement from the Mughal period to the British colonial era.

b) NCC: Adaptive Reuse of Neglected Heritage

The abandoned structure near the NCC building could be repurposed as a cafe, catering to the local student population and generating revenue.

c) Art Deco District

The street at Lothian Road and Bada Bazar road has various Art Deco buildings which have been neglected for some time. Focus should be given to refurbishing the facades of these neglected structures by installing proper hoardings and signage along the entire street.

d) Traffic Management for Nicholson Road

The parking issue can be resolved by making Nicholson Road a non-motorized vehicle zone, facilitating pedestrian movement. Additionally, an automated parking system in the bus parking area could be proposed to address parking concerns.

e) Fortification Wall

The historic dilapidated wall should be consolidated using appropriate conservation repair strategies. The cleanliness of the wall could also be enhanced by providing trash cans and public toilets at the site. A bicycle track could be introduced to improve mobility along the wall and bollards installed to prevent encroachments by vehicles.

f) Heritage Walks

Heritage walks can be conducted through the zone, focusing on neglected heritage. Designing various walks to shed light on both built and unbuilt aspects of local heritage would contribute to raising awareness about North Shahjahanabad. Themed walks could explore topics such as the Rebellion of 1857, Art Deco and Industrial Heritage, and the lesser-known area of North Shahjahanabad.

g) Informational and Directional Signage

Installing directional and informational signage at protected, listed and unlisted monuments like the Fortification Wall, Baradari, Bengali Club and the Art Deco buildings would help to generate awareness and address the information gap regarding the value and significance of these sites.

h) Recognition of North Shahjahanabad in the Master Plan Delhi (MPD)

While the MPD has classified Shahjahanabad as a significant zone, a similar designation should be granted to North Shahjahanabad to ensure its distinctive recognition.

Conclusion

Delhi is a thriving city that houses the remnants of over a thousand years of architecture in various states of preservation. The area of North Shahjahanabad, with its rich history and lasting legacy, continues to shape the cultural and historical landscape of this Indian city. North Shahjahanabad has evolved over time, most significantly in the aftermath of historical events like the Rebellion of 1857, which changed the spatial character of parts of the walled city. During this period, many of its grand structures and gardens were destroyed or repurposed. However, the urban landscape and monumental buildings of the British era remain intact across much of the city. North Shahjahanabad is a melting pot of cultures and traditions, known for its diverse population. The narrow lanes of Old Delhi are lined with temples, mosques, churches and gurdwaras, reflecting India's religious pluralism.

North Shahjahanabad holds a special place in the history and culture of Delhi and India as a whole. Its architectural marvels, cultural diversity, culinary traditions and historical significance continue to make it a captivating and vibrant part of the city. All of the proposals and strategies outlined in this chapter would make a significant contribution to maintaining the area's authenticity in both structure and design. While Shahjahanabad is no longer an imperial capital, it is an important commercial sector, and these proposals seek to overcome its contemporary challenges and enhance the urban environment.

The twentieth and twenty-first centuries have been characterised by the rapid development of science, technology and social systems but also by a desire to consciously preserve the valuable parts of our past and present for future generations. Heritage has always existed, but it is now consciously preserved and researched. The increasing visibility and significance of heritage has heightened its influence in culture and politics, which can be observed at all levels of society.

Heritage can be used in a variety of ways to achieve various objectives. When dealing with cultural heritage, it is important to consider three crucial dimensions: the wide range of potential heritage objects and phenomena, the level of society at which heritage is being managed and the values upon which the definition of heritage is based.

Interventions to conserve architectural landmarks and upgrade the infrastructure of heritage cities facing urbanisation challenges are of immense importance. Special attention is needed to conserve the urban tissues shaping the unique sense of place and character in these environments. This chapter emphasises the revitalisation of the lost identities of old heritage cities, which can guide developers and stakeholders towards a more socio-economically sustainable development approach. In addition, this supports the preservation of the symbolic significance of heritage buildings and the city's distinctive sense of place. The economic strategies for urban regeneration projects can utilise urban heritage centres to promote sustainable urbanisation and inclusive growth. If harnessed properly, urban heritage, nature and culture can act as catalysts for socio-economic and environmental development through tourism, commercial use and higher land

and property values, thereby generating revenue for maintenance, restoration and rehabilitation.

Bibliography

Azhar, Uzma, 'Shahjahanabad: Physical vis-a-vis Socio-Cultural Space' (17 October 2018), *Sahapedia*, sahapedia.org/shahjahanabad-physical-vis-vis-socio-cultural-space

Badshah, Akhtar, *Interventions into Old Residential Quarters* (Cambridge, MA: Massachusetts Institute of Technology, 1983).

Das, Sanjay, 'Time to Re-imagine the Urbanscape' (12 June 2020), *Hindu Business Line*, https://www.thehindubusinessline.com/opinion/time-to-re-imagine-the urbanscape/article31805877.ece#

Delhi Urban Arts Commission, *Rejuvenation of Shahjahanabad* (New Delhi: DUAC, 2017), https://duac.org.in/Upload/City%20Level%20Studies/Site%20specific%20design%20for%20wards/653954173410426.pdf

Elseragy, Ahmed and Elnokaly, Amira, 'Heritage-led Urban Regeneration as a Catalyst for Sustainable Urban Development', in *HERITAGE 2018*, ed. by R. Amoêda, S. Lira, C. Pinheiro, J. M. Santiago Zaragoza, J. Calvo Serrano and F. García Carrill (Granada: Editorial Universidad de Granada, 2018), https://core.ac.uk/download/pdf/163028369.pdf

Getty Conservation Institute, *Historic Urban Environment Conservation Challenges and Priorities for Action* (Los Angeles, CA Getty Conservation Institute, 2010), https://www.getty.edu/conservation/publications_resources/pdf_publications/historic_urban_environment.html

HCC Heritage Conservation Committee, https://hccdelhi.in/u/Default

Hosagrahar, Jyoti, *Indigenous Modernities: Negotiating Architecture and Urbanism* (New York: Routledge, 2005), https://doi.org/10.4324/9780203022733

Mukherji, Amit and Rawat, Indu, *Compilation on Heritage of Delhi* (New Delhi: Heritage Conservation Committee, 2012), https://hccdelhi.in/Upload/Link%20Page/Compilation%20of%20HCC/783144217514590.pdf

Rajeev, Sethi, 'Art for the Sake of Urbanscape' (27 June 2014), *The Hindu*, https://www.thehindu.com/opinion/op-ed/Art-for-the-sake-of-urbanscape/article11640724.ece

Rao, Sanah Devika, *Interactive Museum: Shahjahanabad Ki Haveli* (2017), https://www.behance.net/gallery/56221609/Interactive-Museum-Shahjahanabad-Ki-Haveli

Singh, Ajit, *Confrontation, Comparison and Reconstruction of the Walled City of Shahjahanabad* (Cambridge, MA: Massachusetts Institute of Technology, 2006).

Thurley, Simon, Walley, Mark and Peace, Liz, 'Heritage Works: The Use of Historic Buildings in Regeneration. A Toolkit of Good Practice' (2013), *Academia*, https://www.academia.edu/30421656/The_use_of_historic_buildings_in_regeneration_A_toolkit_of_good_practice

UNESCO, 'Tentative List: Delhi – A Heritage City' (22 May 2012), *UNESCO*, https://whc.unesco.org/en/tentativelists/5743/

11. The Historic Urban Landscape Approach as a Tool for Port Said Heritage Conservation

Amany Abdelsadeq S. Hussein

Introduction

Cities worldwide have been shaped by their people, through the successive layering of their values, traditions and experiences. The traditional view of heritage limited to historical monuments has changed. Nowadays, urban heritage represents the largest category on the World Heritage List, and many cities around the globe recognise the importance of preserving urban heritage as the core of the city's identity and as a catalyst for development through cultural tourism and commercial activities. However, cities face numerous pressures and challenges in conserving their historic areas. The Historic Urban Landscape approach to heritage conservation, which United Nations Educational, Scientific and Cultural Organization (UNESCO) adopted in 2011, is considered a shift from the traditional emphasis on monument conservation towards a broader recognition of urban contexts, including their social and economic aspects.

In Egypt, the urban heritage of the late nineteenth and early twentieth century has suffered for decades from a lack of maintenance, primarily due to state negligence and the vagueness of laws governing the preservation of built heritage. Moreover, the preservation strategy of the nineteenth and twentieth centuries poses a direct threat to

 https://doi.org/10.11647/OBP.0412.11

Egyptian architectural heritage. This strategy is rooted in an approach which isolates buildings from their context without considering the urban system as a whole, eventually leading to the destruction of these historic structures. The city of Port Said is an obvious example of this problem. Despite Egyptian Cabinet decrees in 2009 and 2011 that led to the registration of 644 buildings with unique architectural styles as historic structures, the city is witnessing an increasing trend towards the demolition of these buildings.

This chapter suggests applying the Historic Urban Landscape approach for conserving and managing historic areas in Port Said. The chapter begins by reviewing the history of the city, its urban structure and architectural significance. This is followed by a brief overview of the current socio-economic challenges threatening its urban heritage and the heritage initiatives that have evolved over the past two decades. Finally, the chapter concludes by offering a roadmap for implementing the Historic Urban Landscape approach in Port Said.

Literature Review

Urban heritage, encompassing both tangible and intangible elements, strengthens cities' identities and is considered a key asset for city branding and economic development.[1] The tangible heritage of cities, which includes natural landscapes, monuments and historic urban centres, creates a sense of place, serving as markers of history and nourishing cultural activities like festivals and other practices. Intangible heritage includes social practices handed down from generation to generation, like oral traditions, rituals and performing arts. Intangible heritage is considered the living component of urban heritage as it forms the city's cultural identity and passes local traditions on to new generations.[2]

Urban heritage can contribute to the economic and social development of the urban community. Cultural and creative industries can serve as powerful tools for income generation and employment creation, thus

1 UNESCO, *Culture Urban Future: Global Report on Culture for Sustainable Urban Development* (Paris: UNESCO, 2016), p. 19.

2 Eduardo Rojas, 'Urban Heritage for Sustainable Development', in *Culture: Urban Future; Global Report on Culture for Sustainable Urban Development*, ed. by I. G. Bokova (Paris: UNESCO, 2016), pp. 193–99 (p. 193).

contributing to poverty reduction.[3] However, under the pressures of urbanisation, mass tourism and the commercial exploitation of heritage, cities face a variety of challenges. Addressing these challenges requires effective planning and resource management to achieve a balance between tourism promotion and heritage conservation.

The Recommendation on the Historic Urban Landscape, adopted on 10 November 2011 during the 36th session of UNESCO's General Conference, responds to the need to frame urban heritage conservation within the planning and implementation of urban development agendas. This approach considers urban heritage a social and economic asset for urban development and aims to enhance its sustainability by considering local community knowledge, socio-economic factors and environmental concerns.[4]

The major cities in Egypt, namely Cairo, Alexandria and Port Said, boast an unrivalled urban heritage that dates back to the late nineteenth and early twentieth centuries. Since 1867, these cities have witnessed substantial urban modernisation efforts following trends in the re-planning of industrial European cities. Ismail Pasha, the ruler of Egypt at the time, proposed a transformation from local Islamic urban forms to European-style districts with large, arcaded boulevards, open gardens and French- and Italian-style buildings.[5] Ismail Pasha's successors also adopted this vision of modernisation during the monarchical era. European architects came to work in major Egyptian cities, leaving an indelible architectural legacy in the region.[6] However, the architectural style in Port Said is unique in Egypt, characterised by the remarkable

3 UNESCO, *Culture Urban Future*, p. 20.

4 UNESCO, *Records of the General Conference, 36th session, Paris, 25 October—10 November 2011, v. 1: Resolutions* (Paris: UNESCO, 2011), https://unesdoc.unesco.org/ark:/48223/pf0000215084.page=52

5 Mohamed El Amrousi, 'Imperial Sanctuaries: Arab Urban Enclaves on the East African Coast', in *Colonial Architecture and Urbanism in Africa—Intertwined and Contested Histories*, ed. by Fassil Demissie (Farnham: Ashgate Publishing Limited, 2012), pp. 67–84.

6 James Moore, '"The Alexandria You Are Losing"? Urban Heritage and Activism in Egypt since the 2011 Revolution', *Journal of Eastern Mediterranean Archaeology & Heritage Studies*, 5.3–4 (2017), 427–44, https://doi.org/10.5325/jeasmedarcherstu.5.3-4.0427

homogeneity of facades with high wooden verandas, combined with an expansive variety of designs.[7]

The urban heritage of Port Said has been the subject of numerous urban studies. Dalila ElKerdany explained the urban morphology of the European and Arab quarters and discussed the socio-economic factors that threaten its urban heritage.[8] Inken Baller analysed the architectural and urban characteristics that make the city deserving of World Culture Heritage status.[9] Mohamed El-Amrousi studied Port Said as one of the colonial urban laboratories for intertwining European and Islamic architecture.[10] Naglaa Megahed explored the richness of the city's architectural heritage and the various approaches to urban heritage conservation in this context.[11] Céline Frémaux and Mercedes Volait discussed the cosmopolitan features in the architecture and planning of the Suez Canal cities.[12] Sawsan Noweir analysed the evolution of Port Said, highlighting the potential for urban tourism.[13] Claudine Piaton studied the specificities of wooden verandas in Port Said, reminiscent

7 *Port-Saïd: Architectures XIXe–XXe siècles*, ed. by M. L. Crosnier-Leconte, G. Ghitani and N. Amin (Cairo: IFAO, 2006).

8 Dalila ElKerdany, 'Port Said: A Cosmopolitan Heritage Under Threat', in *Revitalizing City Districts: Transformation Partnership for Urban Design and Architecture in Historic City Districts*, ed. by Hebatalla Abouelfadl, Dalila ElKerdany and Christoph Wessling (Cham: Springer International Publishing, 2017), pp. 15–33, https://doi.org/10.1007/978-3-319-46289-9_2

9 Inken Baller, 'Strategies for the Preservation of the Heritage of the Suez Region and Port Said as World Heritage Site', in *Revitalizing City Districts: Transformation Partnership for Urban Design and Architecture in Historic City Districts*, ed. by Hebatalla Abouelfadl, Dalila ElKerdany and Christoph Wessling (Cham: Springer International Publishing, 2017), pp. 35–51, https://doi.org/10.1007/978-3-319-46289-9_3

10 El Amrousi, 'Imperial Sanctuaries'.

11 Naglaa Ali Megahed, 'Heritage-Based Sustainability in Port Said: Classification of Styles and Future Development', *Archnet-IJAR: International Journal of Architectural Research*, 8.1 (2014), 94–107.

12 Céline Frémaux and Mercedes Volait, 'Inventing Space in the Age of Empire: Planning Experiments and Achievements along Suez Canal in Egypt (1859–1956)', *Planning Perspectives*, 24.2 (2009), 255–62, https://doi.org/10.1080/02665430902734350

13 Sawsan Noweir, 'Devenir patrimonial contre développement urbain: l'exemple de Port-Saïd', *Autrepart: Revue de sciences sociales au Sud*, 33 (2005), 109–26, https://doi.org/10.3917/autr.033.0109

of the tropical architecture widespread in European colonies yet unparalleled in height anywhere else in the world.[14]

Proceeding from this body of literature, this chapter proposes a roadmap for applying the Historic Urban Landscape approach as an alternative strategy for conserving urban heritage in Port Said. The chapter analyses the urban and architectural characteristics of the city and discusses the current socio-economic challenges and civil society initiatives to identify potential stakeholders and suitable strategies for conserving Port Said's historic areas.

Port Said: The Cosmopolitan City

Port Said was founded on 25 April 1859 as the main construction camp for accommodating the workers digging the Suez Canal. The city was named after Khedive Muhammad Saīd Pasha, who granted a concession to the French diplomat Ferdinand de Lesseps for the realisation of the canal project. The city was situated as the northern port, along a narrow strip of land separating the Mediterranean from Lake Manzala at the eastern edge of the Nile Delta. Constructed on a bed of earth dredged from the canal's excavation,[15] Port Said was the first Egyptian city to be built from scratch without any pre-existing settlements.[16]

By the late nineteenth century, the Suez Canal had become a vital artery of trade between Europe and Asia, with Port Said serving as a crucial nodal point in transportation networks[17] and the largest coal-bunkering station in the world.[18] The city's port exported cotton and rice from the eastern delta and following the completion of the railway

14 Claudine Piaton, 'Port Said—Decaying Wooden Verandas Tell the Story of a City', *Al Rawi: Egypt's Heritage Review*, 3 (2011), 22–29.

15 Lucia Carminati, 'Port Said and Ismailia as Desert Marvels: Delusion and Frustration on the Isthmus of Suez, 1859–1869', *Journal of Urban History*, 46.3 (2020), 622–47 (pp. 627–29).

16 ElKerdany, 'Port Said', p. 15.

17 Valeska Huber, 'Connecting Colonial Seas: The International Colonization of Port Said and The Suez Canal during and after the First World War', *European Review of History: Revue européenne d'histoire*, 19.1 (2012), 141–61 (pp. 145–46), https://doi.org/10.1080/13507486.2012.643612

18 Valeska Huber, *Channelling Mobilities—Migration and Globalisation in the Suez Canal Region and Beyond, 1869–1914* (New York: Cambridge University Press, 2013), https://doi.org/10.1080/13507486.2012.643612

between Cairo and Ismailia in 1904, Port Said became Egypt's second most important port after Alexandria.

Along with providing opportunities for investment in wholesale import, ship repair and trade, Port Said became a tourist destination for travellers en route between Europe and the colonies in Africa, Asia and Australia. Situated at the canal's entrance, Port Said was the first port of call after leaving Europe, making it a quasi-obligatory stopover for steamers to stock up on coal and provisions during their journeys.[19] With its several hotels and entertainment facilities like the Grand Casino and Eldorado theatre,[20] Port Said was perceived as, in the words of Rudyard Kipling, 'the exact division between east and west'.[21]

This economic prosperity sparked rapid development in Port Said, attracting Egyptian bourgeois families from Cairo and Alexandria, peasants from the nearby Delta villages and Egyptian labourers who remained in the city after excavating the canal.[22] The city also drew European immigrants, mainly from Greece, Italy, Malta, England and France. Europeans comprised eighteen percent of the population in 1917,[23] working mainly in the maritime and mercantile sectors.

The Historic Urban Form of Port Said

In 1861, the Suez Canal Company (SCC) initiated an urban plan that reflected French colonial planning principles and separated the European quarter, encompassing housing and community services

19 Valeska Huber, 'Cosmopolitanism on the Move: Port Said around 1900' (20 June 2017), *Global Urban History*, https://globalurbanhistory.com/2017/06/20/cosmopolitanism-on-the-move-port-said-around-1900/

20 Stefanie Anna Maria Wladika, 'Port Said—No Future without the Past: Integrated Rehabilitation Concept for the Urban Heritage' (master's thesis, Ain Shams University and University of Stuttgart, 2015), p. 43, https://iusd.asu.edu.eg/wp-content/uploads/2015/11/3rdInt_Wladika.pdf

21 Quoted in Huber, *Channelling Mobilities*, p. 37.

22 Christine Hegel Cantarella, 'Notable Families and Capitalist Parasites in Egypt's Former Free Zone: Law, Trade, and Uncertainty', in *Anthropology of the Middle East and North Africa—Into the New Millennium*, ed. by Sherine Hafez and Susan Slyomovics (Bloomington, IN: Indiana University Press, 2013), pp. 165–84.

23 *The Census of Egypt: Taken in 1917* (Cairo: Ministry of Finance—Statistical and Census Department, 1917).

for European staff, from the Arab village for Egyptian labourers.[24] The European quarter (Ifrang in spoken Arabic) was built along the bank of the canal as the city's facade with its European architecture, while the Arab village was built to the west, far from the canal,[25] and separated by Muhammad Ali Pasha Street.[26]

The master plan of the European quarter followed the hygienic urban planning principles of the time, with its grid pattern of perpendicular streets.[27] The urban grid was oriented parallel to the canal to the east and the coastline of the Mediterranean Sea in the north.[28] This design was intended to allow fresh air and sunlight into the streets to minimise the risk of epidemics, while shading pedestrians from the sun with tree-lined streets.[29]

The European quarter had a cosmopolitan character, with apartment blocks and villas featuring European architectural styles. The structures were surrounded by gardens, monumental churches for each Christian denomination and wide boulevards bearing the names of foreign, Ottoman and monarchical rulers. There were three categories of streets: thirty-metre-wide boulevards with arcades, avenues with widths of twelve to fifteen metres avenues and ten-metre-wide local streets.[30]

The Arab village remained fairly destitute until a great fire destroyed a large portion of it in 1884. Thereafter, a public hygiene project to rebuild

24 ElKerdany, 'Port Said', p. 15; Claudine Piaton, 'European Construction Companies in the Towns along the Suez Canal', in *Building beyond the Mediterranean: Studying the Archives of European Businesses (1860–1970)*, ed. by Claudine Piaton, Ezio Godoli and David Peyceré (Arles: Publications de l'Institut national d'histoire de l'art, 2012), pp. 92–103, https://doi.org/10.4000/books.inha.12729

25 Mostafa Mohielden Lotfy, 'Biographies of Port-Said: Everydayness of State, Dwellers, and Strangers' (master's thesis, The American University in Cairo, 2018), https://fount.aucegypt.edu/cgi/viewcontent.cgi?article=2393&context=etds

26 Lucia Carminati, 'Dividing and Ruling a Mediterranean Port-City: The Many Boundaries Within Late 19th century Port Said', in *Controversial Heritage and Divided Memories from the Nineteenth Through the Twentieth Centuries: Multi-Ethnic Cities in the Mediterranean World*, ed. by Marco Folin and Heleni Porfyriou, 2 vols. (New York: Routledge, 2020), II, pp. 30–44 (p. 32).

27 Céline Frémaux, 'Santé et hygiénisme dans les villes du canal de Suez', *Égypte/Monde arabe*, 3.4 (2007), 75–101, https://doi.org/10.4000/ema.1759

28 Wladika, 'Port Said', p. 57.

29 Frémaux, 'Santé et hygiénisme'.

30 El Amrousi, 'Imperial Sanctuaries', p. 73; ElKerdany, 'Port Said', p. 20; Wladika, 'Port Said', p. 57.

the Arab quarter took place in 1885.[31] The Arab quarter was planned according to a grid pattern for sanitation purposes. The main streets were fifteen metres wide, flanked by arcades, while the secondary streets were ten metres wide with alleys measuring between four and six metres for garbage collection and communal use, specifically by women.[32] The streets bore the names of the governorates from which Egyptian immigrants originated.[33] The building plots were very small (thirty to fifty metres)^2 in order to ensure they remained affordable for Egyptians.[34] While the urban landscape of the Arab quarter lacked gardens or open spaces, Egyptians gathered frequently for social and religious ceremonies. These gatherings gave rise to the distinct musical genre known as Simsimiyya.[35] In 1920, a playground (Al-Masry Club) and a public garden (Saad Zaghloul Garden) were established to the north, on land newly formed from coastal accretion brought about by the western breakwater.

The Historic Architecture of Port Said

The SCC was responsible for planning and determining the architectural styles in canal towns until the canal's inauguration in 1869, when the Egyptian government incorporated them into Egyptian common law. This placed the towns under the government's jurisdiction, subject to

31 Claudine Piaton, 'Port Said: Cosmopolitan Urban Rules and Architecture (1858–1930)', in *Revitalizing City Districts: Transformation Partnership for Urban Design and Architecture in Historic City Districts*, ed. by Hebatalla Abouelfadl, Dalila ElKerdany and Christoph Wessling (Cham: Springer International Publishing, 2017), pp. 3–14, https://doi.org/10.1007/978-3-319-46289-9

32 Noweir, 'Devenir patrimonial'; Frémaux, 'Santé et hygiénisme'; Wladika, 'Port Said', p. 59.

33 Lotfy, 'Biographies of Port-Said', pp. 27, 28.

34 Piaton, 'Port Said: Cosmopolitan Urban Rules', p. 6.

35 ElKerdany, 'Port Said', p. 18; Lotfy, 'Biographies of Port-Said'; Simsimiyya is a folk music genre originating from the Suez Canal cities characterized by local collective singing accompanied by the simsimiyya instrument. A simsimiyya band typically contains a simsimiyya player and a chorus group, with the accompaniment of other instruments, handclapping and the dance known as the 'bambutiyya'. During this dance, the dancer imitates a bumboat man selling his goods to sailors on ships or the gestures of fisherman. Simsimiyya songs in Port Said are deeply tied to the city's locality and reflect a strong sense of place, with metaphors from the surrounding nature, including the moon, pigeons, nightingales and other elements.

the Tanzim, an Egyptian administration that set planning regulations.[36] Ismail Pasha also mandated the co-management of the new towns by introducing a commission comprised of members of the Egyptian government and members of the Anglo-French SCC.[37] In 1911, a city council was established to take charge of the city's urban administration. The council was composed of eleven elected members and five chosen members; half of the council members were Egyptians, and the other half were Europeans.[38] This collaboration resulted in a well-organised city with high aesthetic standards enforced through strict building rules and specifications. However, the identity of each quarter depended upon the communities who lived there.

The cosmopolitan nature of Port Said was reflected in the variety of different architectural styles employed by European architects, which gave the city a hybrid urban identity. The architecture in the European quarter (Ifrang) followed popular Neo-Classical trends, with the Beaux Arts style imbuing the quarter's architecture with a French character.[39] However, different architectural styles were sometimes used as expressions of patrons' origins;[40] for instance, the Italians utilised the Neo-Venetian Gothic style[41], the Shaftesbury Building was built in an English architectural style and there was also the Rococo Revival.[42] The churches adopted the Neo-Romanesque and Neo-Classical styles.[43] The Moorish revival style was utilised on a grand scale in administrative buildings like the Suez Canal Administration building, with its three

36 Piaton, 'Port Said: Cosmopolitan Urban Rules', p. 4, 5; Céline Frémaux, 'Town Planning, Architecture and Migrations in Suez Canal Port Cities: Exchanges and Resistances', in *Port Cities: Dynamic Landscapes and Global Networks*, ed. by Carola Hein (Abingdon: Routledge, 2011), pp. 156–73.

37 Piaton, 'Port Said: Cosmopolitan Urban Rules', p. 5; Frémaux and Volait, 'Inventing Space', pp. 259, 260.

38 Piaton, 'Port Said: Cosmopolitan Urban Rules', p. 9.

39 Beaux Arts, the predominant architectural style in mid-nineteenth-century Europe, was adopted by the French in their colonies. This style combined classical details with modern lines and materials like iron and glass.

40 Frémaux, 'Town Planning', p. 159.

41 The Neo-Venetian Gothic style originated in Venice as a revival of medieval Gothic architecture with its ornate patterns and lancet windows.

42 The Rococo Revival incorporated elements of the Rococo style, including curves and floral ornamentation.

43 The Neo-Romanesque style was inspired by the medieval Romanesque architecture, with its high towers and tiled roofs. The Neo-Classical style revived Roman classical architecture, including columns and other elements.

green domes.[44] For the SCC, this style was a means of demonstrating dominance while also appealing to Egyptians by expressing respect for local traditions.[45]

After the reconstruction of the Arab quarter in 1885, the SCC imposed strict codes for building materials and aesthetics that were enforced by the Egyptian authorities. Before any construction could begin, a permit was required from the city commission—or after 1911, from the city council. Such measures helped to maintain the architectural quality of the city.[46] The architecture in the Arab quarter exhibited European influences in its balance and symmetry,[47] while also integrating Islamic motifs, adapted to modern needs.

Port Said developed a special architectural typology generated by the integration of European architectural styles, Islamic ornamentation and the tropical architectural elements from the initial phase of the city's construction.[48] This architectural typology was embodied by the high wooden verandas of residential buildings, as most buildings in Port Said at the time had three to four floors due to the high cost and scarcity of suitable land for construction.[49]

These verandas offered an ecological solution for the hot climate, shading building facades from the sun while allowing air circulation for ventilation.[50] Although verandas were typical of nineteenth-century tropical architecture as they were favoured by Europeans inhabiting the hot climates of overseas colonies, they were typically made mostly of cast iron and rarely more than two storeys high. In contrast, the verandas

44 The Moorish revival style drew from Islamic architecture, popularised by Europe's fascination with the Orient in the mid-nineteenth century.

45 ElKerdany, 'Port Said', p. 24.

46 Mohamed El Amrousi, 'Beyond Muslim Space: Jeddah, Muscat, Aden and Port Said' (PhD thesis, University of California, Los Angeles, 2001).

47 ElKerdany, 'Port Said', p. 21.

48 El Amrousi, 'Imperial Sanctuaries', p. 71–72; Claudine Piaton, 'Architecture patronale dans l'isthme de Suez (1859–1956)', *Annales islamologiques*, 50 (2016), 11–53, https://doi.org/10.4000/anisl.2112; The city's first constructions, built between 1859 and 1869, had a seaside resort aesthetic with tiled roofs and surrounding wooden verandas to provide shade from the sun. However, these buildings were replaced in the 1880s.

49 Piaton, 'Port Said—Decaying Wooden Verandas'.

50 Baller, 'Strategies for the Preservation', p. 43.

in Port Said, with their wooden construction and exceptional height, are not seen anywhere else in the world (see Figure 11.1).[51]

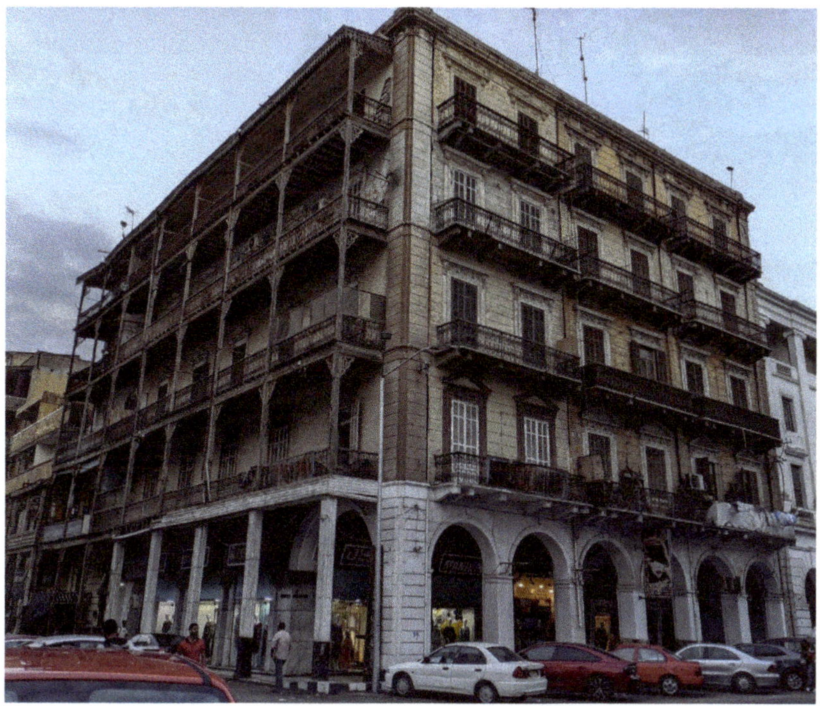

Fig. 11.1 Four-floor-high wooden verandas in the Ifrang quarter. Author's photograph, 2020, CC BY-NC-ND.

The detailing of verandas was influenced by Islamic ornaments but standardised and prefabricated according to modern standards. This architectural typology is present in both Arab and European quarters, but with variations according to the preferences of the inhabitants. In the European quarter (Ifrang), verandas were spacious with delicate ornaments (see Figure 11.1), while in the Arab quarter, verandas were narrower and partly enclosed with mashrabiya-like lattices that could be raised or lowered according to inhabitants' privacy needs (see Figure 11.2).[52]

51 Piaton, 'Port Said—Decaying Wooden Verandas'.
52 Baller, 'Strategies for the Preservation', p. 43; ElKerdany, 'Port Said', p. 21–23.

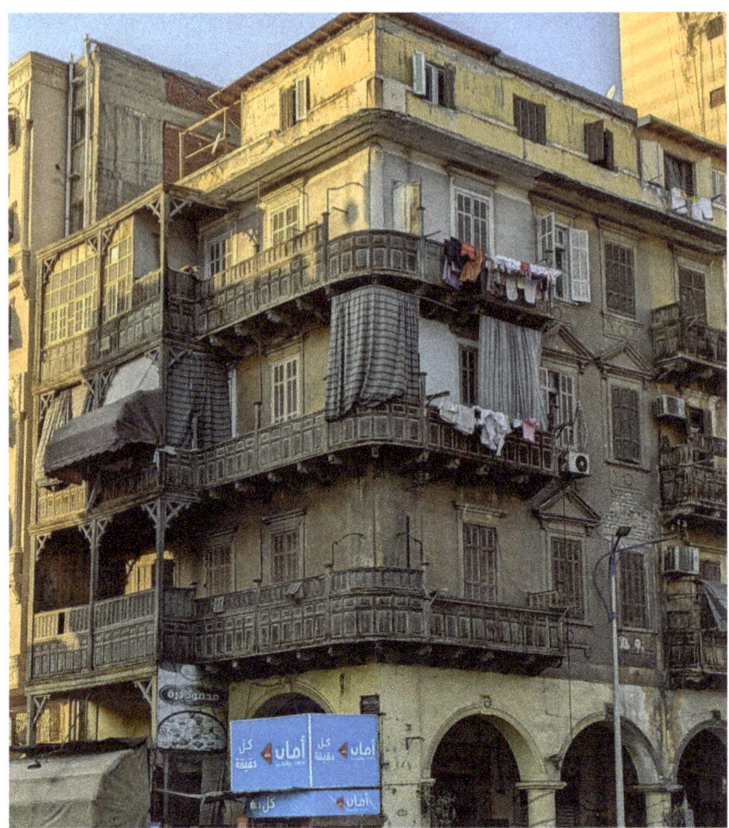

Fig. 11.2 Partly closed wooden veranda in the Arab quarter. Author's photograph, 2020, CC BY-NC-ND.

The combination of arcades along main streets and wooden verandas on secondary streets fostered a complementary relationship between architecture and street hierarchy. Each street corner presented a different scenario depending on its location: open, rounded, or closed angle arcades; a brick arcade and a wooden veranda; or two wooden verandas. The distinctive appearance of each intersection signalled the transition from one urban level to another, giving each street its own identity and displaying a wealth of architectural expressions.[53] Despite the vast diversity of their ornamentation, thanks to the talented woodworkers from the nearby city of Damietta, these wooden verandas lend Port Said a unique air of homogeneity.[54]

53 Noweir, 'Devenir patrimonial'.

54 Piaton, 'Port Said—Decaying Wooden Verandas'.

During the 1920s and 1930s, Port Said experienced growth in all directions. The city gained significant land to the north due to the coastal accretion brought about by the western breakwater. Furthermore, the Arab quarter grew considerably, reclaiming land on Lake Manzala to the south and west but retaining its boundary along Muhammad Ali Street.[55] After the First World War, the SCC needed more workshops and housing for its employees. As a result, Port Fouad, a new quarter on the eastern bank of the canal opposite Port Said,[56] was constructed. Port Fouad was inaugurated in 1926, and its master plan incorporated some attributes of the Garden City with its large boulevards, diagonal streets and vast green areas. Port Fouad is famous for the villas of SCC workers, inspired by workers' houses in the mining village of Dourges in northern France but adapted to the climate of Egypt and decorated by red fired bricks in Neo-Moorish style (see Figure 11.3).[57] Modern architectural styles appeared during this period. While the City Council banned wooden verandas in 1921, the European quarter and Port Fouad became experimental grounds for the Art Deco style.[58] New buildings were constructed of reinforced concrete with rectangular forms, clean lines and unornamented facades.

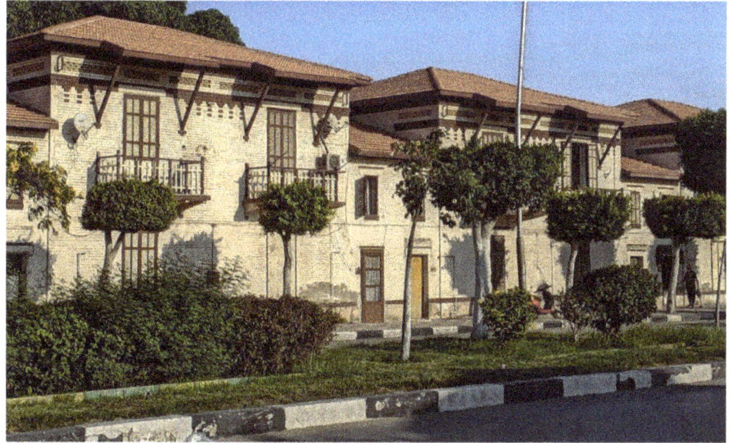

Fig. 11.3 SCC workers' villas in Port Fouad. Author's photograph, 2020, CC BY-NC-ND.

55 Noweir, 'Devenir patrimonial'.
56 Piaton, 'Port Said: Cosmopolitan Urban Rules', p. 11.
57 Piaton, 'Architecture patronale'.
58 Piaton, 'Port Said: Cosmopolitan Urban Rules', p. 8; Wladika, 'Port Said', p. 61.

Port Said: The Valiant City

After the War of 1956,[59] foreigners, fearing the loss of their investments due to nationalisation policies, sold their properties and businesses to Egyptians and left the city.[60] Consequently, Port Said's cosmopolitan era came to an end as the city transformed into a modern Egyptian city and a model of nationalism. The European quarter officially became the Al-Sharq quarter, and the monarchical street names were renamed after Arab and Nasser regime figures. The local authorities built a new quarter, Al-Manakh, to provide social housing for workers and war survivors, dominated by typical apartment blocks with austere architecture and low-quality construction.[61]

After only ten years, Israel seized the Sinai Peninsula and occupied the eastern bank of the Suez Canal in the Six-Day War of June 1967. Port Said was evacuated in 1969, and its people fled to Cairo and towns in the Nile Delta. Following the war of October 1973, Israeli forces withdrew into Sinai, and Port Saidians began to return home. The city was degraded after five years of abandonment, and the Israelis had destroyed entire residential blocks.[62]

The main political objective in 1975 was to achieve the reconstruction of the canal cities as quickly as possible. In rehabilitating the old quarters of Port Said, the planners sought to preserve the old city's grid plan and the style of the arcaded buildings to maintain the character and continuity of these quarters. To accommodate the growing population, the planners had to expand the city to the southwest, utilising land artificially reclaimed from Lake Manzala to build three new quarters, leaving the Mediterranean coastline free for recreational development.

---

59 The War of 1956, also known as the Suez Crisis or the tripartite aggression on Egypt, followed the decision of President Gamal Abdel-Nasser to nationalise the Anglo-French Suez Canal Company. Britain and France attacked Port Said on 29 October 1956 in an effort to re-occupy the Suez Canal. Under intense pressure from the United States, Soviet Union and United Nations, British and French forces withdrew from Port Said on 22 December 1956 and the Suez Canal came under full Egyptian management.

60 Cantarella, 'Notable Families'.

61 Mohamed Elshahed, 'Revolutionary Modernism? Architecture and the Politics of Transition in Egypt 1936–1967' (PhD thesis, New York University, 2015).

62 Frédérique Bruyas, 'Aménagement de la ville de Port-Saïd, le point de vue de l'architecte', *Egypte monde arabe*, 1.23 (1995), 131–68, https://doi.org/10.4000/ema.969

For financial expediency and efficiency, the new quarters were planned according to the modern neighbourhood unit concept, as the grid pattern and arcaded buildings were deemed too expensive.[63]

Port Said: The Duty-Free City

In 1975, President Sadat designated the entirety of Port Said as the first duty-free zone in Egypt. This was part of the vision of Port Said and the canal towns as centres for Egyptian development and counterweights to Cairo and Alexandria.[64] After this declaration, Port Said experienced a dramatic rise in trade and imports. The city became a hub for Egyptians seeking to buy imported goods. The duty-free status attracted unskilled labour from other governorates, causing the city's population to double in the last quarter of the twentieth century.[65]

The economic boom precipitated by duty-free status accelerated the transformation of the built environment. The Arab quarter became a major textile market where commerce occupied the entire ground level, with arcades and side streets converted into open markets closed to traffic. However, over the course of thirty years, the massive crowds of shoppers and the area's transformation into a market and depository weakened the Arab quarter, hastening its decline.[66]

Duty-free status changed the economic and social climate of Port Said. Although the city thrived, ranking first among Egyptian cities on the Human Development Index, it also attracted activities like smuggling and illegal trade. In 2002, the government declared that nearly all duty-free zone privileges in the city would be gradually phased out, except for those promoting manufacturing. Since 2009, Port Said has been in the grips of an economic depression.[67]

63 Ibid.; Michael Welbank and Anthony Edwards, 'Port Said: Planning for Reconstruction and Development', *Third World Planning Review*, 3.2 (1981), 143-60.

64 Bruyas, 'Aménagement de la ville'; Welbank and Edwards, 'Port Said', p. 144.

65 Cantarella, 'Notable Families', p. 183.

66 Noweir, 'Devenir patrimonial'.

67 Cantarella, 'Notable Families'.

Port Said Today

By the beginning of the twenty-first century, Port Said had become a city without a hinterland. It forms a peninsula hemmed by the Mediterranean Sea to the north, the Suez Canal to the east and Lake Manzala to the south and west. The scarcity of available land has led to sky-rocketing land prices and increasing pressure on the historical complexes in the Ifrang and Arab quarters, where real estate investors began demolishing historic structures and replacing them with aesthetically poor high-rise buildings.[68]

Several local associations have made efforts to protect the unique urban heritage of Port Said. In 2002, the Alliance Française, the Port Said-based French Cultural Association, embarked on an advocacy campaign to preserve the city's urban heritage, collaborating with the École de Chaillot to document more than four hundred historic buildings.[69] In 2008, several local cultural organisations launched a public campaign titled 'The Civil Campaign for Protecting Port Said's heritage'. They organised forums and consultations with academics and government officials to advocate for the preservation of the urban heritage of the city. These efforts resulted in the declaration of Cabinet Decree No. 1947 in 2009 and Cabinet Decree No. 1096 in 2011, which recognised 644 buildings in Port Said as historic structures. Of these buildings, 340 (51.8%) were located in the Ifrang quarter (officially Al-Sharq quarter), 139 in Port Fouad (21.5%), 106 in the Arab quarter (16.5%) and 59 in the Al-Manakh quarter (9.2%).[70]

Despite the Cabinet decrees and the various campaigns to preserve Port Said's historic buildings, these structures continue to be demolished. According to a field survey conducted by Stefanie Wladika in 2015, only four years after the Cabinet decrees, twenty-four historic buildings had been razed to the ground. Furthermore, over half of the historic buildings in the Arab quarter and about twenty-five percent of historic buildings in the Ifrang quarter are in poor condition, while the historic

68 Noweir, 'Devenir patrimonial'; ElKerdany, 'Port Said'.

69 Jasmin Shata, 'Urban Stress Relief in Heritage Sites as a Sustaining Approach—The Case of Port Said' (master's thesis, Ain Shams University and University of Stuttgart, 2016), pp. 62, 63, https://iusd.asu.edu.eg/wp-content/uploads/2017/08/14-Shata.pdf

70 Megahed, 'Heritage-Based Sustainability', p. 102.

buildings owned by the Suez Canal Authority are well-conserved under its full supervision.[71]

The rapid demolition of historic buildings has led to the loss of architectural treasures and a conspicuous transformation of the built environment in several zones. This is especially true along the canal and main streets, where high-rise buildings have now replaced or concealed the historic wooden structures. The facades of these new buildings are unpleasantly incongruent in dimensions and styles. The densification process has also altered the land use rate and negatively affected the urban fabric and infrastructure of historic quarters. This systematic disfigurement of the city has stemmed from the uniform application of local building codes throughout the city without any distinction between quarters. If this trend continues, Port Said risks permanently losing its unique urban character.

Applying the Historic Urban Landscape Approach in Port Said

The discipline and practice of urban heritage conservation have evolved in recent decades from a monument-centred notion of heritage, in which cities were divided into separate conservation areas, to an alternative approach that looks beyond the preservation of the built environment and embraces a broader notion of heritage.

The Historic Urban Landscape approach promotes functional diversity and social development within cities by recognising regional contexts. This approach aims to enhance the public use of urban spaces and provides tools for managing transformations in the built environment to ensure that any intervention in a historical setting is harmonious with the existing heritage. UNESCO has identified seven steps for cities to implement the Historic Landscape Approach in their urban contexts:[72]

71 Wladika, 'Port Said', p. 84.

72 UNESCO, *New Life for Historic Cities: The Historic Urban Landscape Approach Explained* (Paris: UNESCO, 2013), p. 16, https://whc.unesco.org/uploads/activities/documents/activity-727-1.pdf

1. Undertake a Full Assessment of the City's Natural, Cultural and Human Resources

According to the Recommendation on the Historic Urban Landscape approach, the historic urban landscape includes: the site's topography, geomorphology, hydrology and natural features, its built environment, both historic and contemporary, its infrastructures above and below ground, its open spaces and gardens, its land use patterns and spatial organization, perceptions and visual relationships. It also includes social and cultural practices and values, economic processes and the intangible dimensions of heritage as related to diversity and identity.[73]

The local authorities in Port Said must undertake the full documentation and mapping of natural and cultural urban assets in order to understand the complex layering of the city, identify its values, and present them comprehensively. Documenting the state of urban heritage and its evolution is crucial for developing necessary protective procedures.

2. Use Participatory Planning and Stakeholder Consultations to Decide on Conservation Aims and Actions

The valuation and assessment of urban heritage should not be limited to the decisions of a select few social actors. It is necessary to engage diverse stakeholder groups in these decision-making processes, as the conservation of urban heritage is not only a concern of the cultural elite but has become a concern of a broader range of social actors. This includes all those interested in its economic and social values, such as local government entities, NGOs, heritage users, entrepreneurs, property owners and culture producers.

Participatory planning empowers stakeholders to identify multiple values in their urban areas, incorporating their views to develop visions, goals and action plans for the preservation of their heritage. Stakeholder consultations facilitate dialogue between groups with conflicting interests and encourage learning from local communities.

73 UNESCO, *Records of the General Conference*, p. 52.

3. Assess the Vulnerability of Urban Heritage to Socio-economic Pressures

Urban growth in Port Said is proceeding on an unprecedented scale, transforming the city's urban image. The unmanaged urban densification process jeopardises the city's sense of place, the urban fabric's functionality and Port Said's identity. This threat calls for strong urban policies to protect the city's identity and requires the approval and support of all stakeholders.

Moreover, rents in historic residential buildings can be as low as less than half a US dollar per month as a result of a rent-blocking law dating back to the Nasser era.[74] These derisory rental prices for historic residences leave landlords without sufficient income to maintain their properties.[75]

Restricting financial gain from heritage properties can compel owners to abandon these properties, leading to their deterioration and demolition. Urban heritage conservation can only be viable if heritage property owners benefit from the conservation. On the other hand, market-driven processes of heritage regeneration may lead to the displacement of lower-income residents. Urban heritage conservation policies must be socially sensitive and ensure inclusive regeneration practices.

4. Integrate Urban Heritage into a Wider Framework of City Development

It is essential that all stakeholders realise the value of urban heritage and its contribution to the city's socio-economic development. If urban heritage is properly managed, new functions like services and tourism can emerge and contribute to the city's economic diversity.

Urban heritage conservation must be integrated into the urban development process through heritage, environmental and social impact assessments during decision-making processes. Public institutions responsible for urban heritage should be integrated into decision-making and local agenda development and must transition

74 Moore, '"The Alexandria You Are Losing"'.
75 ElKerdany, 'Port Said'; Noweir, 'Devenir patrimonial'.

from preserving monumental heritage to sustainably utilising the broad range of urban heritage assets.

5. Prioritise Policies and Actions for Conservation and Development

Official conservation efforts and regulatory frameworks for heritage preservation have been geared towards preserving monuments attributed to Egypt's primary historical eras, namely the Ancient Egyptian, Coptic, and Islamic periods, often at the exclusion of modern urban heritage. Present socio-economic challenges require adopting new policies that recognise this heritage and maintain a balance between economic and cultural values in urban environments.

It is thus incumbent upon the national government to integrate urban heritage conservation into national policy planning and incorporate heritage conservation strategies into development agendas. Existing laws must be amended to explicitly include modern urban heritage as one of Egypt's primary historical values, and regulatory systems should adopt legislative measures for conserving tangible and intangible heritage attributes. Regulations regarding the use of tangible private heritage should reflect local conditions and progress towards flexible frameworks that promote regeneration and the sensible adaptive reuse of heritage for current needs. At the same time, these regulations should ensure that heritage assets are well managed and effectively utilised to avoid the irreparable loss of heritage assets. Furthermore, legal amendments are necessary to encourage private sector and landlord investment in conservation projects. This could include tax exemption schemes and other flexible financing options to foster local investment.

Local authorities cannot enforce these laws without delineating institutional responsibilities, improving the efficiency of urban governance and bolstering capacities for urban heritage conservation. The traditional approach of comprehensive conservation should be reinforced regarding monuments and public spaces of national importance.

6. Establish Appropriate (Public-private) Partnerships and Local Management Frameworks

Urban heritage conservation is not solely the responsibility of the government; it requires a blend of effective public governance, efficient markets and engagement from all social actors. National cultural entities provide the legal and operational frameworks for heritage conservations. The government's task is to build quality infrastructures and public spaces in heritage areas and establish a flexible urban management structure to regulate private investments in these areas.

With the under-developed management institutions in Port Said, ad hoc solutions can be implemented, such as designating urban heritage areas as special districts with special construction regulations supported by national government institutions.

7. Develop Mechanisms for the Coordination of the Various Activities between Different Actors

Urban heritage conservation must shift away from reliance on the government towards mechanisms that coordinate the contributions and perspectives of all local actors. National and local NGOs can participate in developing tools and disseminating best practices for urban heritage conservation, while academic and research centres can develop scientific research on various aspects of urban heritage. Government entities remain instrumental in the development, implementation and assessment of conservation policies. Particularly at the local level, authorities have an important role to play in preparing urban development plans which align with the heritage values of their communities. Development foundations can harmonise their development projects in urban areas with the Historic Urban Landscape approach.

Conclusion

The study of Port Said's architectural and urban features reveals the richness of its architectural heritage and the uniqueness of its urban character, underscoring the city's potential to become a prominent tourist destination in Egypt. However, the current urbanisation trends in the city are destroying its architectural character rather than strengthening it. The Historic Urban Landscape approach presents an effective solution for conserving the city's urban heritage and leveraging it as an asset for the sustainable development of Port Said. By encouraging private sector and landlord investments in the rehabilitation of historic buildings, it is possible to spur the city's economic development through promoting urban tourism and commercial activities. Additionally, this approach contributes to social development by creating jobs, thus aiding poverty reduction. There are also considerable environmental benefits in reusing historic buildings, which were designed to be climatically suitable, rather than constructing new modern buildings that consume more energy.

According to the Historic Urban Landscape approach, the conservation of the urban heritage in Port Said should be incorporated into a comprehensive development plan at the city level. In this plan, heritage complexes would be designated as 'historic districts' within a larger agglomeration, subject to special construction regulations. In this way, these historic districts can be integrated into current development projects. Local authorities should foster the participatory dimension of the heritage conservation process by collaborating with the local community to explore possible strategies for conserving urban heritage. They must also communicate with the stakeholders behind local initiatives, who can offer valuable expertise and innovative solutions in promoting cultural heritage.

At the national level, it is necessary to reform the legal and regulatory frameworks governing heritage conservation. The existing laws must be amended to recognise modern urban heritage as one of Egypt's primary historical values. Amendments should promote the restoration and adaptive repurposing of heritage as well as encourage private sector investments in conservation projects.

Bibliography

Baller, Inken, 'Strategies for the Preservation of the Heritage of the Suez Region and Port Said as World Heritage Site', in *Revitalizing City Districts: Transformation Partnership for Urban Design and Architecture in Historic City Districts*, ed. by Hebatalla Abouelfadl, Dalila ElKerdany and Christoph Wessling (Cham: Springer International Publishing, 2017), pp. 35–51, https://doi.org/10.1007/978-3-319-46289-9_3

Bruyas, Frédérique, 'Aménagement de la ville de Port-Saïd, le point de vue de l'architecte', *Egypte monde arabe*, 1.23 (1995), 131–68, https://doi.org/10.4000/ema.969

Cantarella, Christine H., 'Notable Families and Capitalist Parasites in Egypt's Former Free Zone: Law, Trade, and Uncertainty', in *Anthropology of the Middle East and North Africa—Into the New Millennium*, ed. by Sherine Hafez and Susan Slyomovics (Bloomington, IN: Indiana University Press, 2013), pp. 165–84.

Carminati, Lucia, 'Dividing and Ruling a Mediterranean Port-City: The Many Boundaries Within Late 19th century Port Said', in *Controversial Heritage and Divided Memories from the Nineteenth Through the Twentieth Centuries: Multi-Ethnic Cities in the Mediterranean World*, ed. by Marco Folin and Heleni Porfyriou, 2 vols. (New York: Routledge, 2020), II, pp. 30–44.

Carminati, Lucia, 'Port Said and Ismailia as Desert Marvels: Delusion and Frustration on the Isthmus of Suez, 1859–1869', *Journal of Urban History*, 46.3 (2020), 622–47, https://doi.org/10.1177/0096144218821342

Crosnier-Leconte, M., Ghitani, G. and Amin, N., eds., *Port-Saïd: Architectures XIXe–XXe siècles* (Cairo: IFAO, 2006).

El Amrousi, Mohamed, 'Beyond Muslim Space: Jeddah, Muscat, Aden and Port Said' (PhD thesis, University of California, Los Angeles, 2001).

El Amrousi, Mohamed, 'Imperial Sanctuaries: Arab Urban Enclaves on the East African Coast', in *Colonial Architecture and Urbanism in Africa—Intertwined and Contested Histories*, ed. by Fassil Demissie (Farnham: Ashgate Publishing Limited, 2012), pp. 67–84.

ElKerdany, Dalila, 'Port Said: A Cosmopolitan Heritage Under Threat', in *Revitalizing City Districts: Transformation Partnership for Urban Design and Architecture in Historic City Districts*, ed. by Hebatalla Abouelfadl, Dalila ElKerdany and Christoph Wessling (Cham: Springer International Publishing, 2017), pp. 15–33, https://doi.org/10.1007/978-3-319-46289-9_2

Elshahed, Mohamed, 'Revolutionary Modernism? Architecture and the Politics of Transition in Egypt 1936–1967' (PhD thesis, New York University, 2015).

Frémaux, Céline, 'Santé et hygiénisme dans les villes du canal de Suez', *Égypte/Monde arabe*, 3.4 (2007), 75–101, https://doi.org/10.4000/ema.1759

Frémaux, Céline, 'Town Planning, Architecture and Migrations in Suez Canal Port Cities: Exchanges and Resistances', in *Port Cities: Dynamic Landscapes and Global Networks*, ed. by Carola Hein (Abingdon: Routledge, 2011), pp. 156–73.

Frémaux, C. and Volait, M., 'Inventing Space in the Age of Empire: Planning Experiments and Achievements along Suez Canal in Egypt (1859–1956)', *Planning Perspectives*, 24.2 (2009), 255–62, https://doi.org/10.1080/02665430902734350

Huber, Valeska, 'Connecting Colonial Seas: The International Colonization of Port Said and The Suez Canal during and after the First World War', *European Review of History: Revue européenne d'histoire*, 19.1 (2012), 141–61, https://doi.org/10.1080/13507486.2012.643612

Huber, Valeska, *Channelling Mobilities—Migration and Globalisation in the Suez Canal Region and Beyond, 1869–1914* (New York: Cambridge University Press, 2013), https://doi.org/10.1080/13507486.2012.643612

Huber, Valeska, 'Cosmopolitanism on the Move: Port Said around 1900' (20 June 2017), *Global Urban History*, https://globalurbanhistory.com/2017/06/20/cosmopolitanism-on-the-move-port-said-around-1900/

Lotfy, Mostafa M., 'Biographies of Port-Said: Everydayness of State, Dwellers, and Strangers' (master's thesis, The American University in Cairo, 2018), https://fount.aucegypt.edu/cgi/viewcontent.cgi?article=2393&context=etds

Megahed, Naglaa A., 'Heritage-Based Sustainability in Port Said: Classification of Styles and Future Development', *Archnet-IJAR: International Journal of Architectural Research*, 8.1 (2014), 94–107, https://www.archnet.org/publications/9097

Moore, James, '"The Alexandria You Are Losing"? Urban Heritage and Activism in Egypt since the 2011 Revolution', *Journal of Eastern Mediterranean Archaeology & Heritage Studies*, 5.3–4 (2017), 427–44, https://doi.org/10.5325/jeasmedarcherstu.5.3-4.0427

Noweir, Sawsan, 'Devenir patrimonial contre développement urbain: l'exemple de Port-Saïd', *Autrepart: Revue de sciences sociales au Sud*, 33 (2005), 109–26, https://doi.org/10.3917/autr.033.0109

Piaton, Claudine, 'Port Said—Decaying Wooden Verandas Tell the Story of a City', *Al-Rawi: Egypt's Heritage Review*, 3 (2011), 22–29.

Piaton, Claudine, 'European Construction Companies in the Towns along the Suez Canal', in *Building beyond the Mediterranean: Studying the Archives of European Businesses (1860–1970)*, ed. by Claudine Piaton, Ezio Godoli and David Peyceré (Arles: Publications de l'Institut national d'histoire de l'art, 2012), pp. 92–103, https://doi.org/10.4000/books.inha.12729

Piaton, Claudine, 'Architecture patronale dans l'isthme de Suez (1859-1956)', *Annales islamologiques, 50* (2016), 11–53, https://doi.org/10.4000/anisl.2112

Piaton, Claudine, 'Port Said: Cosmopolitan Urban Rules and Architecture (1858–1930)', in *Revitalizing City Districts: Transformation Partnership for Urban Design and Architecture in Historic City Districts*, ed. by Hebatalla Abouelfadl, Dalila ElKerdany and Christoph Wessling (Cham: Springer International Publishing, 2017), pp. 3–14, https://doi.org/10.1007/978-3-319-46289-9_1

Rojas, Eduardo, 'Urban Heritage for Sustainable Development', in *Culture: Urban Future; Global Report on Culture for Sustainable Urban Development*, ed. by I. G. Bokova (Paris: UNESCO, 2016), pp. 193–99.

Shata, Jasmin, 'Urban Stress Relief in Heritage Sites as a Sustaining Approach—The Case of Port Said' (master's thesis, Ain Shams University and University of Stuttgart, 2016), https://iusd.asu.edu.eg/wp-content/uploads/2017/08/14-Shata.pdf

The Census of Egypt: Taken in 1917 (Cairo: Ministry of Finance—Statistical and Census Department, 1917).

UNESCO, *Records of the General Conference, 36th session, Paris, 25 October—10 November 2011, v. 1: Resolutions* (Paris: UNESCO, 2011), https://unesdoc.unesco.org/ark:/48223/pf0000215084.page=52

UNESCO, *New Life for Historic Cities: The Historic Urban Landscape Approach Explained* (Paris: UNESCO, 2013), https://whc.unesco.org/uploads/activities/documents/activity-727-1.pdf

UNESCO, *Culture Urban Future: Global Report on Culture for Sustainable Urban Development* (Paris: UNESCO, 2016), https://unesdoc.unesco.org/ark:/48223/pf0000245999?posInSet=1&queryId=c5c18968-cce2-406c-aa33-a21371d22f90

Welbank, M. and A. Edwards, 'Port Said: Planning for Reconstruction and Development', *Third World Planning Review*, 3: 2 (1981), 143-60, https://doi.org/10.3828/twpr.3.2.a217921vl8352128

Wladika, Stefanie A., 'Port Said—No Future without the Past: Integrated Rehabilitation Concept for the Urban Heritage' (master's thesis, Ain Shams University and University of Stuttgart, 2015), https://iusd.asu.edu.eg/wp-content/uploads/2015/11/3rdInt_Wladika.pdf

12. Old City Atmospheres in the Age of Globalisation

Irina Oznobikhina

Introduction

Efforts to formulate basic foundational principles for approaching the cultural value of the built environment at the international level arise from current historical, political, social and cultural considerations. Within a rapidly developing design and technology industry, the issues of environmental protection and public sphere reform require specific contextual solutions. These solutions merit careful consideration in order to protect and simultaneously develop the urban landscape without risking the loss of essential cultural places and local identities.

The cultural heritage of the past and the rapid technological development of the future are intertwined within the process of globalisation, where the significant value of old cities is often underestimated. The focus of contemporary urban theorists is not limited to environmental problems, as they also seek methods for preserving cultural monuments and shed light on the ways contemporary cities are planned and governed. As 'rational' planning guided by market-led strategies remains a leading trend, atmospheric considerations related to the historical and sacred architecture of old cities is undeservingly neglected.

Within the architectural fabric of old towns, there is an entire class of building compositions designed to provide access to tangible cultural heritage while maintaining the intangible and spiritual essence of urban settings with its associated practices. The architectural sphere

 https://doi.org/10.11647/OBP.0412.12

is still dependent on social, economic and political factors, perpetually opposed to the ideological weight of prevailing technological trends and capitalistic schemes. Drawing attention to the significance of old cities and cultural heritage is imperative to bring them out of the shadows cast by the rapidly changing digital urban reality and into public discourse.

Maintaining atmospheres necessitates distinguishing the atmospheric features of cultural heritage from the disciplinary framework of architectural history and descriptive case studies. Alongside the concept of local identity, cultural uniqueness is based on many factors, including natural features and the built environment. As crucial elements of a cohesive whole, historical and contemporary land-use models, spatial organisations and visual representations should not be neglected, especially within the contemporarily globalised world. The local identity of each city encompasses the seemingly intangible and transient sphere of the urban commons as well as cultural heritage sites, historical monuments and sacred architecture. These elements provide a deep sense of anamnestic habitualness, transferring connections with the past into a rapidly evolving future. Local identity and a sense of place generate an atmosphere of pre-reflective experience and the desire to rediscover historical parts of cities.

This chapter explores old city atmospheres, investigating the significance of authentic first-person experiences determined by one's bodily disposition and embodied presence in this space. This research examines the intrinsic correlation between place and atmosphere, enriching the (neo)phenomenological method with enactivist theory. The (neo)phenomenological paradigm is not as vague as it may initially seem, and its utility has been proven in many applied human sciences, including architecture, geography, sound studies and urban planning. However, methodologies used in urban studies remain constrained by cognitive and qualitative origins, often leading to predictable outcomes. The combination of methods within this research endeavours to integrate concepts, enabling the investigation of phenomena that defy explanation within the exclusive scope of conventional representational theory, with special focus on the affectivity of atmospheres.[1] Indeed, as unexpected

1 Derek McCormack, 'Engineering Affective Atmospheres on the Moving Geographies of the 1897 Andrée Expedition', *Cultural Geographies*, 15 (2008),

externalities of urban digitalisation and original atmospheres of old cities, such phenomena lie beyond what can be described by discursive and comparative methods alone. The benefits of this methodological combination form the core of this research, offering critical analysis of old city atmospheres.

At a more detailed level, the urban landscape, with its innumerable interconnected streets, squares, public spaces, residential quarters, functionally designed buildings and touristic routes, determine the city's image and, crucially, its atmosphere, which represents its genuine identity. While atmosphere is still a controversial concept evading clear definition and ontological clarity, there is a broad awareness of its essential features, especially within disciplines such as architecture and urban design. However, several questions remain as to atmosphere's role in old cities and architecture, its location, its individual and collective perception, the affective quality of its experience and the source of its significance for urban dwellers. The critical and ultimate question to emerge from this inquiry is how to save the old city atmosphere and integrate it into the contemporary urban context of a rapidly changing technological world. All these questions will be addressed within this chapter.

Affective Turn vs. Digital Turn

Digital communication and global technological development are steadily transforming our world, generating an increasing amount of data that opens an unexplored horizon of new discourses and levels of value creation. Digital technologies are systematically changing our way of life and the spaces we inhabit with a multitude of new digital services, facial recognition systems, artificial intelligence programs, machine learning, big data and the internet, among other indicators of the 'digital turn'.[2] Rather than analysing the reasons, social factors and inevitable political manipulations to come,[3] this chapter shifts focus

413–30.

2 James Ash and Agnieszka Leszczynski, 'Digital Turn, Digital Geographies?', *Progress, Human Geography*, 42 (2016), 25–43.

3 Anna Artyushina, 'The EU Is Launching a Market for Personal Data. Here's What that Means for Privacy' (11 August 2020), *MIT Technology*

from the far-reaching consequences of urban digitalisation to investigate the way they affect the atmospheres of old cities.

The natural interests of large digital corporations (LDCs) lie in major profit increases and value surplus rather than the functional improvement and sustainability of urban environments. For companies like Amazon, Google, Microsoft and others, contemporary urbanity offers fertile ground for monopolisation and the strengthening of market positions through the range of services and technologies available to enhance their influence. In this context, user-friendliness, convenience and the utility of innovations supported by LDCs are some of the most effective tools for developing 'surveillance capitalism'.[4] This manipulative practice encourages market-led land-use paradigms and increases unforeseen risks within the urban planning sphere.[5] It is important to emphasise that apart from personal data and statistics, the main manipulation objective of LDCs is the atmosphere, as the atmosphere[6] of place is sounder than the product itself.[7]

Among recent 'turns', there has also been a so-called 'affective turn' in the humanities.[8] The past decade has witnessed a growing interest in the concepts of atmosphere and affect for their potential to unify groups of people, furnishing a common reality for the 'perceiver and the perceived'.[9] This interest extends across various fields, particularly in sound studies, architecture, urban planning and geography. A key

---

Review, https://www.technologyreview.com/2020/08/11/1006555/eu-data-trust-trusts-project-privacy-policy-opinion/

4 Shoshana Zuboff, *The Age of Surveillance Capitalism—The Fight for a Human Future at the New Frontier of Power* (London: Profile Books, 2019).

5 Constance Carr and Markus Hesse, 'Sidewalk Labs Closed Down—Whither the Google City?' (2020), *Regions*, https://doi.org/10.1080/13673882.2020.00001070

6 See Gernot Böhme, *Critique of Aesthetic Capitalism* (Milano-Udine: Mimesis International, 2017).

7 Philip Kotler, 'Atmospherics as a Marketing Tool', *Journal of Retailing*, 49 (1974), 48–64.

8 See Patricia Ticineto Clough, and Jean Halley, *The Affective Turn: Theorizing the Social* (Durham, NC: Duke University Press, 2007); Tonino Griffero, *Atmospheres: Aesthetics of Emotional Spaces* (London, New York: Routledge, 2014); Tonino Griffero and Marco Tedeschini, eds., *Atmosphere and Aesthetics: A Plural Perspective* (Cham: Palgrave Macmillan, 2019); Dylan Trigg, 'The Role of Atmosphere in Shared Emotion', *Emotion, Space and Society*, 35 (2020), https://doi.org/10.1016/j.emospa.2020.100658

9 Gernot Böhme, 'Atmosphere as the Fundamental Concept of a New Aesthetics', *Thesis Eleven* 36 (1993), 113–26; Brian Massumi, *Politics of Affect* (Cambridge, MA: Polity Press, 2015); Jan Slaby and Rainer Mühlhoff, 'Affect', in *Affective Societies:*

focus from urban and sonic perspectives is cultivating a critical dialogue between theoretical explorations and empirical fieldwork.[10]

Recent analyses of urban environments[11] and architectural settings have argued that atmosphere constitutes a fundamental aspect of the human experience of the world, affecting the mood and well-being of all who perceive it and shaping pre-reflective experiences and emotional states. The concept of atmosphere is closely tied to notions developed by Martin Heidegger—*Stimmung* [mood] and *Befindlichkeit* [affective situation], referring to a specific sense of being-in (a mood) that can be understood as affective tonality infused into a space.[12] This 'all-encompassing world orientation' can be likened to other concepts unstructured within strict conceptual language frames, such as *Stimmung*, ambiance or aura. Gernot Böhme deals with this issue in his book *Atmospheric Architectures: The Aesthetics of Felt Spaces*, defining the phenomenal role atmospheres play in architecture and aesthetics and providing solid practical as well as theoretical grounding:

> Sensing our own presence is simultaneously to sense the space in which we are present. Where we are (where we find ourselves) can still be interpreted topologically, as positioning in space. And indeed, in sensing our bodily presence, both the distances to things (or, better put, their oppressive closeness or their receding expanse) and the geometry of space come into play.[13]

Böhme aptly observes that this process is better understood in the sense of *bewegungsanmutungen* [movement impressions], such as rising or weighing down. We can sense not only what kind of space surrounds us but also its characteristics and, significantly, its atmosphere. For such an assessment of architectural space, this suggests that one

---

Key Concepts, ed. by Jan Slaby and Christian von Scheve (New York: Routledge, 2019), pp. 27–41.

10 Jurgen Hasse, *Atmosphären der Stadt. Aufgespürte Räume* (Berlin: Jovis, 2012); Federico De Matteis, 'The City as a Mode of Perception: Corporeal Dynamics in Urban Space', in *Handbook of Research on Perception-Driven Approaches to Urban Assessment and Design*, ed. by F. Aletta and J. Xiao (Hershey: IGI Global, 2018), pp. 434–57, https://doi.org/10.4018/978-1-5225-3637-6.ch018

11 Jean-Paul Thibaud, 'Frames of Visibility in Public Places', *Places*, 14 (2001), 42–47.

12 Romano Pocai, *Heideggers Theorie der Befindlichkeit: sein Denken zwischen 1927 und 1933* (Munich: Verlag Karl Alber, 1996).

13 Gernot Böhme, *Atmospheric Architectures: The Aesthetics of Felt Spaces* (London: Bloomsbury Academic, 2017), p. 74.

must physically enter a space in order to 'attune' to it.[14] In this way, atmospheres constrain, infuse and define not only inhabited space but also its temporal dimension, enveloping human values and cultural premises in accordance with the material environment. This illustrates atmospheres' historical particularities and reveals their temporal meaning. As Mikkel Bille, Peter Bjerregaard and Tim Sørensen note, atmospheres 'are at the same time a product of the past and future'.[15] Anticipation and recollection of atmospheres represent the extremes of these temporalities in terms of atmosphere creation in architecture and urban planning. Moreover, this extends to human collectives, easily enfolding crowds and affecting them as a whole. While a wide range of literature illuminates the salient characteristics of atmosphere as a concept, the experience of the subject and the in-between space where atmosphere lies, a notion of such ambiguity seems nearly impossible to grasp.

Architects and designers skilfully navigate the task of affecting moods, feelings and behavioural patterns through the material environment. This gives rise to an array of practical, ethical and philosophical questions concerning the role of atmospheres in different spheres of human life. Some of these questions are raised in this chapter in the specific context of old city architecture in times of technological progress and urban development, particularly concerning the critical shifts in urban planning that threaten cultural heritage objects.

Recalling the introduction, we turn to the subject of atmosphere as an affective dimension with certain aspects that may be manipulated with the aim of 'selling' products, events or even places. The impact of such commercial manoeuvres on human behaviour underscores the controversial distinction between experience perceived as authentic and that which ultimately turns out to be synthetic. This is illustrated in an example provided by Bille, Bjerregaard and Sørensen, citing the geographer Tim Edensor, describing the lack of atmosphere at a new Manchester football stadium.[16] The increasingly commercialised

14 Ibid., p. 75.

15 Mikkel Bille, Peter Bjerregaard and Tim Flohr Sørensen, 'Staging Atmospheres: Materiality, Culture, and the Texture of the In-between', *Emotion, Space and Society*, 15 (2015), 31–38 (p. 34).

16 Ibid.

management of football clubs aims to recreate the original experience at matches by generating the proper atmosphere. However, the genuine atmosphere is created in advance as crowds of fans gather prior to the match, even before they enter the stadium, due to the collective energy—the atmosphere—they produce.

Indeed, there is a dense atmospheric tension between the newly designed stadium atmosphere and the atmosphere generated and energetically supported by fans. This absence of the 'specific' and 'matching' atmosphere appears to come not from technological innovation but from simple subterfuge, as LDCs attempt to influence urban planning and commercialise places, launching products and collecting data to support strategic sales mechanisms rather than the well-being of humans and the environment. The rest is affective memory: when people refer to the 'old' times nostalgically, they do not express a longing for the 'old' but for the more vibrant. The sense of place is always marked by time, activated by the presence of the human body—'the old stadium' with packed terraces of standing crowds that had the power of stirring a 'dense atmosphere'. Changes and renovations can lead to the attenuation of an environment's natural atmosphere. Furthermore, the 'smart city', a leading concept in contemporary urban planning, is associated with a lack of atmosphere as well as new political dimensions and structures.

In light of these considerations, Böhme's remarks about the pervasive side of atmospheric production are quite insightful. Atmospheres tend to emerge naturally with various qualities, in contrast to conventional presumptions of an established and regulated production process. At the same time, Böhme and his followers approach the practice of 'staging' atmospheres as a historic example of how production can engender experiences of narrative setting, akin to the theatre.

In an article on staging atmospheres, another German philosopher, Peter Sloterdijk, makes a shrewd prediction about increasing attention to atmosphere production in the future. He emphasises that future societies will have to recognise their artificiality, as the majority of things 'must be produced technically, and the metaphorical atmosphere as much as the physical atmosphere'.[17] He claims that atmosphere and

17 Peter Sloterdijk, *Neither Sun nor Death* (Los Angeles, CA: Semiotext(e), 2011), p. 245.

sociability have always been manufactured as a collective activity, producing 'a resonance between those who live together'.[18]

This leads to the question of the authentic experience of a place. Scholars from various disciplines apply a multiplicity of approaches to investigate atmosphere as a means by which space can transform into a place with a concrete purpose and the potential to influence its inhabitants in different ways. From the historical, urban and phenomenological perspectives, atmospheres broaden the scope of leading paradigms and methods. Collective and individual experience emerge as an exchange between sociality and detachment in people's ability to attune to place.

In Edensor's view, atmospheres tied to the past are far denser than recent ones, possibly due to the density of emotional layers deposited by individuals and events in their temporal context. When the authenticity of human experience coincides with the purpose of a place, it evokes powerful emotions that not only charge the atmosphere but also become embedded in the place itself. The human body, as a threshold for memories, can be easily affected by atmosphere, thus old cities become enveloped by the flickering past and haunting memories.

Understanding the relationships between urban planning, politics and technological innovation is crucial to mitigate the uncertainties and ecological, ethical and political problems that may arise in the near future. Inhabiting and attuning to a space minimally requires having access to 'a space' to inhabit and attune to. In the twenty-first century, space in which to reflect is increasingly scarce. Technological progress, globalisation and the constant flow of information disrupt human rhythms, hindering the ability to react to external stimuli and causing anxiety, depression and detachment. This all stems from the suffocating mechanisms of capitalism that impose product essentiality and technological 'smartness' by selling illusory experiences through staged or technological atmospheres.

18 Ibid., p. 246.

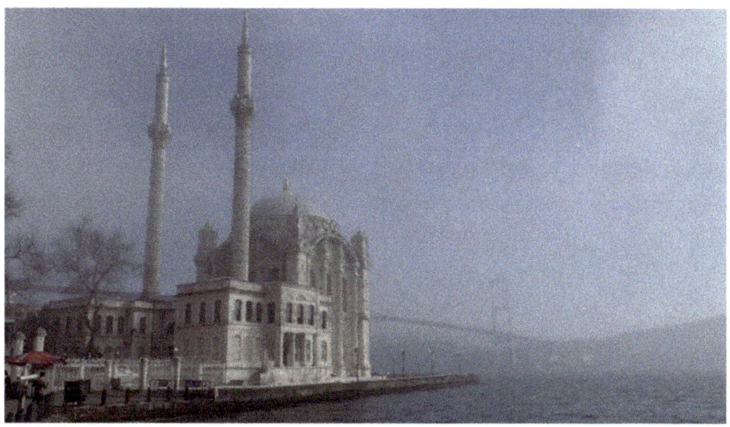

Fig. 12.1 Ortaköy Mosque or Grand Imperial Mosque of Sultan Abdümecid designed in the Neo-Baroque style as an example of a unique atmospheric architectural masterpiece with a distinctive view of the Bosporus Strait and Bridge connecting the European and Asian parts of the city. Author's photograph, 2021, CC BY-NC-ND.

Thus, the 'smartness' of the environment does not always lead to improvement, and it is crucial to maintain the cultural heritage of cities by protecting the historic centres from total demolition or major reconstructions. In light of the historical roots and concept of atmosphere, it is essential for contemporary architecture and urban practices to embrace atmospheres' potential to create places in the authentic sense of the term, fulfilling purposes beyond consumerism dogmas.

Approaching the Spaces Affectively: Atmospheres of Old City Architecture

All attempts to describe the architecture of the past point to the indomitable quest for a spiritual ideal, which cannot be said for the developmental trajectory of contemporary architecture. However, it is worth noting that architecture is generally dependent on certain practical considerations including era, place, climate, context, technical means, construction materials and the structure's main objective and plan. At the same time, a well-designed architectural construction is always more than a mere material representation of an idea, just as profound works of art always convey something beyond their apparent subject matter or physical essence.

This passage is devoted to the (neo)phenomenological analysis of old city architecture, seeking to uncover the particularities of the architecture's corporeal experience. Initially, the phenomenological project of German philosopher Hermann Schmitz was designed to rediscover the key philosophical principles to revitalise dominant Western European thought beyond the subject-object and mind-body split that arose with works of Plato and René Descartes. In this context, blind spots emerge in the perceptible *Leib* [felt body] and corporeal communication, as well as affective involvements as atmospheres, atmospheric sensoriums, sensory perceptions and other significant situations as well as things. Schmitz focuses on affectively tonalised impressions and emotional states as the basis of spontaneous life experiences, which are considered both objects of study and holistic methods within the theoretical framework of (neo)phenomenology aimed at rediscovering human existence.[19]

Schmitz's understanding of space as creating a 'schema' or map that determines location is crucial for the present research. According to him, the focus on the Greek understanding of space and geometry had a substantial impact on how human beings navigate different areas, overlooking the multi-layered, non-Euclidean affective space. Let us briefly examine how Schmitz introduces his atmospheric space theory in order to unveil its significance for architecture and urban planning.

Schmitz identifies *Ortsraum* [locational space], where places, 'mutually determined by the positions and distances of objects situated on them',[20] are physically accessible and familiar. The body cannot be defined without using lines and areas in a three-dimensional volume. However, Schmitz goes further in his queries and asserts that there are area-less spaces, providing the examples of sound or weather. According to this idea, the place these spaces occupy is not three-dimensional due to the absence of edges or lines. In this sense, their typology is composed of natural conditions rather than simply psychological or philosophical predispositions that arise from cognitive processes.

19 See Hermann Schmitz, *System der Philosophie: Band III. Der Raum: Teil 2. Der Gefühlsraum* (Bonn: Bouvier, 2005).

20 Hermann Schmitz, 'Atmospheric Spaces', trans. by Margret Vine, *Ambiances* (2016), 1–11, https://doi.org/10.4000/ambiances.711

There are two neglected yet crucial types of area-less spaces for Schmitz: the felt body space and the affective spaces as atmospheres. The felt body is not a lived body as it may go beyond the skin of one's *Körper* [material body] and can be described without referencing the five senses and the original body schema[21]—the representation of one's physical body, gained from experiential awareness.

Notably, felt bodies can be interconnected incorporeally through a common vitality in the *Einleibung* [en-corporation] —another term Schmitz develops through deriving it from psychology where the term 'encorporation' literally means 'to integrate' something into one's bodily schema—perceivable on one's own felt body and on figures one interacts with or encounters. This notion is of crucial importance because, if Schmitz is correct, then building qualities and characteristics are experienced bodily.

We now turn to Schmitz's notion of atmosphere, central to the present chapter, which does not necessarily address human emotions infused into space but implies a certain affective quality of lived space. Atmospheres are defined as 'area-less space in the sphere of that which is experienced as being present'.[22] In this sense, atmospheres of the felt body differ from atmospheres of emotion, buildings and weather. Atmospheres of emotion can either be merely perceived or can move one in a corporeally perceptible way. In this case, they are felt in affective collision as one's own emotions.

'Emotional' space has a separate place in Schmitz's theory, appearing as *Gefühlsraume*—a concept which is criticized[23] for lacking a clear

---

21 The term was coined by Shaun Gallagher in his work *How the Body Shapes the Mind*. Jan Slaby provides a profound distinction between body schema and body image: 'The crucial distinction is the one between body image and body schema. The body image is the conscious image or percept that a person has of her own body—the way the body appears in her perceptual field. The body schema, on the other hand, is the way the body shapes and constraints the perceptual field—this term refers to the structure one's body imposes upon experience'. Jan Slaby, 'Affective Intentionality and the Feeling Body', *Phenomenology and the Cognitive Sciences*, 7 (2008), 429–44. See Shaun Gallagher, *How the Body Shapes the Mind* (New York: Oxford University Press, 2005).

22 Hermann Schmitz, 'Atmospheric Spaces', trans. by Margret Vince, *Ambiances* (2016), 1–11, https://doi.org/10.4000/ambiances.711, p. 5.

23 Jens Soentgen, 'Probleme und Perspektiven der Schmitz'schen Gefühlsphilosophie', *Synthesis Philosophica*, 33 (2018), 343–57, https://doi.org/10.21464/sp33203

definition. While this term indeed merits revaluation, the concept itself is beneficial to delineate 'climatic' and affectively charged spaces akin to weather, that 'umstrukturierung der konstellation des gefühlsraums' [restructure the constellation of the emotional space].[24] Many of the emotional atmospheres that he describes manifest optically or acoustically. Others are recalled as phantasms that can be haunting, alongside emotions or memories that one never 'sees or hears, not even when visualising them, and which nonetheless move one in a *corporeally* tangible way, such as when without any discernible cause, one is overcome by a sense of happiness or sinks into melancholy or despair'.[25]

Atmospheres can imbue locational space to the extent that a person can shape their own emotional space from emotions accessed at particular locations. Within an enclosed space, emotions are moulded by the building's qualities, which can be both physically sensed and derived from the object.

On account of this proximity to the felt body, emotions are imprinted on felt-bodies as contours (going beyond the subject-object split) that are endowed with such qualities, just as they move felt bodies. En-corporation allows emotion to be perceived through such contours or to be assimilated by a conscious or unconscious being communicating corporeally as their own emotion. The intentional incorporation of such features into suitably designed objects leads to the formation of atmospheres of emotion within the enclosed space, attuning occupants and/or visitors to these atmospheres. Approaching places experientially, it is impossible to reduce them to a concept defined merely by space, without an embodied focus and bodily dynamics, which would compromise the affectivity. Therefore, we experience places affectively and our bodies, in turn, have the capacity of place orientation, enabling us to act, live and move in a given environment.

Old cities, with their historical sites, boulevards and piazzas, serve as the 'beating heart' of urban structure. They are considered sources of the authentic and dense atmospheres which define cities' unique characters and personalities. For example, religious architecture, a notable feature of this historic fabric, does more than simply fulfil the basic need for shelter from the elements. Rather, they embody the art of capturing

24 Schmitz, *System der Philosophie*, p. 152.
25 Schmitz, 'Atmospheric Spaces', p. 9.

emotional atmospheres and refining them so as to enable individuals to attune in accordance with his or her corporeal mood. Architects, therefore, approach religious constructions to invoke sublime feelings of inspiration. This is what Juhani Pallasmaa calls 'the eternal and unblemished world of beauty'.[26]

Architectural settings may vary depending on city types and building purposes, just as interior artefacts and elements can exude certain atmospheres. For example, the Gothic masterpiece of Saint Bavo Cathedral in Ghent, Belgium, contains a prominent Ghent altarpiece hidden deep within the heart of the church which radiates a gilded aura and contributes to the site's distinctive atmosphere. More generally, the presence of an archaic Gothic church piercing through an urban landscape not only fosters feelings of a connection with the past and the cosmos, in the Greek sense, but also instils a sense of spirituality and the sublime essence of existence itself. These architectural experiences project our focus and thoughts beyond the utilitarian sphere of building construction and globalised urban processes rooted in capitalistic structures.

For much of the past century, as the need for urban planning alternatives arose from the overpopulated conditions of nineteenth-century industrial cities, the authenticity of old city cultural centres have been called into question. Atmospheres, with their inherent nuance, do not appear viable for contemporary architecture. Commenting on this, Juhani Pallasmaa observes: 'modernity resists tradition, whereas ambience and atmosphere often arise from layering things, particularly a sense of time and deterioration. These are qualities that have been all but erased from the modern conception of aesthetic ideas...'[27] Pallasmaa goes on to cite the young architect Alvar Aalto: 'most people, but especially artists, principally grasp the emotional content in a work of art. This is especially manifest in the case of old architecture'.[28]

26 Juhani Pallasmaa, 'Light, Silence, and Spirituality in Architecture and Art', in *Transcending Architecture. Contemporary Views on Sacred Space*, ed. by Julio Bermudez (Washington DC: Catholic University of America Press, 2015), pp. 19–32 (p. 22), https://doi.org/10.2307/j.ctt130h9f6.7

27 Juhani Pallasmaa, 'Atmosphere as a Modernist Blind Spot', *Environmental & Architectural Phenomenology*, 27 (2016), 3–4 (p. 4), https://newprairiepress.org/cgi/viewcontent.cgi?article=1018&context=eap

28 Ibid.

The question remains as to how contemporary architects should deal with emotion-laden spaces and how to preserve the atmospheres of old cities—a subject to which we will now turn.

Against Disembodiment: Enactivism and Environmental Humility

The phenomenon of place undoubtedly has deep historical roots, with numerous scholars having approached this theme, including Christian Norberg-Schulz, Edward Casey, Bernd Jager and Dylan Trigg, among others. Urban design practices, informed by places' practical aims, functionality and qualitative characteristics, have been explored through various methodologies, and the study of emotional architecture from a phenomenological perspective is not at all new. However, the aim to illuminate the salient structures of places using (neo)phenomenology broadens the traditional three-dimensional taxonomy of space by delineating the character of place through the concept of atmosphere.

Emotionally charged spaces can be experienced individually and collectively. Authentic experience is derived from the outside world and, despite our bodily presence in it, is always pre-reflective. Architecture affects us; the environment shapes our being and the way we perceive it. In other words, perception is 'what one does'[29] rather than what happens to them. However, when it comes to affect, there is an additional element of being engaged and feeling certain emotions, i.e. the activity of being passive in one's own bodily experience, whether consciously or not. As Maurice Merleau-Ponty noted, the primacy of embodied perception and 'radical reflection'[30] provides access to the pre-reflective mode of being. While he did not have the opportunity to prove this idea scientifically, it has since become evident that as the present temporality inhabited by the being, the body is not merely a physical point between past and future, but a transitive process of immediate and mediate memories and projections.

Recent approaches in cognitive science have examined the correlation between the world and cognitive processes. Eleanor Rauch, Francisco

29 Alberto Perez-Gomez, *Attunement* (Cambridge, MA: MIT Press, 2016), p. 195.
30 Cited from ibid., p. 222.

Varela and Evan Thompson introduced the term neurophenomenology in the book *The Embodied Mind* (1991), a major contribution to enactivist theory, which claims that cognitive processes arise through embodied actions in correlation with the environment. Enactive views and embodied perception are focal points for understanding atmosphere and its significance for contemporary urban planning and the preservation of old city atmospheres. Human consciousness, in constant interrelation with and able to attune to the environment, is framed by the city and its architectural settings. At the same time, it is not simply an object that shapes the lives of urban dwellers and their intentions. Hence, intentional actions require both perception and emotion and, as we have seen, bodily engagement.

On one hand, places hold special meanings for their inhabitants, rooted in nostalgic memories of events and situations that transpired within their boundaries and affects spatially diffused into the environment. Although places are bound up with memories, they cannot be reduced to such, given the conscious mind's openness to the external world and one's physical presence in it. 'For all its internal differences, one of the features that define phenomenology's treatment of place is a commitment to the belief that lived spatiality is not a container that can be measured in objective terms, but an expression of our being-in-the-world',[31] asserts British philosopher Dylan Trigg, following Merleau-Ponty's idea of the correlations between subjects and spaces.[32] In this context, being-in-the-world refers to inhabiting a specific location, with all of the bodily particularities integral to finding oneself in that place. This marks the beginning of human experience, where life acquires spatial characteristics.

Trigg develops his own phenomenology of place based on the theory of Merleau-Ponty. He argues that our orientation and experience are fundamentally affective. For example, Trigg describes Merleau-Ponty's journey through Paris, where he experienced the unity in the 'city's whole being'.[33] The style of Paris is not simply perceived through

31 Maurice Merleau-Ponty, *Phenomenology of Perception*, trans. by Donald Landes (London: Routledge, 1962), p. 293, cited in Dylan Trigg, *The Memory of Place* (Athens, OH: Ohio University Press, 2013).

32 Merleau-Ponty, *Phenomenology of Perception*, p. 294.

33 Ibid., p. 328.

its constitutive parts but rather 'there is present a latent significance, diffused throughout the landscape or the city'.[34] Notably, this 'style' can also be approached as an atmosphere and explored through its capacity to be grasped by the lived body.[35] Merleau-Ponty experiences a continuous line from one place to another, grounded in the 'certain style' of Paris. Thus, the perception of lived space is not a particular cluster of neural connections or simple acts—it is 'the energy with which he tends toward a future through his body and his world'.[36] This passage is crucial for Trigg's theory as well as for the present chapter. Merleau-Ponty draws attention to the relationship between one's experience of place and affective states that sculpt that experience, defining places by their affective relationship with their inhabitants. The present study contends that this affectivity emerges as atmosphere.

Within this context, identifying the in-between space where atmospheres are located proves difficult. Although straightforward answers and clear definitions are elusive, certain considerations can delineate its critical features. Our bodies orient us in place, as the means by which we move, dwell and experience the world. In this process, our perception of a given environment proceeds from an embodied grasp of the world. This corporeal correlation reveals place as temporally and spatially singular. Atmosphere occupies the space between wild being, in the Merleau-Pontean sense, and our bodily experience of the environment, with the intelligence of the body enabling the coexistence of body and place. The bodily experience of an unfamiliar place may precede our comprehension due to its pre-reflectivity and initial, nascent feeling. In order to grasp the atmosphere of a place, one must not only be present physically with the spatio-temporal dimensions of one's *Körper* [body] but also possess the capacity within one's lived body to be affected by it. The *Leib* [felt body] is a substrate of *Verspürgen* [immediate feelings] and reflects them in the sphere of the real, physical body. Thus, the in-between is a place rather than being defined in terms of 'orientation toward a point either far away or close by'.

34 Ibid.

35 Joel Krueger, 'Enactivism, Other Minds, and Mental Disorders', *Synthese*, 198 (2019), 365–89, https://doi.org/10.1007/s11229-019-02133-9

36 Merleau-Ponty, *Phenomenology of Perception*, p. 330.

If we were to conflate the outer edges of space without situating ourselves on this ambiguous ground, the result would be a rigid determination of place. Such conflation leads to an abstraction of place, producing a sedimented notion that separates place from its otherness. Yet, place is neither fixed nor exact, and before cultural, ethical and sociological judgments are applied, its genesis is a phenomenal appearance in time and space.[37]

Notably, in-between places cannot be described in terms of Euclidian geometry, occasioning a Schmitzean understanding of space. This implies that places of cultural heritage are not merely historical monuments or ruins; they embody the architecture of memory, directly accessible through our bodies. The experience of place is activated through bodily motion that 'literally absorbs the contours and textures of the environment in the absolute here'.[38] Following Trigg's concept, the body initiates insight into something that eventually becomes familiar but, at first glance, carries what he defines as an 'aura of strangeness'.[39] Furthermore, Edensor's football stadium example illustrates that atmosphere cannot be understood only through isolated instances extracted from the wider context, as nostalgia is an integral component of the match-day atmosphere, connecting it to the past. Edensor argues that such connections to the past create more potent and concentrated atmospheres.

To purposefully reinforce an atmosphere, one must also move through it. This idea aligns with theories from urban geography and environmental psychology that regard city strolling as an endeavour, exploration and lifestyle. The journey through an old city reveals a pair of binary oppositions—nearness and distance, intimacy and publicity—which, like atmosphere, can be perceived both collectively and individually. Safeguarding cultural heritage objects, such as old towns, religious edifices and architectural ensembles, entails preserving the past embodied in stone and manifested as atmosphere. This is one of the urgent tasks facing contemporary urban planners and architects

37 Trigg, *Memory of Place*, p. 135.

38 Ibid., p. 113. Absolute here is described in this passage as 'the confluence between the place and the physical body through which one catches sight of things in their incipient being visible'.

39 Ibid., p. 136.

and gives rise to the important question of whether the preservation of authenticity is possible during the Anthropocene, amidst late capitalism and technological progress.

Conclusion

This chapter has explored the conceptual framework of atmospheres as affectively tonalised environments in order to illuminate the significance of old cities in urban and architectural contexts. This was achieved through the implementation of a (neo)phenomenological approach enriched by enactivist methods.

The first part of the chapter focused on old cities and their preservation amidst rapid globalisation, technological advancement and urban development. Trends in urban renovation and digitalisation are threatening the authenticity and cultural heritage of old cities, requiring a new paradigm for considering the value of cultural heritage and approaches to its preservation. The present research contends that the concept of atmosphere is crucial in developing such a paradigm, as the atmospheric characteristics of old cities are an integral component of local identities and shape how residents and visitors alike experience these urban environments. In this context, the concept of atmosphere, increasingly prominent in spatial arts, urban planning and sound studies, illuminates the affective dimension of old cities as an essential component of urban spaces.

The design of atmosphere is beyond the structural, linguistic and other representational cognitive or language-based approaches, as revealed by the present research. Moreover, the existing theoretical assumptions of many philosophical surveys on atmospheres were found insufficient, prompting a critical examination of these theories through a fresh perspective. Notably, the (neo)phenomenological methods of Schmitz and Böhme, who introduced the concept of feelings as atmospheres, were analysed. These authors are frequently referenced in atmosphere research, yet often without adequately explaining the concept's significance or acknowledging that atmosphere is not merely a tool but a separate dimension with a certain affective quality.

This chapter has analysed potential approaches to atmospheres, particularly in the context of old cities as vanishing elements of contemporary urban landscapes. Moreover, it has explored environmental and bodily conditions and the possibility of attuning to certain places through enactivism. Examining natural felt bodily dispositions reveals the significance of atmospheres beyond symbolic representations, as spaces that unfold 'in-between' while simultaneously embracing cities in their entirety. Contemporary urban development trends rooted in functionality and neoliberal thinking erode authentic cultural experience, making it imperative to preserve old cities and their atmospheres.

Bibliography

Artyushina, Anna, 'The EU Is Launching a Market for Personal Data. Here's What that Means for Privacy' (11 August 2020), *MIT Technology Review*, https://www.technologyreview.com/2020/08/11/1006555/eu-data-trust-trusts-project-privacy-policy-opinion/

Ash, J. and Leszczynski, A., 'Digital Turn, Digital Geographies?', *Progress, Human Geography*, 42 (2016), 25–43.

Bille, M., Bjerregaard, P. and Sørensen, T. F, 'Staging Atmospheres: Materiality, Culture, and the Texture of the In-between', *Emotion, Space and Society*, 15 (2015), 31–38.

Böhme, Gernot, 'Atmosphere as the Fundamental Concept of a New Aesthetics', *Thesis Eleven* 36 (1993), 113–26.

Böhme, Gernot, *Atmospheric Architectures: The Aesthetics of Felt Spaces* (London: Bloomsbury Academic, 2017).

Böhme, Gernot, *Critique of Aesthetic Capitalism* (Milano-Udine: Mimesis International, 2017).

Carr, C. and Markus, H., 'Sidewalk Labs Closed Down—Whither the Google City?' (2020), *Regions*, https://doi.org/10.1080/13673882.2020.00001070

Clough, P. T. and Halley, J., *The Affective Turn: Theorizing the Social* (Durham, NC: Duke University Press, 2007).

De Matteis, Federico, 'The City as a Mode of Perception: Corporeal Dynamics in Urban Space', in *Handbook of Research on Perception-Driven Approaches to Urban Assessment and Design*, ed. by F. Aletta and J. Xiao (Hershey: IGI Global, 2018), pp. 434–57, https://doi.org/10.4018/978-1-5225-3637-6.ch018

Gallagher, Shaun, *How the Body Shapes the Mind* (New York: Oxford. University Press, 2005).

Griffero, Tonino, *Atmospheres: Aesthetics of Emotional Spaces* (London, New York: Routledge, 2014).

Griffero, T. and Tedeschini, M., eds., *Atmosphere and Aesthetics: A Plural Perspective* (Cham: Palgrave Macmillan, 2019).

Hasse, Jurgen, *Atmosphären der Stadt. Aufgespürte Räume* (Berlin: Jovis, 2012).

Kotler, Philip, 'Atmospherics as a Marketing Tool', *Journal of Retailing* 49 (1974), 48–64.

Krueger, Joel, 'Enactivism, Other Minds, and Mental Disorders', *Synthese*, 198 (2019), 365–89, https://doi.org/10.1007/s11229-019-02133-9

Massumi, Brian, *Politics of Affect* (Cambridge, MA: Polity Press, 2015).

McCormack, Derek, 'Engineering Affective Atmospheres on the Moving Geographies of the 1897 Andrée Expedition', *Cultural Geographies*, 15 (2008), 413–30.

Merleau-Ponty, Maurice, *Phenomenology of Perception*, trans. by Donald Landes (London: Routledge, 1962), p. 293.

Pallasmaa, Juhani, 'Light, Silence, and Spirituality in Architecture and Art', in *Transcending Architecture. Contemporary Views on Sacred Space*, ed. by Julio Bermudez (Washington DC: Catholic University of America Press, 2015), pp. 19-32, https://doi.org/10.2307/j.ctt130h9f6.7

Pallasmaa, Juhani, 'Atmosphere as a Modernist Blind Spot', *Environmental & Architectural Phenomenology*, 27 (2016), 3–4, https://newprairiepress.org/cgi/viewcontent.cgi?article=1018&context=eap

Perez-Gomez, Alberto, *Attunement* (Cambridge, MA: MIT Press, 2016).

Pocai, Romano, *Heideggers Theorie der Befindlichkeit: sein Denken zwischen 1927 und 1933* (Munich: Verlag Karl Alber, 1996).

Scheler, Max, *Der Formalismus in der Ethik und die materiale Wertethik. Neuer Versuch der Grundlegung eines ethischen Personalismus* (Bern: Francke, 1954).

Schmitz, Hermann, *System der Philosophie: Band III. Der Raum: Teil 2. Der Gefühlsraum* (Bonn: Bouvier, 2005).

Schmitz, Hermann, 'Atmospheric Spaces', trans. by Margret Vince, *Ambiances* (2016), 1–11, https://doi.org/10.4000/ambiances.711

Slaby, Jan, 'Affective Intentionality and the Feeling Body', *Phenomenology and the Cognitive Sciences*, 7 (2008), 429–44.

Slaby, J. and Mühlhoff, R., 'Affect', in *Affective Societies: Key Concepts*, ed. by Jan Slaby and Christian von Scheve (New York: Routledge, 2019), pp. 27–41.

Sloterdijk, Peter, *Neither Sun nor Death* (Los Angeles, CA: Semiotext(e), 2011).

Soentgen, Jens, 'Probleme und Perspektiven der Schmitz'schen Gefühlsphilosophie', *Synthesis Philosophica*, 33 (2018), 343–57, https://doi.org/10.21464/sp33203

Thibaud, Jean-Paul, 'Frames of Visibility in Public Places', *Places*, 14 (2001), 42–47.

Trigg, Dylan, *The Memory of Place* (Athens, OH: Ohio University Press, 2013).

Trigg, Dylan, 'The Role of Atmosphere in Shared Emotion', *Emotion, Space and Society*, 35 (2020), https://doi.org/10.1016/j.emospa.2020.100658

Uhrich, S. and Benkenstein, M., 'Sport Stadium Atmosphere: Formative and Reflective Indicators for Operationalizing the Construct', *Journal of Sport Management*, 24 (2010), 211–37.

Zuboff, Shoshana, *The Age of Surveillance Capitalism—The Fight for a Human Future at the New Frontier of Power* (London: Profile Books, 2019).

Conclusion: Sustainability in the Age of Globalisation

Lilia Makhloufi

The case studies presented in this volume have been analysed by researchers and practitioners from diverse backgrounds and countries. The contributors, including architects, civil engineers, urban planners, sociologists and philosophical anthropologists, sought to investigate different urban contexts and their heritage to understand the stakes of conservation, management and development in a globalised world. Through an interdisciplinary approach, this book explores aspects of urban heritage at four key levels: city, neighbourhood, building and landscape.

The book's first half prioritises perspectives on urban heritage, with architects, civil engineers and sociologists focusing on the sustainability of historic cities and, in particular, their urban development processes. They underscore the historical and cultural richness of these cities and their significance in people's lives. Moreover, the contributors evaluate the sustainability of traditional neighbourhoods, shedding light on the specificities of their urban formation and transformation over time. By analysing the conditions of the past, they seek to inform the present and the future.

The book's second half shifts the focus to perspectives on architectural heritage. Architects, urban planners and philosophical anthropologists prioritise the sustainability of old buildings, particularly their facades and envelopes. They analyse and assess selected buildings according to

 https://doi.org/10.11647/OBP.0412.13

climatic objectives and design parameters. Furthermore, the contributors emphasise the enduring presence of history in urban and architectural landscapes, the cultures of local communities and the development of the built environment. In approaching these topics, the contributors consider the architectural process and cultural context as interconnected with the environmental context.

In the twenty-first century, sustainable development is an essential element in the consideration of urban life, evincing the need for 'development that meets the needs of the present without compromising the ability of future generations to meet their own needs'.[1] Along with its environmental facets, sustainable development also includes human development, values and cultures.

Researchers recognise that cities are progressively affected by regional, interregional, national and international economic conditions. At the crossroads of expertise and initiatives, urban areas foster education and innovation, encouraging economic growth.

This reality becomes especially striking in the context of globalisation, as financial markets subtly push towards uniformity for the sake of cost-efficiency. This trend is also apparent in architecture, where it threatens the cultural diversity of cities. Breaking away from repetitive architecture can appear to be a daunting task in light of the stringent economic system of the construction industry and the constraints of prefabrication processes.

In this framework, local life and its spatial dimension are uniquely situated to support identity. A locality's evolution should be driven by the population's needs and their motivation to collectively organise to express their values. This approach considers economic factors, the broader cultural context and the choice of local construction materials, prioritising the human aspect of architecture over dominant trends.

Drawing on a range of disciplines, this book demonstrates that historic cities foster diversity and cultural exchange through the continuous development of their urban heritage. Old cities are characterised by the forms and contents of their urban networks, residential and infrastructural building, and urban spaces such as streets, squares and

1 United Nations, *Report of the World Commission on Environment and Development, General Assembly Resolution 42/187* (New York: United Nations, 1987), https://digitallibrary.un.org/record/153026?ln=en

gardens. Urban heritage is perceptible through the five senses and frames the life setting of the local population, interacting with identities, values and cultures. This book investigates the liveability of these built environments and the sustainability of old cities for future generations.

The globalisation of the economy goes hand-in-hand with the global standardisation of architectural production. According to Jean-François Dortier, 'the West had colonised the world previously by strength, producing thus ethnocides. Today, westernisation develops mainly by acculturation, a voluntary adherence'.[2] Thus, the growing resemblance among major international cities testifies to the undeniably homogenising nature of globalisation.

However, urbanism goes beyond the simple material dimension to include social, economic and political considerations. Urban planners recognise that the economic domain is by no means independent from the social and political context nor subject exclusively to its logic. Urban heritage transcends architectural features, requiring cities to establish shared values and consistent institutional practices in order to pursue social objectives with more equal ambition. Lived experiences prove to be considerably more complex, and local populations resist the homogenisation of their ways—and spaces—of life.

The political decisions made today impact the present and future of historic cities in many ways. These decisions shape cultural life through public spaces and the cultural activities that generate urban atmospheres. These cultural elements are an important tool for reinforcing local identity.

Moreover, recent studies have revealed the considerable influence of atmospheres in various fields, especially in architecture and aesthetics. The term 'ambience'—often confined in literature to romantic, seasonal or festive atmospheres—has emerged in recent years as a relevant instrument for spatial analysis and design and a foundation for various theoretical and operational practices.

For architects, this approach to the built environment involves considering all sensations—sound, light, odours, texture and heat, among others. Cultural ambiences contribute to reviving interest in

2 Jean-François Dortier, 'Vers une uniformisation culturelle?' (March 2007), *Sciences Humaines*, http://www.scienceshumaines.com/10-questions-sur-la-mondialisation_fr_279.htm

local values and preserving the richness of local life, as communities cherish that which is specific to their local cultures in contrast to global influences.

Therefore, for sake of present and future generations and the long-term liveability of cities, the urban field must devote greater attention to the local aspects of contemporary cities in defiance of the ideology of globalisation. To preserve identity and economic aspirations, architectural practices must be localised to specific places, empowering diverse expressions as an alternative to the totalitarian features of the so-called global city.

Index

About the Team

Alessandra Tosi was the managing editor for this book.

Monica Hanson-Green performed the copy-editing.

Adèle Kreager performed the proof-reading and Anja Pritchard provided editorial assistance.

Annie Hine indexed this book.

The authors created the Alt-text.

Jeevanjot Kaur Nagpal designed the cover. The cover was produced in InDesign using the Fontin font.

Cameron Craig typeset the book in InDesign and produced the paperback and hardback editions. The text font is Tex Gyre Pagella and the heading font is Californian FB.

Cameron also produced the PDF, and HTML editions. The conversion was performed with open-source software and other tools freely available on our GitHub page at https://github.com/OpenBookPublishers.

Jeremy Bowman produced the EPUB edition.

Raegan Allen was in charge of marketing.

This book was peer-reviewed by two referees. Experts in their field, these readers give their time freely to help ensure the academic rigour of our books. We are grateful for their generous and invaluable contributions.

This book need not end here...

Share

All our books — including the one you have just read — are free to access online so that students, researchers and members of the public who can't afford a printed edition will have access to the same ideas. This title will be accessed online by hundreds of readers each month across the globe: why not share the link so that someone you know is one of them?

This book and additional content is available at:
https://doi.org/10.11647/OBP.0412

Donate

Open Book Publishers is an award-winning, scholar-led, not-for-profit press making knowledge freely available one book at a time. We don't charge authors to publish with us: instead, our work is supported by our library members and by donations from people who believe that research shouldn't be locked behind paywalls.

Why not join them in freeing knowledge by supporting us:
https://www.openbookpublishers.com/support-us

You may also be interested in:

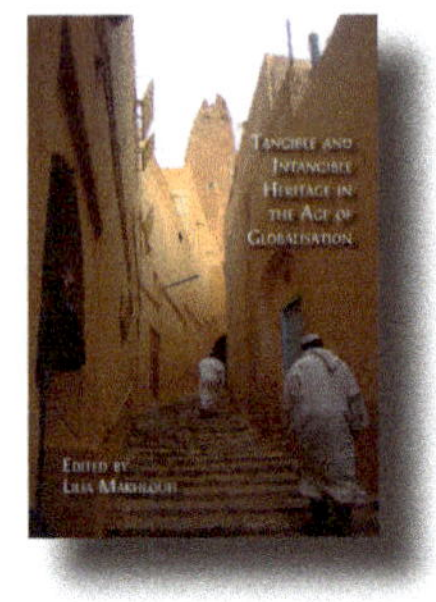

Tangible and Intangible Heritage in the Age of Globalisation

Lilia Makhloufi (Ed.)

https://doi.org/10.11647/obp.0388

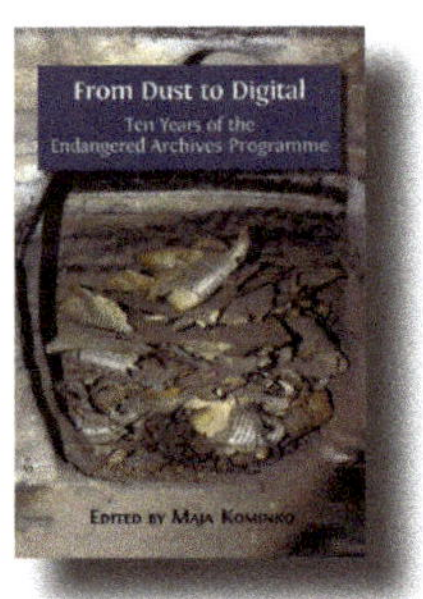

From Dust to Digital

Ten Years of the Endangered Archives Programme

Maja Kominko (ed.)

https://doi.org/10.11647/obp.0052

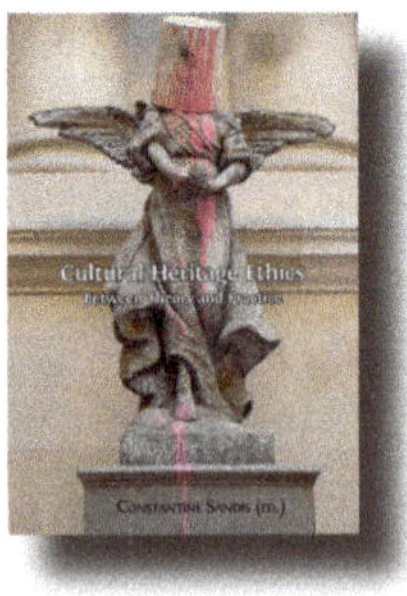

Cultural Heritage Ethics

Between Theory and Practice

Sandis Constantine (ed.)

https://doi.org/10.11647/obp.0047

www.ingramcontent.com/pod-product-compliance
Lightning Source LLC
LaVergne TN
LVHW052350100826
845147LV00013B/801

9781805113409